NO SHELF
REQUIRED 2

NO SHELF REQUIRED 2

Use and Management of Electronic Books

Edited by Sue Polanka

AMERICAN LIBRARY ASSOCIATION
Chicago   2012

SUE POLANKA created the award-winning blog No Shelf Required, about the issues surrounding e-books for librarians and publishers. Polanka has been a reference and instruction librarian for over twenty years at public, state, and academic libraries in Ohio and Texas and is currently the head of reference and instruction at the Wright State University Libraries in Dayton, Ohio. She edited *No Shelf Required: E-books in Libraries* (ALA Editions, 2011) and *E-Reference Context and Discoverability in Libraries: Issues and Concepts* (IGI Publishing, 2012). She has served on *Booklist*'s Reference Books Bulletin Editorial Board for over ten years, serving as chair from 2007 to 2010. Her column on electronic reference, "Off the Shelf," appears in *Booklist* quarterly. Sue was named a 2011 *Library Journal* Mover and Shaker.

Printed in the United States of America

16 15 14 13 12   5 4 3 2 1

Extensive effort has gone into ensuring the reliability of the information in this book; however, the publisher makes no warranty, express or implied, with respect to the material contained herein.

ISBNs: 978-0-8389-1145-7 (paper); 978-0-8389-9382-8 (PDF); 978-0-8389-9385-9 (ePub); 978-0-8389-9383-5 (Mobipocket); 978-0-8389-9384-2 (Kindle). For more information on digital formats, visit the ALA Store at alastore.ala.org and select eEditions.

Library of Congress Cataloging-in-Publication Data
No shelf required 2 : use and management of electronic books / edited by Sue Polanka.
     p.   cm.
 Includes bibliographical references and index.
 ISBN 978-0-8389-1145-7 (alk. paper)
 1. Libraries--Special collections--Electronic books. 2. Electronic books. 3. Libraries and electronic publishing. I. Polanka, Sue. II. Title: No shelf required two.
 Z692.E4N62 2012
 070.5'73--dc23
                                                                2011040497

Text design in Charis SIL by Karen Sheets de Gracia.
Cover design and composition by Casey Bayer. Cover image © pressureUA/Shutterstock, Inc.

⊗ This paper meets the requirements of ANSI/NISO Z39.48–1992 (Permanence of Paper).

CONTENTS

ACKNOWLEDGMENTS

This book would not have been possible without the contributions of twenty knowledgeable, creative, and talented people. I thank the contributors: Amelia Brunskill, Sarah Twill, Ken Petri, Lisa Carlucci Thomas, Amy Kirchhoff, Alice Crosetto, Steve Kelley, Sylvia Miller, Michael Porter, Matt Weaver, Bobbi Newman, Tom Peters, Joseph Sanchez, Jessica Grim, Allison Gallaher, Carolyn Foote, Jennifer LaGarde, Christine James, Buffy Hamilton, and Kathy Parker. I would also like to thank three other individuals who contributed their expertise in a variety of ways: Piper Martin, Kathryn Reynolds, and James Galbraith. Finally, I thank the people who support me the most: my wonderful family, my encouraging boss, and my energetic staff.

INTRODUCTION

D ecember 2010 was a major turning point for the e-book market. When e-reader prices dropped in preparation for the holidays, record numbers of devices were sold (Minzesheimer 2011). In fact, the demand for content was so intense that the Barnes & Noble servers crashed on Christmas Day (Carnoy 2010). This rising e-book trend charged into 2011 and thus far shows no sign of retreat. In March the Barnes & Noble Nook surpassed Amazon's Kindle in sales (Chan 2011), and the much awaited Apple iPad2 was also released. Amazon reached another milestone in April, announcing that digital book sales now exceeded sales of all print titles, both hardcover and paperback combined (Stevens 2011). But the surefire sign that e-books had reached the tipping point came in February when the Association of American Publishers declared—for the first time ever—that e-books ranked as the number one format among all categories of trade publishing (Sporkin 2011).

Many librarians predicted this growth trend and were prepared with downloadable e-book content and device lending programs. *Library Journal*'s 2010 survey of e-book use in libraries found that 94 percent of academic, 72 percent of public, and 33 percent of school libraries had existing e-book collections (Polanka 2011). Device lending, while not as widespread, was offered by 12 percent of academic, 5 percent of public, and 6 percent of school libraries (Polanka 2011). Preliminary reports of *Library Journal*'s not-yet-released 2011 survey indicate 93 percent of libraries are experiencing an increased demand for e-books. Because e-books are now mainstream, libraries have adapted by offering new expanded digital content, device lending programs, and new services.

E-book content, devices, and services have created challenges for libraries as well as opportunities. Increasingly librarians find themselves being forced to deal with issues of licensing, digital rights management, and accessibility, plus device and format incompatibility. At the same time they are acknowledging and implementing new, innovative services in device use and lending, training, and support of self-publishing. *No Shelf Required 2* examines how libraries are using and managing e-books and e-reading devices. It expands well beyond the boundaries of the first volume, with sixteen completely new chapters from twenty new contributors. It includes contributions from academic, school, and public librarians; faculty; and vendors. The reader is invited to read the entire work or select chapters that stand on their own. Some important topics may be visited more than once, but in different contexts.

No Shelf Required 2 begins with an examination of the digital library. Ameila Brunskill debates how new technologies have altered the relationship between libraries and their print collections and questions whether e-books are a true replacement for print. She presents the digital-but-not-bookless library through real-world examples from Cushing Academy in Ashburnham, Massachusetts; Stanford University Engineering Library; University of Texas at San Antonio Applied Engineering and Technology Library; and the University of Texas at Austin undergraduate library.

Chapters 2 through 7 spotlight different perspectives on e-book access. In chapter 2, social work professor Sarah Twill brings her nonlibrarian's perspective to e-books. Twill examines both the impact of household income and access to digital technologies on the adoption of electronic content and discusses implications for libraries. She discusses the case example method *Can the Jones Family Participate in Digital Technologies?* Twill encourages librarians and social service providers to collaborate in order to bridge the digital e-book divide.

In chapter 3, Ken Petri discusses e-book and e-book reader accessibility issues and the Americans with Disabilities Act. He looks at the costs involved in converting print books into more accessible e-books, and the legal environment surrounding e-book accessibility. Petri examines various degrees of accessibility in e-book formats, devices, and software and provides strategies for publishers, libraries, and software and device makers on how to provide mainstream e-books accessible to all.

Chapter 4 explores access to e-books in the rapidly developing mobile environment. Lisa Carlucci Thomas discusses the impact of e-books and mobile devices on libraries, suggesting that libraries remain flexible as e-books continue to evolve. Thomas summarizes a research study on mobile access to e-books at Yale that found that 84 percent of their one million–book collection could be accessed on Apple iOS devices and 24 percent on dedicated e-reader devices.

Amy Kirchhoff asserts that perpetual access to e-books should not be ignored in chapter 5. Kirchhoff focuses on preservation requirements for permanent access to content along with specific challenges of preserving e-books, including digital rights management, legal issues, and the packaging of e-books.

In chapter 6, Alice Crosetto discusses weeding electronic content. She insists that e-books are long overdue for evaluation and weeding. Crosetto hypothesizes that e-books are not weeded because they do not occupy valuable shelf space. However, she cautions against ignoring this practice, citing out-of-date content and cluttering of the online catalog as concerns. She examines the similarities and differences of weeding print versus electronic books.

Chapter 7 completes the focus on e-book access with a discussion of resource description and access (RDA), the new cataloging code set to replace AACR2. Steve Kelley defines RDA for noncatalogers and describes how RDA provides a necessary foundation for building better data structures that will change the capabilities of future cataloging systems. RDA will provide future access to e-books through the online catalog. It will most likely provide the next step toward integrating library resources with the much heralded Semantic Web.

The publishing world is beginning to embrace enhanced e-books, those with multimedia features, internal and external links, or a combination of nontext features. In chapter 8, Sylvia Miller uses examples from the social sciences and humanities fields to explore the current landscape of enhanced e-books. She contemplates a future where enhanced formats are the norm.

Chapter 9 takes a more in-depth look at e-books in the public library environment. Michael Porter, Matt Weaver, and Bobbi Newman survey new developments in the use of e-readers in libraries, staff training for these new technologies, and budgeting for e-content. This chapter also includes a special report by Michael Porter, who provides a compelling look at the controversial HarperCollins decision to limit an e-book purchase to twenty-six circulations.

In chapter 10, Thomas Peters expands on the 2010 Chief Officers of State Library Agencies (COSLA) report about the future of public libraries. The report discusses seven areas of action; Peters's chapter focuses on the fifth action item: *help local authors and support self-publishing.* His chapter suggests that libraries should be zones for content creation, independent publishing, and print-on-demand services.

Joseph Sanchez insists in chapter 11 that libraries in this digital environment get control, stay relevant, and push the envelope to their advantage. He encourages libraries to develop their own content management systems to host local content rather than outsource access to large vendors. Sanchez shares his experience with such a project at Red Rocks Community College in Colorado, chronicling the progression of events that led to its decision to host e-book content locally.

Lending e-reading devices is a growing trend in libraries. In chapter 12, Jessica Grim and Allison Gallaher explain the planning and implementation of an iPad loaner program at the Oberlin College Library in Ohio. They describe pilot and full programs in detail, share assessment data, and explore future plans.

The final four chapters focus on e-book integration in school libraries and classrooms. Carolyn Foote begins in chapter 13 with an overview of the state of technology in the school library and its impact on leading and learning. She discusses the very real need for e-books and encourages librarians to take a leadership role adopting e-books in the school. Foote also foresees a myriad of obstacles as well as choices to be made along the way.

Three specific examples of e-book integration in school libraries and classrooms follow. First is from Jennifer LaGarde and Christine James in chapter 14. The librarian-teacher duo adopted Nook readers for a seventh-grade English classroom. The chapter chronicles their journey of collaboration and discovery, providing details on budgeting, connecting e-readers to the curriculum, selecting devices and content, training students, and discussing lessons learned and possible future steps.

In chapter 15, Buffy Hamilton provides a detailed description of a Kindle pilot program at the Unquiet Library in Georgia. She shares her experience developing circulation procedures and purchasing content, offering best practices and recommendations for libraries who wish to adopt similar programs. Hamilton shares student responses to the program and anticipates its future direction.

Kathy Parker documents the success of an e-reader pilot program in a rural Illinois school system in chapter 16. This program implemented eighteen Kindle 2 devices with second-grade reluctant readers. She gives details of the program planning, implementation, student selection, assessment, and best practices.

Though this book was written in the first half of 2011, every effort was made to ensure the accuracy of its content. But because the e-book playing field is constantly changing, any predictions are, at best, tenuous. Using and managing e-books and e-readers in any setting is challenging to say the least, much like chasing a moving target. Librarians must be resilient, for as the pace of change continues to quicken, they need to manage—and not be managed by—e-books and their progenies.

REFERENCES

Carnoy, David. 2010. "Barnes & Noble's Nook Server Woes Rectified." *CNet News,* December 29, http://news.cnet.com/8301-17938_105-20026729-1 .html.

Chan, Rodney, 2011. "Nook Outnumbers Kindle in March, says Digitimes Research." *DigiTimes,* April 26, www.digitimes.com/news/ a20100426VL204.html.

Minzesheimer, Bob, and Carol Memmott. 2011. "Week after Holidays, E-book Sales Outdo Print." *USAToday,* January 5, www.usatoday.com/life/books/ news/2011-01-05-1Aebooksales05_ST_N.htm.

Polanka, Sue. 2011. "Library Journal Publishes E-book Survey Results—Sample Data Here," www.libraries.wright.edu/noshelfrequired/2011/02/09/ library-journal-publishes-library-ebook-survey-results-sample-data-here/.

Sporkin, Andi. 2011. "Popularity of Books in Digital Platforms Continues to Grow, According to AAP Publishers February 2011 Sales Report,"

Association of American Publishers, April 14, www.publishers.org/press/30/.

Stevens, Tim. 2011. "Kindle Books Officially Take Over Print Sales at Amazon, Pulp Starts Making Retirement Plans." *Engadget,* May 19, www.engadget.com/2011/05/19/Kindle-books-officially-take-over-print-sales-at-amazon-pulp-st/.

1

Going Digital but Not Bookless

Physical, Digital Library Spaces

AMELIA BRUNSKILL

I n 2009, Syracuse University's Bird Library had reached 98 percent of its capacity. To create more space within the building, administrators proposed moving thousands of books to a storage facility in Patterson, New York. This proposal sparked protests by students and faculty, culminating in more than 200 people attending the university senate meeting designated for the discussion of this proposal. An article discussing these events described the protestors as "want[ing] the library to remain a library, at least in the way that many of us traditionally define it" (Kirst 2009).

That sentence neatly encompasses an attitude held by many: that a plentiful supply of print books is essential for defining a space as a library. Under this logic, by proposing to substantially reduce its print collection, the Bird Library was endangering its very status as a library.

Yet, even here we have the caveat of "at least in the way that many of us traditionally define it." We have an acknowledgment that the print-centric definition is a traditional one and that there could be a future in which libraries' identities are not shaped around their physical collections.

This potential future: physical spaces without books that are still libraries is an intriguing but daunting prospect. If we have little—or no—physical materials, then what will define these spaces as libraries? What will people do there, and what will we as librarians do in them?

In order to explore these questions, we will start by considering how, over time, new technologies have shifted the relationship between libraries and their print collections. Then we will explore both the case against, and for, electronic books as substitutes for print ones. The bulk of this chapter will be devoted to looking at libraries that are challenging the centrality of print materials. Some of these libraries are new spaces; others are existing spaces that have been radically transformed; but together they provide a sense of the scope of the challenges and opportunities in moving away from a print-centric definition of library spaces. In looking at these spaces, we will explore the implications of what these libraries are doing and to what extent they should be viewed as merely interesting anomalies or as potential templates for the libraries of the future.

HISTORY

In 1885, Reuben A. Guild, a librarian at Brown University, published an essay on the history of the library at his institution. He wrote earnestly about the success of his proposal for the library, which included "open shelves, where the books can be readily handled by all, and quite well-lighted alcoves, with convenient tables and seats, inviting to study and research" (Guild 1885, 221). While all this conforms nicely with today's norms for library spaces, this proposal reads as positively revolutionary after Guild leads the readers through some of the prior statutes for the library, including one that warned against lending titles, cautioning that "we have been too well taught what ruin and destruction the frequent lending of books has introduced" (Guild 1885, 218).

Guild's essay is an excellent reminder that while libraries have a long lineage, most modern libraries have little in common with their ancestors. While the preservation of manuscripts was once the primary goal of a library, with patrons' convenience and comfort barely warranting consideration, many libraries now prioritize patrons above collections. This change in priorities has been facilitated by society's ability to efficiently and cheaply mass-produce texts and has resulted in greater access, with fewer restrictions, for a larger and more inclusive set of users.

Although free circulation of titles has not been controversial in most libraries for quite some time, the decreasing price of books and the increasing focus on patrons have also led to other, more recent, shifts. One example, simultaneously superficial and revealing, is libraries' relationship to food. Once shunned as the natural enemy of the printed word, food and beverages have become increasingly permissible in libraries' spaces. The formal inclusion of food and drinks through the creation of library cafés has gone from being shocking to being an almost mandatory part of any new library building or major renovation. The rules and policies that were created to guard expensive, rare materials are now increasingly relegated to those few spaces that still contain such materials.

Assumptions about print materials are being continually tested by advances in available technology. In 2001, Nicholas Baker, author and self-appointed library critic, remarked that "we're always going to have shelves full of books because it would be monumentally expensive to scan those things" (Baker 2001). But less than ten years later, the Google Books project had digitized untold shelves of books from major research libraries. While the accompanying lawsuit for this project has still not been settled, access to these virtual shelves of titles is now squarely a legal rather than a technological concern.

Changes in technology are also providing new options for content acquisition and access. Libraries can use existing approval plans to populate their catalogs with relevant e-book titles—titles that will be purchased only when, or if, they are accessed by a patron. If users would prefer to browse a print copy of a digital book, then the Espresso Book Machine can print out a perfect-bound paperback in mere minutes. While most libraries are only considering whether to experiment with patron-driven acquisition of e-books and only a very limited number actually own an Expresso Book Machine, these innovations represent possibilities that, until recently, few would have anticipated. The recent boom in e-reader purchases represents another technology, although available in some form for some time, that has now found a niche and a price point where it has implications for our assumptions about how users access library content.

With new technological capabilities come new options for how to develop libraries' collections and how to structure physical library spaces. As more materials are digitized or simply born digital—and methods for accessing this content are refined—the role of large print collections becomes less obvious, and some of the traditional rationales for the supremacy and need of print materials will begin to falter. All these changes are laying the groundwork for a potentially radical shift in the ever-evolving relationship between libraries, materials, and their patrons.

DISADVANTAGES OF E-BOOKS
(OR: PUT DOWN THOSE MATCHES)

Of course, simply because a format is new does not make it better. We, as a profession and as a society, have had thousands of years to become proficient with creating, accessing, organizing, and preserving print books— and by comparison, e-books (recent interlopers that they are) have many wrinkles that remain to be ironed out.

The problem of the long-term support and preservation of digital content, despite the promise of projects like HathiTrust, is still far from being resolved, and even the meaning of perpetual access for digital texts is unclear when so much of their functionality is dependent on proprietary platforms. The digital rights management setting for e-books can take away any potential gray area for fair use and often errs on the side of allowing very limited copying, downloading, or printing. Within the last two years we have witnessed two extremely unnerving examples of the power that providers can wield over their e-book content, with Amazon first yanking illegitimate versions of *1984* from Kindles (Stone 2009) and then HarperCollins deciding to limit circulation of its e-books to a mere twenty-six checkouts (Hadro 2011), leading both individual libraries and consortiums to boycott its products.

While pricing of e-content would intuitively be much lower than its print counterparts, this is actually another variable that can work in favor of print content. Individually purchased e-books are often more expensive than their print counterparts, particularly in the academic realm, with price tags that are often tethered to hardcover prices even after paperback editions are available. E-book packages may be considerably less expensive on a per-book basis but also begin taking on the unsavory undertones of the "big deals" where quantity can begin to exceed quality.

E-books also rely on people being able to access them through a technological device, and at least their original download requires a device with access to the Internet. Not everyone has this, let alone an e-reader that allows for an optimal reading experience of this digital content. E-book content is not democratic—a better, more flexible reading experience of this content can be purchased, plus the price is not cheap and the learning curve for these devices is not minimal.

Perhaps most important for this chapter, however, e-books suffer from simply not being print books. People like print books. They like the way they smell and feel, how they give libraries a sense of gravitas, and how they present a physical embodiment of scholarship and creativity. People rally around print books; it is difficult to imagine e-books inspiring the same level of loyalty. When Newport Beach library system in California announced this March that they were looking into changing one of their branch libraries into a primarily digital space, there was an immediate uproar (CBS 2011). Due to the vehemence of the response, these plans have since been suspended. By contrast, the cancelation of electronic resources has never come close to inspiring this level of response.

Even if all these hurdles are either ignored or successfully bypassed, there are still obstacles to moving toward a largely or completely digital collection. The most daunting obstacle is that some content, both new and old, is still simply not available for purchase in digital form. Some content simply has not been digitized yet, and other content that is available in digital form is still not available for individual purchase. Even titles that are sold electronically may become available only considerably after their print release, leaving librarians who would prefer to purchase the content electronically in a quandary as to whether to wait or satisfy patrons more immediately with the print edition. Even a strong desire to remove print from a library can easily be stymied by a combination of technological restrictions, cost, public reaction, and endless logistics and frustrations.

THE IMPETUS FOR PAPERLESS LIBRARIES

Given the concerns regarding e-books, why would libraries consider drastic reductions of their existing print collections to rely instead on digital content? Despite their flaws, e-books do have enormous potential in terms of convenience and access, providing the ability to access book content as one does electronic journal articles: from anywhere with an Internet connection, without regard to who else happens to be looking at it at the same time. They cannot be misshelved, lost, or misplaced. While an additional level of computer error is added, the removal of most human error is enormous.

Also, they take up no physical space—and space is quite simply an asset of enormous value. Most libraries now serve a much wider variety of user needs than simply providing raw content, and these needs—from community and social gatherings, computer access, job-seeking assistance, and tutoring—all take space. The very considerable amount of space that books take up, once a nonnegotiable cost of providing access to this content, can now be reconsidered.

A recent Council on Library and Information Resources report actually explored the literal cost of keeping print books. One passage is particularly germane:

> The argument in favor of moving toward digital versions of books and sharing both electronic and print collections is further enhanced when we recognize that university libraries tend to be located on prime real estate, and that there are uses of central campus stack space—for classrooms, study, offices, and enhanced library services, among others—that would be far more valuable than using that space to store materials most of which are used rarely, provided that access to the materials in aggregate could still be provided reliably. (Courant and Nielsen 2010)

The idea that other uses of a library space might take precedence over the housing of physical collections is not an easy pill to swallow but can be seen as part of the larger continuum of valuing user needs over collections.

This passage also touches on the sad truth that in most libraries the titles that circulate represent a relatively small percentage of the collection. When space is at a premium, it is difficult to justify maintaining large, just-in-case print collections. Supporting the long tail is much easier when the content is digital and does not require a physical infrastructure and staff time for its maintenance.

EXPERIMENTS WITH MOVING AWAY FROM PRINT COLLECTIONS

Over the last decade, many libraries have begun seriously reassessing the primacy of print materials in certain areas of their collections.

Periodicals and reference texts have been particularly likely candidates for this assessment, and many print periodical collections and reference stacks have subsequently been weeded dramatically in favor of their online counterparts.

It is a much more limited number of libraries, however, that have explored what sort of spaces and services they might have if they dramatically decrease their entire print collection or even decide to go without any physical collections at all. We will be looking at four different scenarios where libraries have made this decision. Each of the profiled libraries has had a different initial set of circumstances and undertaken different approaches, but each provides a window into how a less print-focused space can serve its users.

CUSHING ACADEMY: WIPING THE SLATE CLEAN

> [T]he information within that library space became rather small relative to all the information that was available to the students and faculty.
>
> *Tom Corbett, executive director of the library, Cushing Academy (School Library Journal 2010)*

Given the furor that any weeding can provoke, what happens when a library decides to not just trim their collection but to remove the vast majority of the books from their shelves?

When Cushing Academy, a prep school in Ashburnham, Massachusetts, announced that they were drastically reducing their collection of print books, there was an outcry. A letter of protest published in *School Library Journal* was particularly emphatic, stating that "a school library's most important goals are to support the academic curriculum, to teach information literacy, and to foster a love of reading. None of these goals can be reached without printed books" (Gray and Barnett 2009).

To be accurate, the library did not remove all of their print books. They kept fiction, art books, and donated nonfiction for an overall total of approximately 5,000 remaining titles. Still, it was a drastic change for the library, and the majority of books—about 15,000—were withdrawn from the library and either distributed to departments within the school or donated to local schools and nonprofits.

After the emptied book stacks were removed, additional reference and circulation stations were added, and the library staff was increased by 25 percent to provide additional support to students navigating their collection of digital resources. In a talk dedicated to this project, Tom Corbett, the executive director of the library, explained that Cushing Academy's status as a one-laptop-per-student institution had a considerable impact on the feasibility of this project, as did Cushing's ability to provide enough e-readers in the library—now almost 200—so that hardware would not be an impediment to students' ability to access e-books.

Students and faculty are actually encouraged to request specific titles to load onto the library's e-readers, and over the last three semesters almost 1,000 titles have been purchased for this purpose. Library staff have found that students enjoyed the serendipity of browsing through the unique set of titles contained on each e-reader, and students report using the dictionary feature much more frequently in the e-reader than in the print alternative. After the initial setup cost of the devices, the library is spending roughly the same amount of money as they did for print titles while being able to more immediately fulfill patron requests.

In terms of the library space itself, Corbett commented via e-mail that

> the use of our library's physical space has changed dramatically. It's a very popular gathering space where group work and the drinking of lattes are very much encouraged. . . . We're now less concerned with providing a quiet space to accommodate users who can only do their work here since students can do their "library work" anywhere. (Tom Corbett, personal communication, 2011)

He elaborated that users that do wish to use this space for more quiet work can check out noise-canceling headphones or use one of the designated quiet study rooms but that the space is not focused around supporting quiet individual study.

The transformation of the library at Cushing was not necessitated by financial or space concerns but to instead better align the library with the perceived needs of its students and the future of reading and accessing content. Corbett's statement at the beginning of this section highlights an interesting and universal development, that a library's physical content is now but a fraction of the information that library patrons have access to, both in terms of library content and in terms of the rich amount of content made available online.

Although he has led Cushing's metamorphosis, Corbett expresses hope that "the digital lending process will be more mature and inclusive by the time most libraries move to a primarily digital approach." Even with this caveat, he commented that "once the information we provide is unbundled from a physical device I believe we could witness a true library resurgence."

STANFORD UNIVERSITY'S ENGINEERING LIBRARY: NEW BUILDING, NEW GOALS

It is about the service around the digital content as much as picking the right digital content.

Helen Josephine, head of the engineering library at
Stanford University (personal interview, 2011)

In August 2010, Stanford's new engineering library, the Frederick Emmons Terman Engineering Library, opened in the Jen-Hsun Huang School of Engineering Center.

At 6,000 square feet, this new space is just over one-third the size of the old engineering library, a space that is currently slated for demolition due to structural issues. However, in addition to housing materials from that previous, much larger space, it also houses materials previously shelved in the physics library and the math and computer sciences library. The combination of a much smaller footprint and expanded discipline coverage could have easily resulted in a cramped space, but the new space does not suffer from such a predicament. This result did not come from mere weeding, though; instead, this is the result of years of planning for this space to become, eventually, a digital materials–only space.

Helen Josephine was hired to lead the move to the new space back in 2007. No stranger to this kind of effort, Josephine previously headed a similar project for the corporate library at Intel, involving the consolidation of several libraries and the exploration of electronic alternatives for existing print collections.

Starting in the July after Josephine arrived at Stanford, print materials were shipped to an off-campus storage space in Livermore, California. As of March 2010, 36,000 monographs, 6,000 reference titles, and 8,000 dissertations had been moved into this storage space.

Currently, the new library contains approximately 20,000 print books, including commonly accessed textbooks, student theses, and dissertations. Select print titles will continue to be added to the collection, but the primary focus is on adding to the electronic collection and moving print titles to off-site storage as digital editions become available. They are currently investigating the feasibility of trying to reduce the amount of print materials by 25 percent every eighteen months.

The new library has a strong emphasis on teaching and providing support for learning about electronic resources and is staffed by four librarians and three full-time library assistants. Librarian offices are not separated out and walled off, as in the previous building, but are open to users—who are encouraged to interact with them and ask questions. The new space also has more outlets, to allow more students to bring in their laptops.

In February 2011, the library opened the Gadget Bar, which provides users with access to a number of e-readers, including the Kindle 3, Kindle DX, and Sony Reader Touch. Some e-readers are reserved for in-library use, but others are loaned for four weeks at a time, preloaded with select titles. The library hopes to add additional types of e-readers to the Gadget Bar, requesting to purchase Xooms and Nooks.

In a conversation about this new space, Josephine emphasized that a very strong digital presence is critical in order to go to a more electronically oriented collection. To this end, they were careful to do a lot of research about their users prior to opening the library to learn what resources their patrons were using and how the library's website was being utilized. She commented that the problem with having less, but still some, physical content is that users sometimes think that the physical content is all that is available to them. She elaborated that having some physical content almost distracts from the wealth of digital content.

Communication and teaching—through both the website and the in-person services—are clearly a critical part of making a space with fewer digital materials successful. Without the print collection, it is not immediately obvious what materials the space can provide. When content can be accessed outside of the physical space, then the services begin to literally define the space. In Stanford's new engineering library, the space is not a library because it has books but because it helps users find and access a wide range of materials and supports a variety of users' scholarly and intellectual needs.

THE UNIVERSITY OF TEXAS AT SAN ANTONIO'S AET LIBRARY: NEW SPACE, NO PRINT

> We decided we would prioritize services in the way that the engineers and scientists use them and that is using the digital media first and then supplementing with the physical items that are actually less used.
>
> Dr. Krisellen Maloney, dean of libraries, University
> of Texas at San Antonio (UTSA 2010)

The Applied Engineering and Technology (AET) Library is an eighty-person-capacity library located on the second floor of the University of Texas at San Antonio's new AET building. This library, which opened in September 2010, contains no print books.

The library sprang forth from a situation many libraries would envy: an academic department proactively inviting the library into their building. Indeed, both the dean of libraries and the dean of the College of Engineering were instrumental in developing the initial concepts for the space.

The two librarians who currently help staff this area—the science librarian and the engineering librarian—were also involved with the initial planning of the physical space, particularly the service desk area, which they helped configure to be a more user-centered and flexible space. Since the library has opened, they have continued to adapt the space based on user feedback. These modifications include replacing some of the original furniture—which was comfortable but provided only limited support for writing—with additional tables and chairs, a change that has proven extremely popular.

There is a strong focus on collaboration in this space, reflected in the fact that this space is not a designated quiet study area. There are three group-study areas that can be used on a first-come basis, and a minimum of two people must use the room. Ellen Lutz, the science librarian, wrote that "the most interesting thing about working in a bookless library is how quickly our students have embraced the space and really made it their own" (personal communication, 2011).

The print materials for engineering and the sciences are still housed in the main library, but there are plans to reduce the amount of print materials in that space as they increase their amount of electronic holdings. Students can request for print titles to be delivered from the main library to the AET Library, where they can then check them out.

E-books play an important role in the library, and the librarians have been focusing specifically on increasing the number of e-books that users have access to in their collections. They are in the process of rolling out an e-reader pilot to see if their users respond positively to reading science and engineering content on these readers.

According to the library's statistics, the questions asked at the service desk are similar to those asked at their other campus libraries, with the majority of questions in the directional and technical categories. They have two librarians that are available for consultations and appointments, and they also have five trained student assistants, all engineering and science majors, that staff their service desk.

The AET Library represents the unusual and desirable situation of having extra space where experiments with new models can take place. It is not a traditional space by design, and no materials needed to be weeded for its creation. Lutz had found that "the biggest opportunity with this space is that, since we don't have physical collections taking up space, we have maximized the amount of space for student use." In response to a question about what makes this space, without books, without any of the traditional accouterments of a library, a library, she replied that "[t]he services we offer define this space as a library."

UNIVERSITY OF TEXAS AT AUSTIN: REMOVING THE BOOKS AND THE DESIGNATION OF "LIBRARY"

> The library is not so much a space where books are held as where ideas are shared.
>
> *Geneva Henry, executive director of the digital library initiative at Rice University, commenting on UT's initiative (Blumenthal 2005)*

In the summer of 2005, the University of Texas at Austin removed almost 90,000 volumes from its undergraduate library. The removal of these books was estimated to provide an additional 6,000 square feet, allowing for additional computing space, a center for writing instruction, and a center for computer assistance and repair.

Five years later, the space houses these and also a liberal arts career services center, a language lab, space for the State of Texas Blind Services, the campus computer store, the ID center, and the iStudio, which is managed by UT's School of Information. But this space is now managed by the Information Technology Services division and is no longer listed as one of the campus libraries.

The former undergraduate library at the University of Texas at Austin no longer calls itself a library but supports a wide array of learning and interaction for students both with one another and with technology, including students who are in the process of earning degrees that may lead to their becoming librarians themselves.

In many ways, this space simultaneously represents the fears and the promise of removing books from a space. By removing print books, a space can be subject to a complete change in identity—and that identity may no longer match most, or even any, definition of a library. However, it can also allow an institution to realign the use of its spaces with the needs of its users.

SUMMARY

Among the libraries discussed in this chapter, the impetus for moving toward more digitally oriented spaces differed considerably. Some were prompted by either losing square footage or gaining a new space; others wanted to repurpose or reinvent the existing space. Two of these libraries removed the majority of their collections: in one case, another was created with no intention of ever adding print materials, and the other case is no longer categorized as a library at all. While there are numerous differences between them, they are all intentionally light on print materials, but far from being "bookless," they provide their users with a wide variety of book content, simply in digital form.

Of these libraries, two are science libraries at academic institutions, another is a former undergraduate library, and the other is the school library at a prestigious prep school. The libraries at Stanford and UTSA both specifically serve academic departments that are much less book-focused than most; UTSA still maintains its print collection for this population in the already existing library. The library at Cushing was able to invest what can be considered an unusual amount in e-readers and new e-content and, as a one-laptop-per-student institution, can make assumptions about technological access that few other libraries could. The University of Texas at Austin experimented with just one library space, with thirteen others remaining throughout the campus. These libraries have a significant amount of resources and serve populations that are particularly equipped and inclined to access content electronically. None of these libraries can be seen as more broadly representative of typical academic or school libraries, let alone public libraries.

While these spaces are moving away from housing print materials, Cushing is unique among them in that the books were removed entirely from the library system rather than being sent to an off-site storage facility or moved into other libraries on campus. Whether this reflects the politics of weeding books entirely from a collection, uncertainties around predicting future user needs, or distrust of digital preservation efforts are not clear. Also interesting is that while money is an enormous concern for most libraries, the libraries in these case studies did not make these changes primarily to save money. Conversely, most of them invested a considerable amount of both money and time in equipment and staff for these spaces.

Even if these libraries are not typical, that does not mean that there is nothing to be learned from their actions. Their interest in their users, their focus on providing content through alternative means, and exploring new modes of providing access are admirable and may represent the logical next stage of the more gradual move to electronic resources that many libraries are already embarking upon.

LOOKING FORWARD

For a library to remove books from its shelves is always controversial, and the more a collection is reduced, the more controversial it becomes. Yet libraries that have chosen to do so offer us some insight into where our future may take us and demonstrate that it is possible for the paring down of print collections to be part of a proactive investment in the direction of the library.

By changing the focus of our collections and our spaces to digital materials, we do risk alienating some of our users. The digital divide should not be taken lightly, and this alone means that there will still very much be a place for print texts in many modern libraries for some time to come. Likewise, there are still very real concerns about how we will be able to access, control, and preserve the electronic content we purchase for our collections. However, in continuing to define our spaces around our print collections we may be devaluing the electronic collections to which we already commit an enormous, and increasing, share of our budgets.

While there are still hurdles to cross before most libraries would, or even should, consider making drastic reductions of their print collections in favor of digital resources, ultimately it is quite promising that a space to gather, research, and ask questions is still valued even when the same content could be accessed anywhere by authorized users. Libraries are still places to focus and to learn, even as their forms and collections shift, and librarians still serve to provide context and guidance for these materials.

REFERENCES

Baker, N. 2001. "Author Says Libraries Shouldn't Abandon Paper: Interview with Jeffery R. Young." *Chronicle of Higher Education,* 47(36), A40, May 18, http://chronicle.com/article/Author-Says-Libraries/2077.

Blumenthal, R. 2005. "College Libraries Set Aside Books in a Digital Age." *New York Times,* May 14, www.nytimes.com/2005/05/14/education/14library.html.

CBS. 2011. "Newport Beach's 'Bookless Library' Plan Blows Up." *CBS Los Angeles,* March 31, http://losangeles.cbslocal.com/2011/03/31/newport-beachs-bookless-library-plan-blows-up/.

Courant, P. N., and Nielsen, M. 2010. "On the Cost of Keeping a Book." In *The Idea of Order: Transforming Research Collections for 21st Century Scholarship,* 81–105. Washington, DC: Council on Library and Information Resources.

Gray, L., Steele, C., and Barnett, C. 2009. "Letter to the Editor." *School Library Journal,* November.

Guild, R. 1885. "The College Library." *Library Journal,* 10, 216–221. Retrieved from books.google.com.

Hadro, J. 2011. "HarperCollins Puts 26 Loan Cap on E-book Circulations." *Library Journal,* February 25, www.libraryjournal.com/lj/home/889452-264/harpercollins_puts_26_loan_cap.html.csp.

Kirst, S. 2009. "Syracuse University Students Reserve the Right to Wander into a Great Read." *Post-Standard,* November 18, www.syracuse.com/kirst/index .ssf/2009/11/syracuse_university_students_r.html.

School Library Journal. 2010. "SLJ Leadership Summit 2010: One Year Later at Cushing Academy," www.schoollibraryjournal.com/slj/home/887504-312/ slj_leadership_summit_2010_one.html.csp.

Stone, B. 2009. "Amazon Erases Orwell Books from Kindle." *New York Times,* July 17, www.nytimes.com/2009/07/18/technology/companies/18amazon .html.

University of Texas at San Antonio (UTSA) Applied Engineering Technology Library. 2010. "UTSA's Aplied Engineering Technology Library," YouTube, October 26, www.youtube.com/watch?v=LaTQCB_4xt4&feature=player _embedded.

2

Do E-books Bridge the Digital Divide?

SARAH E. TWILL

It has become virtually impossible for Americans to succeed without computers and the Internet, and millions of people in the U.S., most of them low-income and disadvantaged individuals, rely on public libraries as their primary access to this essential technology.

Bill and Melinda Gates Foundation (2007)

Library services that involve the provision of information, regardless of format, technology, or method of delivery, should be made available to all library users on an equal and equitable basis.

American Library Association (1993)

Initially, the term *digital divide* referred to access to a computer and modem (U.S Department of Commerce 1998). Today, *digital divide* includes having the aforementioned, as well as access based on gender, age, socioeconomic status, race and ethnicity, literacy, disability, geography, and education (Stevenson 2009). These demographic characteristics are often interrelated and may put individuals at risk of struggling to economically and socially participate in society. As e-books are usually accessed through an Internet connection and either a computer or an e-reader, it is important to understand low-income individuals' ability to purchase these items.

Lack of access to the Internet and a computer renders advances in e-books irrelevant to this segment of the population. This chapter will discuss issues of household incomes and access to digital technology and information, implications for libraries, and how librarians and social service providers can work together to bridge the digital divide so that e-books are more accessible to all.

WHO IS POOR IN THE U.S.?

How to define income, wealth, and poverty is a complex issue debated by economists, social scientists, and the U.S. government. For the purposes of this chapter, some commonly used federal census data will be used to help readers appreciate issues related to income and poverty. To begin to discuss who is economically disadvantaged, let us first examine the median income. The real median household income in the U.S. is $49,777 (DeNavas-Walt et al. 2010). That means that half of U.S. household have incomes greater than $49,777 per year and half make less. People of color and women have lower median incomes. For example, blacks' median income is $32,584, and women's median income is $36,278.

The economic recession beginning in 2007 has impacted the incomes and lifestyles of most Americans but has been especially hard on those living below the median income, some of whom would be classified as living in poverty (DeNavas-Walt et al. 2010). Poverty guidelines are minimum annual incomes used to qualify clients for social welfare services such as Temporary Assistance for Needy Families (TANF—cash

2011 U.S. POVERTY GUIDELINES	Persons in Family	Maximum Household Income
	1	$10,890
	2	$14,710
	3	$18,530
	4	$22,350

TABLE 2.1 *2011 U.S. Poverty Guidelines*

assistance for low-income women with children, sometimes called *welfare*) or Supplemental Nutrition Assistance Program (SNAP—the former food stamps program to provide food assistance to those likely to experience food insecurity). See table 2.1 for the 2011 poverty guidelines (Federal Register 2011) and the median guidelines for comparison.

The poverty threshold is a guideline used by the Census Bureau to determine poverty rates. For practical purposes, when the poverty rate is reported, a reader can assume that the person and/or household fell below the incomes reported above. The 2010 U.S. poverty rate was 14.3 percent and represents 43.6 million people living in poverty (DeNavas-Walt et al. 2010). This is the third consecutive year in which the number of people living in poverty has increased and represents the largest number of people living in poverty in the past fifty-one years. Poverty disproportionately impacts people of color, women, and children under the age of 18.

It is also important to note that some individuals and families who are economically at risk are among the working poor. The U.S. Labor Department (2011) defines *working poor* as "persons who spent 27 weeks in the labor force (that is, working or looking for work) but whose incomes still fell below the official poverty level." The working poor often include individuals working at or slightly above the minimum wage; in addition, these workers may be employed only part-time, typically lack employer-provided health care, and may work multiple minimum wage jobs to make ends meet. An individual working full-time at the federal minimum wage ($7.25) would make approximately $15,000 a year; if this person were supporting two children, the family would still fall about $3,500 under the guidelines for a family of three (Hall 2011). Women—mostly single mothers—and people of color benefit most

TOTAL U.S. POPULATION	
Category	Income
Asians	$65,469
Whites	$54,461
Median Income	$49,777
Men	$47,127
Hispanics	$38,039
Women	$36,278
Blacks	$32,584

TABLE 2.2 *2011 U.S. Median Incomes*

from increases in the minimum wage, which today lacks the real buying value it did in the past (Filion 2010).

DIGITAL DIVIDE

In order to understand low-income individuals' access to e-books, we must first understand their access to the Internet and a computer or e-reader. Without an Internet connection to get an e-book and without a device to read it on, advances in e-books technology has little impact on low- and moderate-income households. Lack of access to e-books may become another way in which economically at-risk individuals are barred from full participation in society.

Libraries are often relied upon to help bridge the digital divide. Becker et al. (2010) examined libraries' role in providing free Internet access. Over 50,000 patrons from over 400 public libraries participated in the project. They found that low-income individuals were frequent library users (defined as visiting the library every day or most days) compared with those with more affluent incomes. Over 75 percent of all library patrons use the public computers to access digital resources during their visit. The authors concluded that low-income and working-poor patrons used library computers and the Internet by a factor of 2.68 compared with more affluent patrons.

For 22 percent of those who used technology at the library, this was their only access to a computer and the Internet (Becker et al. 2010). Some users identified having a computer and dial-up service at home but articulated that the library provided high-speed Internet. Jansen (2010) studied technology ownership and household incomes. Not surprisingly, households with annual incomes over $75,000 owned more technology devices compared with households with incomes less than $30,000. See table 2.3 for electronic ownership comparisons.

Larrison, Nackerud, Risler, and Sullivan (2002) examined how the digital divide impacted welfare recipients. TANF recipients are typically women with children who have little to no income and receive a monthly cash payment. The authors found that single mothers under the age of 25 were the least likely welfare recipients to have a home computer. Those with a high school diploma were twice as likely as those without to own

	Household income over $75,000	Household income under $30,000
Broadband Internet access	87%	40%
Desktop computer	79%	42%
MP3 player	70%	32%
E-reader	12%	3%
Cell phone	95%	75%

TABLE 2.3 *Electronic Ownership by Income*

a computer. In a related study, Larrison, Nackerud, and Risler (2001) also found that older adults on TANF—often grandparents raising grandchildren—had higher rates of computer ownership than younger TANF users and that the computer was used to help the child in their care.

Jackson et al. (2006) studied how Internet use impacted the academic performance of low-income children. The authors concluded that participants who used the Internet had higher GPAs and higher scores on standardized reading tests. The participants used the Internet an average of twenty-seven minutes per day and were more likely to use the Internet to gather information rather than engage in communication activities. Similarly, Finn et al. (2005) examined foster children and families vulnerable to the digital divide. The research project provided a computer and Internet access to the foster families. At the end of the study, foster children thought that they had increased their skills and confidence in using the computer and Internet.

Finally, Hersberger (2002) studied how families living in emergency homeless shelters perceived their access to digital information. None of the shelters in which the participants lived had Internet service. Only six of twenty-five participants had ever sought digital information. Using the Internet was seen by participants as a luxury, as the time it took to overcome transportation barriers and unfamiliarity with the technology was not worth it.

CASE EXAMPLE: CAN THE JONES FAMILY PARTICIPATE IN DIGITAL TECHNOLOGIES?

How much does it cost to participate in digital technologies? A glance at a national big-box electronic store reveals that being digital may be out of the reach of many struggling families. See table 2.4 for prices.

Device	Starting Price
Computer and monitor	$399
Laptop	$259
Software	$100
iPad	$499
Broadband	$20
Dial-up Internet	$10
E-reader	Kindle: $114 Nook: $149 Sony: $129
Smartphone (mobile device)	$100 with two-year activation

TABLE 2.4 *Prices for Technology*

Let's take a look at the Jones family's life situation and finances to determine their digital needs and their ability to purchase them. Grandma Jones is the head of household. She is 57 years old and works as a bus driver for a K–12 school district. She has held the job for two years and earns approximately $26,000 per year. She receives health care benefits from her employer.

Grandma Jones recently called her health insurance company. She wanted to change her primary care doctor and was told to go online to do so. When Grandma Jones said she did not have access to a computer or the Internet, the call representative directed her to visit the library.

Grandma Jones is a high school graduate and thinks education is important. She wants the children in her care to have a better life. One family rule is that the TV cannot be turned on until all homework is done and everyone has read something "for fun" for thirty minutes each day. Grandma Jones relies on the school and public libraries for books and Internet access. The family visits the public library at least once per week for school assignments and to use the computer and Internet.

Three people live in the apartment with Grandma Jones. Granddaughter Brandi is 19 years old and a college student. Brandi receives Stafford loans in the amount of $10,500 per year (tuition is $7,500 per year plus $800 in books and fees) and has a campus job that brings in $355 per month. Brandi is an English major and hopes to become a middle school language arts teacher. The English department received a grant to use e-readers in two courses (for more information, see Behler 2011). Brandi is enrolled in one of the identified courses and was loaned an e-reader preloaded with seven classic novels that would be assigned over the term.

Brandi has a 2001 laptop computer that she won in a school raffle. Brandi uses the laptop to write her term papers. The laptop is not connected to the Internet, nor does the family own a printer. Brandi transfers documents to a flash drive and uses the library computer labs at her university. Brandi is aware that some of the university library's reference books are available in an electronic format. However, because she does not have Internet access at home, e-books do not help her any more than a reference book that doesn't circulate. Brandi also received an e-mail from the campus bookstore regarding electronic textbook rentals. She would like to do this to save money, but again lack of Internet access or an e-reader is a barrier.

Two of Grandma Jones's nieces' children also live with her. Ty and Timone are 11-year-old twin boys who are in the fifth grade. Grandma Jones does not have legal custody of the children, nor does she receive any government benefits for their care. The children are staying with her because her niece has a substance abuse problem and is unable to care for them. Ty is a well-adjusted child who likes school, video games, and basketball. Timone has some academic and social problems. He is assigned to a special education classroom because of a learning disability. Ty and Timone have homework assignments that require them to research topics. Grandma Jones makes the boys read for thirty minutes every day so that they "get smarter." Ty is a good reader and does so willingly. However, Timone reads at the first-grade level and is embarrassed by the picture books that he is forced to use.

Because Brandi was loaned the e-reader as part of her course work, the rest of the family has become intrigued with the device. Grandma Jones has borrowed the e-reader from Brandi and likes that she can change the font size. She likes to read biographies and romances. Ty likes to read and is upset that Brandi's teacher did not assign the Percy Jackson and the Olympians series so that he could read them on the e-reader. He has tried to read one of Brandi's assigned texts but, not surprisingly, found *Emma* "boring." Timone, who struggles in school, has even shown a little interest. He like the e-reader because "the kids at school could not see what I was reading if I used it [the e-reader]. If they couldn't see what I was reading, they would not make fun of me because I can only read the 'baby books.'"

The family income for one month is $2,889 ($1,659 from Grandma Jones's paycheck, $875 in Stafford loans, and $355 for wages for Brandi's campus job). The family's budget for one month is shown in table 2.5.

Based on this budget, the family brings in $2,889 but spends $3,011, leaving a $122 shortfall each month. Their annual income is $34,668, putting them above the poverty line for a four-person household ($22,350) but well below the median income ($49,777). Like many struggling families, the Jones family may cut the food budget to save money, drive less, or make a minimum payment on a bill. They may also use a food pantry in times of need. This budget also assumes that the family avoids unexpected costs such as a car repair or a catastrophic medical emergency. Based on these factors, there is little opportunity for the family to close the digital divide at home. As such, they rely on libraries to meet their digital needs.

E-BOOKS AND ACCESS

Struggling families who are interested in e-books will likely rely on libraries to help meet their needs. E-books are becoming more available in libraries. For example, 94 percent of academic libraries, 72 percent of public libraries, and 33 percent of school libraries offer e-books (Polanka 2011). However, to access e-books, individuals need the Internet and a computer or an e-reader. Libraries have made strides in making computer terminals and Internet access available to patrons. In spite of these gains, for 22 percent of patrons who used technology at the library, the digital divide still exists as the library is their only access to a computer and the Internet

Expense	Monthly Cost
Rent	$750
Utilities (electricity, gas, and water)	$120
Cable	$30

Phone
    Land line (Grandma)
    Smartphone (Brandi)
	
	$15
	$40

Food	$550
Car payment (Brandi)	$250

Car insurance
    Grandma Jones
    Brandi
	
	$22
	$50

Gas
    Grandma Jones
    Brandi
	
	$100
	$150

Health insurance (Grandma) Medical co-pay (Grandma)	$62 $40
Tuition, books, and fees (Brandi)	$692
Charitable donation to the church	$50
Clothing, haircuts, hygiene supplies	$40
Furniture rental	$30
Life insurance (burial—Grandma)	$20

What is missing from this budget:
    Car repairs
    Medical care for all but Grandma
    Entertainment
    Gifts and holidays
    Savings	

TABLE 2.5 *Jones Family Budget*

(Becker et al. 2010). For these users, e-books are rendered irrelevant as soon as they leave the library.

In order to make e-books accessible for all patrons, libraries must provide e-readers for circulation. Today, 12 percent of academic libraries have e-readers with preloaded content available for checkout (Polanka 2011). An additional 26 percent of library respondents are considering adding e-reader circulation. School and public libraries lag behind academic libraries in offering e-reader circulation. Only 6 percent of school libraries and 5 percent of public libraries circulate preloaded e-readers. However, both school (36 percent) and public libraries (24 percent) are considering moving in the direction of e-reader circulation.

If a patron owns her own e-reader but lacks a home computer and Internet access, e-books from the library may still be inaccessible. For example, the public library of this author does not allow e-books to be downloaded on library computers due to software issues (Greene County Public Library 2011). The library specifies that in order to check out an e-book, a patron needs the following: a valid library card, Internet access, a computer or device that meets the system requirements for the type of materials to be downloaded, and free software for the computer or device on which the material will be used.

Smartphones may increase access to e-books for lower-income users. There was the least disparity between individuals with incomes over $75,000 and those with incomes under $30,000 in cell phone ownership (95 percent vs. 75 percent) (Jansen 2010). It should be noted that this research does not distinguish the type of cell phone ownership and it is impossible to identify what percentage of these cell phones are smartphones. However, in a different study, 31 percent of mobile users owned smartphones (Kellogg 2011). Smartphone ownership was also higher among people of color than it was for whites. For smartphone owners, Project Gutenberg provides over 33,000 free titles for the iPhone and the Android (Project Gutenberg 2011). While smartphone owners may have increased access to e-books, some readers will not enjoy reading a book on such a small screen. This may be especially true for academic textbooks. However, a market for e-books that are longer than a magazine article but shorter than a novel is growing in popularity and may provide some access to lower-income users with smartphones (Wortham 2011).

THE JONES FAMILY GOES TO THE LIBRARY

Grandma Jones takes the twins to the public library. She uses the computer station to access her health insurance company's website and change her primary care physician. While there, Grandma inquires about checking out an e-reader. She is told that the library circulates only e-books, not e-readers. Ty is upset, as he was looking forward to getting to try out the new e-readers. At dinner that night, Ty is complaining to Brandi about life not being fair. Brandi knows that the university library has e-readers that can be checked out.

When Brandi goes to school, she tries to check out an e-reader. She is told that the library owns only ten e-readers and that the wait is approximately six weeks. Patrons may check out the e-reader for one week. Brandi reserves one, but Ty is disappointed. At the same time, Grandma Jones calls the boys' teacher and asks if the middle school has e-readers. She is told that the school cannot afford such technology. After about a month, Brandi receives an email that the e-reader is available for pickup from the university library. She checks it out and takes it home to Ty. They learn, however, that the e-reader comes with eighteen preloaded books. The titles include *Full Dark, No Stars* by Stephen King, *Star Wars* by John Miller, and *Hands of Buddha* by Susan Cogan. While there are no Percy Jackson and the Olympians books on the e-reader, Grandma Jones is excited to read a biography or romance. The closest Grandma Jones gets to romance is *Little Women.*

Based on the case example and the availability of e-readers in the Jones family's school and public libraries, e-books are not readily accessible for the members of the family. Only Brandi had some access to an e-reader through a pilot program in the university's English department. Brandi was unable to download additional content to the e-reader, so it did not advance her opportunities to buy or rent electronic textbooks or use e-books that could be accessed from the university or public library. While Brandi's university is advanced by having an e-reader checkout program, the preloaded content may not be appealing to all patrons.

E-READER PRICING AND PATRON AFFLUENCE

E-books and e-readers are gaining in popularity. In 2010, just under 11 million e-readers were sold (Dilworth 2011). Predictions are that in 2014,

72 million will be sold. In addition to purchasing e-readers, people are buying more e-books (Bosman 2010). As a result of demand, experts predict that e-reader prices will fall from an average of $182 to $114 by 2014 (Dilworth 2011). Most recently, Amazon (2011) dropped the price of the Kindle to $114 if the owner is willing to view advertisements as part of the screen-saver feature.

In part, this price reduction may be due to greater library offerings of e-books. The *Library Journal*'s 2010 survey of e-book penetration estimates that approximately 2.5 percent of public libraries' materials budgets are being allocated to e-book purchases or subscriptions for e-books (*Library Journal* 2010). By 2015, the survey predicts, 7.4 percent of materials budgets will be dedicated to e-books. Nearly one-third of respondents thought e-book expenditures would be 10 percent or higher. However, consideration must be given to the fact that not all patrons have the ability to use e-books. In fact, libraries may be catering to affluent patrons (those with computers, Internet access, and e-readers) with the purchase of e-books. A New York City librarian commenting on Random House's library e-book lending policy said, "As our readership goes online, our materials dollars are going online" (Bosman 2011). The clash of spending priorities as libraries battle between "brick and mortar" books or "click and mortar" e-books for their collections impacts poorer patrons' access to library resources and may further exacerbate the digital divide.

For economically struggling families who have access to a computer and the Internet, e-books may be very helpful. E-books give access to patrons twenty-four hours a day. E-books eliminate the need to coordinate trips to the library, thus reducing the cost of time and travel to get there. For example, individuals living in rural communities or those who must work when the library is open may find it easier to access needed information online. Youth may no longer rely on parents to drive them to the library if they can access the reference e-book needed for a school assignment. Patrons with e-readers or smartphones who check out e-books for pleasure reading may avoid the hassle and cost associated with trips to the library. Further, late charges would be eliminated as e-books automatically vanish from e-readers on the due date.

WORKING TOGETHER TO BRIDGE
THE DIGITAL DIVIDE

Librarians and human service providers have a unique opportunity to partner to help close the digital divide for economically struggling patrons who lack access to e-resources. Librarians and social workers have similarities in their professional values and codes of ethics, which promote that individuals should be granted the access needed in order to fully participate in society (ALA 2008; National Association of Social Workers 2008). Both professional organizations have antidiscrimination policies that include issues related to economic status. In addition to the values of the professions, librarians and social workers have some similar skills (e.g., the ability to help others tackle problems, to do more with less, to engage with multiple community groups) that suit us well to work together on closing the digital divide.

There are several ways that librarians and social workers could partner to decrease the digital divide and increase access to e-books. In the short term, improving cross-training and becoming partners in technology grants may increase access for economically disadvantaged patrons. However, in order to eliminate the digital divide and make e-books and the technology needed to use them available to all, librarians and social workers must join as advocates for providing affordable home Internet service.

CROSS-TRAINING

As previously proposed, librarians and social workers have some overlapping professional values and may serve some of the same populations. Social workers often refer clients to the library in hopes that they check out books and movies or participate in other free activities. Typically, this referral occurs without a professional consultation with a librarian. Likewise, conversations with librarians reveal that there is little thought of social workers as potential partners.

There are several additional ways librarians and social workers could come together to serve digitally excluded patrons. Some communities have low-income or homeless coalitions that meet quarterly to discuss issues in the community. This might be a place for librarians and social workers to begin conversations about meeting the technology needs of those who are digitally excluded. Librarians could share information about upcoming programming, while social workers could update librarians about government e-forms (e.g., SNAP or Social Security applications) that people may be accessing at the library. If the library has an e-reader circulation program or access to e-books, librarians could help educate social workers about these offerings so that the social workers could share the information and brochures with their clients. Social workers may be able to help librarians by surveying their clients about the types of materials that they would like to see preloaded onto e-readers. Sometimes social workers recommend popular self-help titles to their clients and could advise librarians about this need.

GRANT PARTNERS

It is likely that librarians and social workers will identify gaps in services. Both librarians and social workers are often put in the position of facing budget cuts and doing more with less. As a result, they often can identify gaps in services and develop creative problem-solving skills. Librarians and social workers could search for and write grants that increase e-book access to those at risk of digital exclusion.

One funding opportunity comes to mind for school librarians and school social workers: Title I funds (money allocated to schools with approximately 40 percent of the student population on free/reduced-price lunches) are used to improve academic and school performance. There are many restrictions and regulations regarding the use of Title I funds; one requirement mandates parental involvement (for more information, see SEDL National Center for Family and Community Connection with Schools 2011). It is possible that the school librarian, school social worker, and reading intervention specialist could look into using funds to purchase e-readers to promote family reading. The new e-reader technology may be seen as more engaging than traditional books and promote family reading time.

ADVOCATES

Finally, librarians and social workers and their respective professional organizations could come together to advocate for policy changes that could help close the digital divide. Stevenson (2009) traces telecommunication policies that moved information access from the public good toward private sector interests. Initially, legislation favored providing universal Internet service that mirrored telephone service provided to all, based on subsidies to low-income and/or rural customers. However, the 1996 Telecommunications Act shifted to a policy of "universal access," which cut home subsidies for the Internet and placed the responsibility of providing Internet access on schools, libraries, and community access centers. Stevenson argues that this policy move hurt low-income individuals by making it socially acceptable to provide limited rather than full (and equal) Internet service. Likewise, in regard to the digital divide, Hick (2006) likens libraries to food pantries—they are both stopgap measures to fill an immediate need, but neither addresses the underlying issues of poverty and access. He proposes that providing computer and Internet access at locations outside one's home is a form of "technological segregation" (64).

Expanding high-speed Internet access to everyone in the country is possible; however, the majority of Americans do not see it as a priority for the federal government (Smith 2010). High-speed Internet at an affordable price is available around the world. For example, the Hong Kong Broadband Network offers a speed of 1,000 megabits a second for about $26 per month (Stross 2011). In contrast, $150 will buy U.S. consumers access at significantly slower speeds. In order to bring down cost and increase speed, the Federal Communications Commission would need to make regulatory changes.

CONCLUSION

E-books are changing the way individuals read books and the ways libraries provide them. E-books have many advantages: reducing the cost of time and travel to and from the library, being more portable than traditional books, providing e-book availability twenty-four hours a day, and allowing synching on multiple reading devices. However, for individuals and families making less than $30,000, e-books may be out of reach. If librarians, social workers, and public policy makers do not attend to access issues, e-books may widen the chasm of the already existing digital divide.

REFERENCES

Amazon. 2011. "Kindle Wireless Reading Device, Wi-Fi, Graphite, 6" Display with New E Ink Pearl Technology—Includes Special Offers & Sponsored Screensavers," www.amazon.com/Kindle-Special-Offers-Wireless-Reader/dp/ B004HFS6Z0/ref=amb_link_356007942_4?pf_rd_m=ATVPDKIKX0DER&pf_ rd_s=center-1&pf_rd_r=0E1ZJVQ205S0RY65P0MY&pf_rd_t=101&pf_rd_ p=1294309222&pf_rd_i=507846.

American Library Association. 1993. *Economic Barriers to Information Access: An Interpretation of the Library Bill of Rights,* www.ala.org/Template.cfm?Section =interpretations&Template=/ContentManagement/ContentDisplay .cfm&ContentID=76532.

―――. 2008. *Code of Ethics of the American Library Association,* www.ala.org/ ala/issuesadvocacy/proethics/codeofethics/codeethics.cfm.

Becker S., M. D. Crandall, K. E. Fisher, B. Kinney, C. Landry, and A. Rocha. 2010. *Opportunity for All: How the American Public Benefit from Internet Access at U.S. Libraries.* Bill and Melinda Gates Foundation, www.gatesfoundation .org/learning/Pages/us-libraries-report-opportunity-for-all.aspx.

Behler, A. 2011. "The Penn State University Sony E-book Reader Project." From *No Shelf Required,* Sue Polanka, ed., 88–90. Chicago: American Library Association.

Bill and Melinda Gates Foundation. 2007. "Foundation Launches New Investments to Help Public Libraries Provide Free, High-Quality Computer and Internet Service," www.gatesfoundation.org/press-releases/Pages/ library-investment-070118.aspx.

Bosman, J. 2010. "Christmas Gifts May Help E-books Take Root." *New York Times,* December 24, www.nytimes.com/2010/12/24/books/24publishing .html.

―――. 2011. "Publisher Limits Shelf Life for Library E-books." *New York Times,* March 15, www.nytimes.com/2011/03/15/business/media/15libraries .html.

DeNavas-Wall, C., B. D. Proctor, and J. C. Smith. 2010. *Income, Poverty, and Health Insurance Coverage in the United States: 2009.* (U.S. Census Bureau Publication No. P60–238). Retrieved from www.census.gov/ prod/2010pubs/p60-238.pdf.

Dilworth, D. 2011. "Global E-reader Sales Expected to Grow to $8.2 billion by 2014." *eBookNewser* (blog), *Mediabistro,* February 9, www.mediabistro.com/ ebooknewser/global-ereader-sales-expected-to-grow-to-8-2-billion-by-2014_ b5800.

Federal Register. 2011. "Annual Updates of the HHS Poverty Guidelines," www
.federalregister.gov/articles/2011/01/20/2011-1237/annual-update-of-the
-hhs-poverty-guidelines.

Filion, K. 2010. "Minimum Wage Anniversary: Still Helping Millions of Workers
Get By, but Just Barely." Economic Policy Institute, www.epi.org/analysis_
and_opinion/entry/minimum_wage_anniversary_still_helping_millions_of_
workers_get_by_but_/.

Greene County Public Library. 2011. "E-book Frequently Asked Questions,"
www.greenelibrary.info/Ebook-FAQ.html.

Hall, D. 2011. "Increasing the Minimum Wage Is Smart for Families and the
Economy." Economic Policy Institute, www.epi.org/analysis_and_opinion/
entry/increasing_the_minimum_wage_is_smart_for_families_and_the_economy.

Hersberger, J. 2002. "Are the Economically Poor Information Poor? Does the
Digital Divide Affect the Homes and Access to Information?" *Canadian
Journal of Information and Library Science,* 27(3), 48–63.

Hick, S. 2006. "Technology, Social Inclusion, and Poverty: An Exploratory
Investigation of a Community Technology Center." *Journal of Technology in
Human Services,* 24(1), 53–67, doi: 10.1300/J017v24n1_04.

Jackson, L. A., A. von Eye, F. A. Biocca, G. Barbatsis, Y. Zhao, and H. E.
Fitzgerald. 2006. "Does Home Internet Use Influence the Academic
Performance of Low-Income Children?" *Developmental Psychology,* 42(3),
429–435. doi: 10.1037/0012–1649.42.3.429.

Jansen, J. 2010. *Use of the Internet in Higher-Income Households.* Pew Research
Center, www.pewInternet.org/Reports/2010/Better-off-households/
Overview.aspx.

Kellogg, D. 2011. "Among Mobile Phone Users, Hispanics, Asians Are Most-
Likely Smartphone Owners in the U.S." *NielsenWire* (blog), February 1,
http://blog.nielsen.com/nielsenwire/consumer/among-mobile-phone-users-
hispanics-asians-are-most-likely-smartphone-owners-in-the-u-s/.

Larrison, C. R., L. Nackerud, and E. Risler. 2001. "A New Perspective on Families
That Receive Temporary Assistance for Needy Families (TANF)." *Journal of
Sociology and Social Welfare,* 28(3), 49–69.

Larrison, C. R., L. Nackerud, E. Risler, and M. Sullivan. 2002. "Welfare
Recipients and the Digital Divide: Left Out of the New Economy?" *Journal of
Technology in Human Services,* 19(4), 1–12.

Library Journal. 2010. *Survey of E-book Penetration and Use in U.S. Public Libraries.*
www.libraryjournal.com/csp/cms/sites/LJ/info/Reportpurchase.csp.

National Association of Social Workers. 2008. *Code of Ethics,* www.naswdc.org/
pubs/code/code.asp.

Polanka, S. 2011. "Library Journal Publishes Library E-book Survey Results—Sample Data Here." *No Shelf Required* (blog), February 9, www.libraries.wright.edu/noshelfrequired/?p=1914.

Project Gutenberg. 2011. "Free E-books by Project Gutenberg," www.gutenberg.org/wiki/Main_Page.

SEDL National Center for Family and Community Connection with Schools. 2011. *A Toolkit for Title I Parental Involvement,* www.sedl.org/connections/toolkit/.

Smith, A. 2010. "Home Broadband 2010." Pew Research Center, www.pewInternet.org/Reports/2010/Home-Broadband-2010/Summary-of-Findings.aspx.

Stevenson, S. 2009. "Digital Divide: A Discursive Move Away from the Real Inequalities." *Information Society, 25,* 1–22. doi: 10.1080/0972240802587539.

Stross, R. 2011. "Cheap, Ultrafast Broadband? Hong Kong Has It." *New York Times,* March 5, www.nytimes.com/2011/03/06/business/06digi.html.

U.S. Department of Commerce. 1998. *Falling through the Net II: New Data on the Digital Divide,* www.ntia.doc.gov/ntiahome/net2/falling.html.

U.S. Department of Labor. 2011. *A Profile of the Working Poor, 2009,* www.bls.gov/cps/cpswp2009.pdf.

Wortham, J. 2011. "Shorter E-books for Smaller Devices." *New York Times,* February 12, www.nytimes.com/2011/02/13/business/13ping.html.

3

Accessibility Issues in E-books and E-book Readers

KEN PETRI

I n the wake of the lawsuits over the accessibility of the Amazon Kindle DX, it was common to see, in the comments to articles and blog posts covering the litigation, statements like the following:

> Before you say "of course this was the right decision," allow me to demonstrate the absurdity of the lawsuits. The basis for the suits was that the Kindle DX was not accessible to the blind. Well, neither are the paper textbooks that the Kindle DX was replacing. Obviously we should stop using them as well (Nate the Great 2010).

The poster's comment reveals a misunderstanding over a fundamental difference between accessing a paper book and an electronic one. To make a paper book accessible to a person with a print disability, its form must be altered—it must have its spine cut off and its pages run through a high-speed scanner and optical character recognition, its digital text content must be edited and logical structure added—and only then can it be output into accessible forms: DAISY book, large print, Braille readable format, and so on. In contrast, the e-book the Kindle DX reads is (at least technically) accessible originally, without any alteration of form. E-books offer something paper books never could: the ability to be fully accessible to people with disabilities, right off the shelf.

In this chapter our focus is primarily on e-books within the context of higher education, and we will emphasize the imminent possibility of e-book accessibility. To begin, we will ask what accessibility is in relation to e-books, discuss the cost of conversion of paper books into accessible e-books, and survey the legal contexts for e-book accessibility. We will then briefly look at some of the major formats for e-books and discuss the degree of accessibility possible in each and after point to resources for current information about some of the various e-book devices and software. Finally, we offer recommendations for some of the stakeholders in e-book creation, adoption, and deployment—publishers, libraries, and software and device makers.

Overall, we want to emphasize a belief that the ultimate marker of success of digital books vis-à-vis people with print disabilities boils down to one word: *mainstream*. Emerging formats and platforms and a propitious legal atmosphere seem to be pointing toward a future in which born-digital books are universally usable—usable regardless of the reader's ability. We are nearing a time when accessible e-books are no longer a socially ghettoizing, inordinately expensive, legally fraught exception but rather represent the status quo of e-books—when the e-book that the nondisabled student buys on the first day of class is the same e-book bought by the student with a print disability, and when the market model of publishers producing and distributing accessible e-books as the norm for all of their e-book publishing coincides with ubiquitous devices and software, all of which are usable enough to accommodate any reader's needs. We are hopeful for the day when a student with a disability sits in a class holding the same device as her nondisabled classmate, both of them interacting with the text and each other fluidly, quickly, and effectively, the only differentiating factor being their individual intellectual grasp of the text.

It might be argued that accessible off-the-shelf e-books are a truly political technology, in that they may have the effect of helping erase the stigma that can accrue to people with disabilities, especially in higher education. Mainstream, accessible e-books can act to level the educational playing field and nullify any competitive disadvantages in knowledge acquisition that a person with a disability may encounter. And when students with disabilities have the same technology as their peers, difference no longer invites invidious comparisons—my peers have the same devices and the same books, the only difference is that that student's book is reading aloud to him, that student's book is highlighting the words as it reads, that student's book is set to display a larger font with higher contrast, and the like. But we are all equally provisioned; we are all "on the same page."

A caveat before beginning: the advance of technology virtually always outpaces a writer's attempt to report on it. And reporting on the technology for e-book accessibility is no exception. We are highly aware that many of the e-book formats we report on below are evolving. In fact, as of May 2011, what in our view is the most promising accessible format specification—EPUB 3—is only at the "working draft" stage and will not reach the status of "final recommendation" until midsummer at the earliest. And there is even more rapid progress—some might call it proliferation rather than progress—in e-book reader devices and software. Because of this, we limit our discussion to a short preamble mentioning some of what we deem the most prominent and up-and-coming technologies and then point to external resources that will be more up to date.

WHAT IS ACCESSIBILITY IN RELATION TO E-BOOKS?

Typically when we refer to the accessibility of an e-book we have a particular category of readers in mind—those with a print disability. A *print disability* is a learning, visual, or physical disability that makes it difficult or impossible to access print text in the standard way provided by paper books—unassisted reading and interaction with a paper text. And an accessible e-book is one that gives to a person with a print disability complete access to all the content and/or functionality of the book, without requiring that person to expend extraordinary effort.

The term *print disability* is not defined within the Americans with Disability Act (ADA) or other broad federal legislation, though many state-sponsored accessible instructional materials (AIM) initiatives and communities of practice have come up with their own definitions. For example, the Maine AIM Community of Practice defines *print disability* as "[a] condition related to blindness, visual impairment, specific learning disability or other physical condition in which the student needs an alternative or specialized format (i.e., Braille, Large Print, Audio, Digital text) in order to access and gain information from conventional printed materials" (AIM for Maine Students with Print Disabilities n.d.). The Advisory Commission on Accessible Instructional Materials in Postsecondary Education (AIM Commission) has perhaps the broadest definition of print disability—and the one that is likely to be definitive in the future (about which more later, when we discuss the AIM Commission). Its working definition reads, "A print disability means, with respect to an individual, a physical or mental impairment that substantially limits the individual in seeing or reading" (Advisory Commission on AIM 2011).

The group of people who would be considered to have a print disability include people who are blind or have other severe visual impairments, including those whose vision impairment is merely the result of aging, people with learning disabilities and other text comprehension issues, and people with injuries (temporary or permanent) or nerve disabilities who cannot hold or manipulate a print book. Taking into consideration the potential for embedded multimedia in e-books, we should probably broaden the scope of print disability—or at least our particular scope in discussing e-book access—to include people who cannot hear an embedded video or audio clip.

People with print and hearing disabilities often use so-called assistive technologies to access e-books. We cannot cover all of these in detail, but we can mention broad categories of assistive technologies that may be used with e-book readers and indicate the prominent software for each in the commercial and open source assistive technology space on Windows and Mac:

- Screen readers (e.g., JAWS, NVDA, VoiceOver): Used by people with severe visual impairments, screen readers provide complete access to all functions of the computer system via keystroke combinations and speech output. Screen reader users also benefit from audio descriptions of video and need complete transcripts of audio.
- Screen magnifiers (e.g., Windows 7 Screen Magnification, ZoomText, MAGic, Mac Zoom): Used by people with moderate to severe visual impairments, screen magnifiers enlarge a portion of the screen, attempting to minimize

distortion. Some magnifiers also have settings for increasing the foreground/background contrast of text and controls, and some have the ability to read aloud controls and selected portions of text.

- Literacy software (e.g., Kurzweil 3000, Read and Write Gold, WYNN): Used by people with learning, cognitive, and reading disabilities, literacy software typically provides many study tools, including but not limited to text-to-speech (TTS) functionality accompanied by word- and/or sentence-level synchronized highlighting, integrated dictionaries and thesauruses, and specialized note-taking, bookmarking, and text/image-highlighting tools.

- Captioning: Used by people who are deaf or hard of hearing, captioning is a synchronized text equivalent of the audio track, typically superimposed over the bottom portion of the video during playback. There are many video implementations that support captioning, and significantly with regard to the e-book space, the World Wide Web Consortium (W3C) is working on specifications for captioning HTML5 video. HTML5 video will be the de facto video implementation within EPUB 3 (more on EPUB 3, below).

- Various low mobility/strength/dexterity "alternative" pointing devices and on-screen keyboards: Used by people with upper-body mobility disabilities, these pointing devices and keyboards provide an alternative means for text input and computer interaction. Examples include head wands and mouth sticks, puff-and-sip switches, oversized trackball mice, speech recognition software, and eye-tracking systems. We might also include native computer settings such as Windows "Mouse Keys," "Sticky Keys," and "Filter Keys," which, respectively, map mouse movements to the keyboard, allow for independent pressing of keys for key combinations, and ignore accidentally repeated keystrokes.

- Speech-to-text/speech recognition (e.g., Windows 7 Speech Recognition, Dragon Dictate): Used by people with a broad range of physical and reading disabilities, speech-to-text allows for a user to dictate via voice and have the dictation appear as text. Full-blown speech recognition systems typically allow for all functionality of a computer to be operated solely by voice.

STANDARDS FOR E-BOOK ACCESSIBILITY

In 1999, the National Information Standards Organization (NISO) authored a list of features for accessible e-book reading devices. (NISO Digital Talking Books (DTB) Standards Committee 1999) Though this document is more than a decade old, its recommendations for features of e-book reader user interfaces and document navigation in some ways reveal how limited current e-book devices are. For example, the NISO DTB guidelines recommend that data tables within books be easily navigable and understandable through speech output. Even highly specialized and disability-oriented e-book readers are weak in this area.

Though the NISO guidelines have not been updated, the W3C has been working on a new version of the User Agent Accessibility Guidelines (UAAG), which became an official recommendation in 2002. The new version, UAAG 2.0, is currently in working draft status (see www.w3.org/TR/UAAG20/); it will likely supersede UAAG 1.0 and aligns closely with the W3C's other major accessibility recommendation, the Web Content Accessibility Guidelines (WCAG) 2.0. UAAG 2.0 focuses on user agents—browsers and other media players—for the Web and provides guidelines on how their interfaces should interact with users so that accessibility for people with disabilities is maximized, regardless of how the user is directly interacting with a user agent's interface or whether the user's experience is mediated by an assistive technology. The first principle of the UAAG holds that user agents should render their content according to the content's specifications rather than in an idiosyncratic manner—that is, that a web browser (or e-book reader?) should display to the user its content exactly how the content specification—the HTML specification, for instance—says it should be displayed. The first principle also states that the user agent's interface should follow accepted conventions for interaction—that is, it should behave in a way that meets with the user's expectations, having had experience with similar interfaces. The other principles outlined in the UAAG mirror WCAG, which we discuss shortly.

Thus even though there are no recently updated accessibility standards or guidelines that specifically reference e-books and e-book readers, there are accessibility standards and guidelines that apply to device/player design and to content rendering. Besides the NISO guidelines and UAAG, the two most generally applicable, well-known standards are Section 508 of the Federal Rehabilitation Act, especially Subpart C, Section 1194.31, "Functional Performance Criteria" (see www.section508.gov/index.cfm?fuseAction=stdsdoc#Functional) and WCAG 2.0 (see www.w3.org/TR/WCAG20/). Section 508 is the most prominent U.S. legal standard, whereas WCAG is the primary international standard for Web accessibility. Meeting Section 508's Functional Performance Criteria demands that a user-facing hardware or software component have at least one mode of operation and information retrieval that does not require vision; that accommodates low visual acuity; that does not require hearing and/or can amplify produced sound to compensate for poor hearing; that does not require fine motor control or simultaneous actions; and that is operable with limited reach and strength. WCAG 2.0 is organized around four broad principles:

1. Perceivable: that "information and user interface components must be presentable to users in ways they can perceive."
2. Operable: that "user interface components and navigation must be operable."
3. Understandable: that "information and the operation of user interface must be understandable."
4. Robust: that "content must be robust enough that it can be interpreted reliably by a wide variety of user agents, including assistive technologies" (W3C 2010A).

Identifying print disabilities with broad functional limitations then, accessible e-books and e-book reading devices should be able to accommodate users with:

- Total or near total visual impairments
- Low vision (moderate to profound visual impairment)
- Any form of color blindness
- Motor disabilities that prevent grasping a book or turning pages/clicking controls to manipulate book functions

- Cognitive disabilities that affect comprehension, including reading problems (e.g., dyslexia) and concentration or attention problems (e.g., ADHD)
- Hearing impairments (deaf or hard of hearing)

Taking into consideration the NISO DTB guidelines, UAAG and WCAG 2.0 principles, and Section 508 performance criteria, each of these functional limitations might be accommodated in various ways within an e-book or e-book platform. We have compiled our own listing of e-book accessibility functional considerations and attributes, elaborating on these guidelines and principles. Due to space considerations for this chapter, we have made this listing available on the Web (see "Functional Criteria for E-book Accessibility," http://wac.osu.edu/ebook-access-overview). Though the attributes required of e-books to satisfy all (or most) of the needs of (most) people with disabilities may be daunting, there are mainstream e-book reading devices and software currently available and e-book formats on the horizon that are well on the road to fulfilling most of the required and desirable functionality.

WHAT CAN E-BOOK ACCESSIBILITY COST?

National population statistics are not fine-grained enough to give us a definitive percentage of Americans with print disabilities; however, we can make a rough estimate that around 5 percent of Americans have a print disability.* If we are close in our estimate, the 5 percent figure in itself may make a compelling argument for the need to create born-digital

---

* The 2008 American Community Survey states that 2.3 percent of U.S. residents report a "visual disability," defined as being blind or having serious difficulty seeing, even when wearing glasses. This same survey states that 6.9 percent have an ambulatory disability ("serious difficulty walking or climbing stairs"), and 4.8 percent have a cognitive disability ("Because of a physical, mental, or emotional condition, does this person have serious difficulty concentrating, remembering, or making decisions?"). Census 2000 lists 2.3 percent of people 16–64 years old as having sensory disability, which is defined as "blindness, deafness, or a severe vision or hearing impairment." And 6.2 percent have a physical disability ("substantial limitation in the ability to perform basic physical activities, such as walking, climbing stairs, reaching, lifting, or carrying"). 3.8% report a mental disability ("difficulty learning, remembering, or concentrating") (Cornell University n.d.). To arrive at our 5 percent estimate, we take the two sets of figures, average and round down, and then take one-third of the amount, to account for the severity of the disabilities. This figure may be low: the slogan of the advocacy organization Reading Rights Coalition is, "We represent 30 million Americans who cannot read print"—that works out to roughly 10 percent of Americans.

accessible e-books. The percentage comes into more stark relief, though, if we examine the costs incurred to provide accessible e-books to postsecondary students. Production of alternative text materials for students with print disabilities cost nearly $130,000 in student and staff labor for the Ohio State University (OSU) Office for Disability Services (ODS) during the 2010 summer and fall quarters. During this period, approximately 1,000 course-related materials were converted. The office incurred $10,000 for books that had to be destroyed for document scanning and optical character recognition in order to be converted. This comes to an average $140 per item. Books, however, take significantly more effort to convert than articles and shorter materials. So it is safe to estimate a minimum average cost of conversion of $400 per book. This number will be lower for novels and other books without complex layouts or graphics. And the number is far higher for books in the science, technology, engineering, and mathematics (STEM) disciplines, which include math and other scientific notation. Of STEM books, the average during the same period was nearly $1,900 per book (OSU ODS, personal communication).

This direct cost figure becomes more compelling, however, when we take into consideration the number of students served. The OSU Office for Disability Services regularly has registered around 1,500 students per quarter. Of those, only a small fraction qualify for alternative print materials—somewhere around forty students per quarter, or eighty students served in the two quarters we are discussing. Using the rounded figure of 250 books at $400 per book and dividing that into the eighty students served, we have a half-year cost per student of $1,250—which translates into an extra $2,500 per student with a print disability per year that must be absorbed by the university. Ultimately, these funds must come from somewhere—state or federal subsidies, or grants, or the pockets of students in the form of tuition hikes. The roughly $200,000 a year that the Office for Disability Services spends solely on textbook conversions could not be completely recovered: accessible e-books cannot deliver all forms of content, there will still be need for Braille for highly complex or intricate math and for music, and there is currently no replacement for tactile graphics for certain applications. Nevertheless, born-digital, from-the-publisher, fully accessible e-books would be able to save significant money and would free up time for alternative media personnel to accommodate an even broader segment of requests more proficiently.

LEGAL CONTEXTS FOR E-BOOK READER ACCESSIBILITY, WITH A FOCUS ON HIGHER EDUCATION

Under the 2004 reauthorization of the Individuals with Disabilities Education Act (IDEA)—federal law that governs how states provide special education, early intervention, and related services for K–12 students with disabilities—legislation was issued that required all state education agencies (SEAs, the entities that oversee education of students through secondary school) to adopt the National Instructional Materials Accessibility Standard (NIMAS) and thereby provide access for students with documented print disabilities to accessible electronic text versions of SEA-adopted textbooks. Since SEAs are required to comply with IDEA and require the textbook publishers they deal with to submit NIMAS files of all approved textbooks as part of their contracts, K–12 textbook publishers have well-honed mechanisms for producing these accessible digital formats. There is also a centralized repository to which publishers can submit NIMAS-conforming file sets. State and local education agencies are encouraged to use this repository. Thus students in K–12 education who have print disabilities that are covered under either IDEA or the more liberal benchmarks of Section 504 of the Federal Rehabilitation Act can expect accessible educational materials in a timely manner.

Students in postsecondary education are not covered under IDEA, and thus there is no requirement that textbooks have readily available accessible versions. However, postsecondary students with disabilities are covered under Section 504 of the Federal Rehabilitation Act and ADA Title II. Section 504 applies to all colleges and universities that take any amount of funding from the federal government. ADA Title II applies to public entities, including all publicly funded postsecondary institutions. Taken together, 504 and ADA Title II cover virtually all U.S. universities and colleges. ADA and 504 are broad civil rights laws that make it illegal to discriminate on the basis of disability. They require that students with disabilities get benefits and services comparable to those enjoyed by nondisabled students and make it illegal to provide an unequal or lower-quality benefit or program. In addition, these laws require that benefits, services, and programs must be "equally effective" for students with disabilities (National Center on Accessible Instructional Materials n.d.; Peer Project 1999).

Regardless of this very high bar of "equally effective," there is no comparable pressure on publishers serving the higher education market to provide richly structured text formats that are originally accessible or that are readily convertible to accessible formats. Publishers of materials for postsecondary education—or higher education imprints within larger publishing houses—thus have not had to adopt methods of production that put as acute an emphasis on accessibility as those serving the K–12 space. Likewise, e-book device and software vendors have been able to back-burner accessible solutions, and higher education institutions have not had to consider institution-wide adoption of accessible electronic textbooks.

Institutions of higher education rely primarily on their disability services (DS) offices to produce accessible electronic versions of textbooks. In doing these conversions, such offices are in a sort of legal hinterland. The well-known Chafee amendment adds a section to chapter 1 of title 17 of the United States Code on copyright (National Library Service 1996). The amendment allows designated "authorized entities" to distribute accessible copies of books to blind people and people with other organic disabilities affecting reading. Problematic is the provision that requires a "physical disability" certified by medical or licensed therapeutic professionals. This can be a limitation in cases where it may be clear to a counselor in a DS office that a student needs an accessible book, but one cannot be provided under law. The National Library Service, Bookshare, APH, and Learning Ally (formerly Reading for the Blind and Dyslexic) are all recognized authorized entities, which are exempt from copyright when they make accessible versions of copyright-protected books (Wikipedia n.d.). These entities are also allowed legally to circumvent digital rights management (DRM)–protected books. In most circumstances, including for fair use, it is illegal to break DRM. The exception is for use by people with documented print disabilities. In this case an authorized entity can circumvent DRM. But as we noted, disability services offices are not considered authorized entities. So although these offices regularly convert materials to accessible versions, there is no clear support of this under law, and the Association of American Publishers (AAP) in 2004 proffered that disability services office conversions were not covered under Chafee. By contrast, the Association on Higher Education and Disability's (AHEAD) position is that such conversion is covered under both fair use and Chafee, and AHEAD cites a

Department of Education Office for Civil Rights ruling supporting that position (Association on Higher Education and Disability 2006).

In any regard, the situation is vexed, and the legal status for conversion to accessible e-text by postsecondary institutions is not entirely clear. Thus it remains that currently the most unequivocally aboveboard means for getting an accessible version of an e-book is through the publisher directly, making it accessible at the point of publication and licensed distribution. However much advocates would like to force the situation, it appears that copyright may trump creation of universally accessible e-books—at least until publishers willingly submit and come to the understanding that accessibility is no threat to the revenues copyright is designed to protect.

Recently, however, a series of lawsuits against colleges and universities is likely to dramatically alter the approach to accessibility taken by e-book publishers, device makers, and software vendors who are serving or would like to serve the higher education market. In fact, these suits have already had significant impact. We are referring, of course, to the legal activity surrounding the Kindle DX pilots launched at a number of U.S. colleges and universities. The controversy over the Kindle actually predates the higher education suits. In 2009, right after the release of the Kindle 2, which had the ability initially to voice the contents of any book, the Authors Guild raised objections that self-voicing was a violation of copyright because it constituted a public performance that diminished the value of audio performances of a book. As the then president of the Authors Guild, Roy Blount Jr., wrote in an op-ed in the *New York Times,* the Authors Guild held "that authors have a right to a fair share of the value that audio adds to Kindle 2's version of books" (Blount 2009). Amazon backpedaled and gave the publisher/copyright holder the ability to choose to enable text-to-speech, at the same time claiming nevertheless that Amazon believed "Kindle 2's experimental text-to-speech feature is legal: no copy is made, no derivative work is created, and no performance is being given" (Stone 2009).

In March 2009, disability rights groups, including the National Federation of the Blind (NFB) and the International Dyslexia Association, sent a letter to publishers HarperCollins, Penguin, Random House, and Simon & Schuster saying, "Should the publishing industry and Amazon accede to the Authors Guild's stance and deny persons with disabilities the service of mobile access to e-books it offers to the public, they will be at risk of violating state civil rights laws that guarantee equal access to persons with disabilities, including the Massachusetts Equal Rights Act, California's Unruh Act, the New Jersey Law Against Discrimination, and the Kentucky Civil Rights Act" (Engleman 2009). The Reading Rights Coalition also published a press release urging authors to allow accessible e-books (Reading Rights Coalition 2009).

In June 2009, the NFB and the American Council of the Blind (ACB) filed suit against Arizona State University in order to prevent deployment of the Kindle DX for use as a means of distributing electronic textbooks at the school. The complaint noted that, though books could be read aloud using built-in text-to-speech, there was no way for a blind user to activate this functionality without help from a sighted person because none of the device's menus were voiced, preventing any access to the advanced reading features of the DX. At the same time NFB and ACB filed complaints with the Office for Civil Rights (OCR) of the Department of Education and the Civil Rights Division of the Department of Justice (DOJ) against five colleges and universities for piloting the DX (National Federation of the Blind 2009). ASU settled with ACB and NFB in January 2010. As part of the settlement, ASU agreed that in any future deployments of e-book readers it would "strive to use devices that are accessible to the blind" (National Federation of the Blind 2010). Later that month, the Department of Justice reached settlements with three of the other schools. The agreements hold that the schools will "not purchase, recommend or promote use of the Kindle DX, or any other dedicated electronic book reader, unless the devices are fully accessible to students who are blind and have low vision. The universities agree that if they use dedicated electronic book readers, they will ensure that students with vision disabilities are able to access and acquire the same materials and information, engage in the same interactions, and enjoy the same services as sighted students with substantially equivalent ease of use" (Department of Justice 2010). In the summer of 2010, just three days after the twentieth anniversary of the ADA, on June 29, the OCR and the DOJ released an open "Joint 'Dear Colleague' Letter: Electronic Book Readers." That letter states that "requiring use of an emerging technology in a classroom environment when the technology is inaccessible to an entire population of individuals with disabilities—individuals with visual disabilities—is discrimination prohibited by the Americans with Disabilities Act of 1990 (ADA) and Section 504 of the Rehabilitation Act of

1973 (Section 504) unless those individuals are provided accommodations or modifications that permit them to receive all the educational benefits provided by the technology in an equally effective and equally integrated manner" (USDOJ and USDOE 2010). Taken together, the settlement letters and the Dear Colleague letter set a very high bar for providing accessible e-books and e-book readers within higher education institutions.

In March 2010, in the time between the settlement of the Kindle suits and the Dear Colleague letter, the print disability advocacy group the Reading Rights Coalition signed a joint statement with the AAP and the Authors Guild, both of which had previously taken strong stands against text-to-speech in e-books. The AAP and the Authors Guild had apparently reversed their position, saying they "believe that the contents of books should be as accessible to individuals with print disabilities as they are to everyone else," and arguing that "[to] that end, these groups agree to work together and through the communities they represent to ensure that when the marketplace offers alternative formats to print books . . . print-disabled consumers can access the contents of these alternative formats to the same extent as all other consumers." In other words, the Reading Rights Coalition joint statement endorses a market model for accessible books, in which e-books are born-accessible from the publisher and are immediately available to accessible e-book readers and devices (Reading Rights Coalition 2010).

The activities of the U.S. Department of Education's Advisory Commission on Accessible Instructional Materials in Postsecondary Education for Students with Disabilities (AIM Commission) seek to provide best practices and recommendations on a legal framework that would guarantee that the sentiments expressed in the Reading Rights Coalition joint statement have weight as part of U.S. policy and law, at least within the postsecondary marketplace. The AIM Commission was established by the Higher Education Opportunity Act of 2008 "to study the current state of accessible materials for students with disabilities in postsecondary education and make recommendations" in a report to Congress "to improve the quality and abundance of accessible instructional materials." Their work involves holding regular meetings, doing primary research, inviting experts and students to give testimony, and drafting recommendations on law and best practices for delivery of accessible instructional materials. Their meetings and the testimony is streamed live to the Web and archived as a public record. In the end, the commission's report to Congress will identify best practices for achieving readily available accessible materials for students with print disabilities at costs comparable to materials for nondisabled students. The commission also will make recommendations on how to "modify the legal definitions of 'instructional materials,' 'authorized entities,' and 'eligible students' to improve services to students with disabilities," while maintaining compliance with copyright (USDOE n.d.).

So, whereas only a few years ago it seemed that the possibility of ubiquitous accessible e-books was scant due to possible copyright issues and publisher pushback, the Kindle cases and the forward-thinking activities of advocates both private and governmental, sometimes in allegiance with publishers, have radically altered the landscape. It now appears likely that publishers will move toward producing accessible e-books as a primary format—some, like O'Reilly, which distributes its e-books in bundles of multiple DRM-free formats, including DAISY, have already demonstrated a clear commitment (Savikas 2010)—and there is some momentum toward enabling text-to-speech for native playback within e-readers (that is, without the assistance of screen readers). Many major publishers still disable text-to-speech—as of May 2011, Doubleday, Hachette, Knopf, Little Brown, Penguin Press, Putnam, Random House, and Vintage typically disallow it. But some, fortunately including education publishers such as McGraw-Hill and Pearson, are enabling text-to-speech.

There is even further momentum at an international level. At the end of April 2011, EDItEUR, an organization of more than ninety members from seventeen countries coordinating standards for e-books and e-book and electronic serial commerce, released "Accessible Publishing: Best Practice Guidelines for Publishers," in partnership with the DAISY Consortium and funded by the World Intellectual Property Organization. The guidelines encourage all publishers to enable text-to-speech and publish in well-structured, accessible e-book formats, including DAISY and EPUB (EDItEUR 2011).

THE PROMISE OF (CERTAIN) FORMATS

In the previous sections we have discussed some aspects of the cost and legal contexts for accessible e-books. Before offering potential approaches for the future for various stakeholders in e-book accessibility—namely libraries, publishers, disability services offices, and software and device makers—it makes sense to survey quickly the current state of the art in e-book formats and e-book reading software and hardware.

PDF

As of May 2011, the International Association for Information and Image Management is nearing completion of the specification of PDF/UA (universal accessibility), which will become an ISO standard. PDF/UA is a subset of the PDF specification, which establishes guidelines that define what PDF components can be included and how they must be implemented in order to maintain document accessibility (see www.aiim.org/Resources/Standards/Committees/PDFUA).

To be minimally accessible, PDF must contain actual text rather than merely images, and that text must be tagged. The tag layer of the PDF provides semantics for the textual content, and it is the tags layer that screen readers and other assistive technologies navigate. Most major desktop publishing software can produce tagged PDF. However, the quality of the tag structures that is exported from these software packages varies widely, and it is advisable to perform manual checks on tagged PDFs. PDF is accessible in a number of e-book readers; however, the richest experience for a screen reader user is probably via access through Adobe Acrobat Reader or Acrobat Professional, which can provide some orientation for the screen reader user even in relatively difficult structures, such as tables.

PDF maintains fidelity in appearance to the printed original. This and the fact that PDF can be opened and viewed on virtually all devices account for its popularity. But PDF can also be set to "reflow," which linearizes the text contents so that users with low vision or who prefer a simplified view have better access.

MOBI/AZW

Kindle on all platforms—PC/Mac and mobile devices and on the Kindle device itself—supports MOBI format books. AZW is Amazon's DRM format. AZW is merely MOBI that has been processed for DRM.

MOBI is a simple book structure. It is a very basic implementation of EPUB, in which an open publication format (OPF) XML file contains pointers to multiple HTML files, which contain the book content. The OPF file also stores metadata about the book—title, publisher, cover location, and so on. MOBI does not contain very much semantic structure, though it does support basic data tables and adding text alternatives to images. As a result of the paucity of structure, the primary mode of getting around within a Kindle e-book is via the table of contents or by skimming though pages, which, of course, doesn't provide very fine-grain navigation.

A long-standing complaint leveled against Kindle devices and software is that books had no page-number equivalents to the print versions. Kindle devices and software register progress within the book by "location" ranges. Recently, however, Amazon has begun mapping pages into Kindle e-books.

MOBI and AZW are very important formats for e-book accessibility, especially considering the size of the Kindle bookstore (900,000-plus books, much larger than authorized entities such as Bookshare, Learning Ally, and APH combined). Add to this the fact that there is some amount of accessibility within the Kindle device and significant accessibility within the laptop-installed Kindle for PC with Accessibility Plugin. Due to the lack of rich semantic and logical structure, however, it is unlikely that accessible e-readers for MOBI and AZW will have a facility of navigation and orientation similar to what is achievable in other formats, such as DAISY and EPUB.

From DAISY to EPUB 3

First published in 1996 and now in its third version, DAISY has long been considered the gold standard for accessible e-book formats. DAISY stands for *Digital Accessible Information System* and is interchangeably referred to as a digital talking book, or DTB. The DAISY specification is maintained by the DAISY Consortium and is an official NISO standard. NIMAS files are an implementation of DAISY. A DAISY book is distributed as a single compressed (zipped) package and consists minimally of a package file (.opf), which contains a manifest of the book contents, metadata about the book, and a "spine" (the default reading order of the files); one or more content files, which are semantically structured XML files that conform to the DTB document type definition; and a Navigation Control File (.ncx), which is the book's detailed table of contents organized hierarchically and which allows e-book readers and assistive technologies to navigate effectively within DAISY books. This semantically rich book structure provides a strong scaffolding for effective text-to-speech and Braille output. And the DTB documents can contain a range of semantic markup, including MathML. In addition, with DAISY it is possible to synchronize prerecorded audio with book contents and package that audio with the book. This facility allows for humans to voice a book and still have sentence-by-sentence playback with highlighting as content is voiced. Some users prefer voice recordings over synthetic speech. It also makes it possible to package very high-quality synthetic voices with books to account for the possibility that the consumer may not have an adequate synthetic voice installed on his computer. Synchronization of prerecorded audio and text is handled by files that align text sentences within the DTB contents with their recorded equivalents.

Over the last two years, key members of the DAISY Consortium—along with people from the digital publishing industry—have been participating in the evolution of the EPUB e-book format. EPUB is considered the international standard for distribution of e-books. The current EPUB specification (version 2.0.1) is generally accessible by e-book readers. Apple's iBooks on iOS devices, for example, consumes EPUB books, and when read using the iOS native screen reader, VoiceOver, a user with disabilities has quite good TTS access to book contents. EPUB, however, does not have the rich structure and semantics of DAISY, nor does it support synchronized prerecorded audio—that is, until now.* The emerging EPUB 3 specification "coincides" with DAISY, incorporating many features of DAISY—albeit in a different form internally—including DAISY's rich navigation structure and its ability to synchronize pre-recorded audio with book text (via what are called "media overlays," in the EPUB 3 spec).

It is unclear whether DAISY will continue to evolve as an independent specification. In fact, with the advent of EPUB 3, it may be that DAISY will become a legacy format, maintained for purposes of backward

---

* EPUB 3 adopts a major subset of the W3C HTML5 syntax and semantics. It will support rich layout and styling, borrowing much of Cascading Style Sheets (CSS) 2 and 3. And it will support embedded multimedia and scripting of interactivity. It also supports in-line MathML for accessible math, and SVG, a graphics specification that allows, among other things, for the ability to enlarge graphics without loss of clarity. See http://idpf.org/epub/30/spec/ for more detail.

compatibility with current DAISY-capable software and devices.* Or, more likely, version 4 of DAISY may continue as primarily an authoring and interchange format, with EPUB as the target distribution format (DAISY Planet 2010). What is clear, though, is that EPUB 3 will emerge incorporating all of the functionality and semantics of DAISY (plus much more!). The accessibility impact of EPUB 3 should not be underestimated. It represents the merger of the dominant, international, mainstream e-book format (EPUB) with the dominant specialized accessibility format (DAISY) and offers improvements to both. If we had to place a bet on what will (very soon!) become the de facto accessible e-book format, we would double-down on EPUB 3.

A NOTE ON THE ACCESSIBILITY OF E-BOOK READING PLATFORMS

As indicated in the introduction to this chapter, rather than catalog mainstream e-book hardware and software, we have opted to point to an external resource, which can be kept more current. We have compiled a "Survey of Common E-book Reader Accessibility" (see http://wac.osu .edu/resources/ebook-access-overview/) to meet this need. The listing is intentionally nonexhaustive, instead opting to concentrate on commonly available, relatively mainstream software and devices. Another good place to track the evolving landscape of e-book reading platforms is the Diagram Center's Product Matrices (http://diagramcenter.org/ index.php?option=com_content&view=article&id=24&Itemid=28), which attempts to provide up-to-date information on the accessibility of a wide range of e-book software and devices. One thing immediately obvious from the list of mainstream e-book devices is how few are accessible. At the time of this writing, only the iPad and the Kindle are considered to

---

* The EPUB 3 changes document suggests the end of DAISY as an independent, evolving specification. In particular, we read, "DAISY DTBook . . . was an alternative syntax to XHTML1.1 for Content Documents . . . in order to provide an option for more semantic, and thus more accessible, content. As HTML5 includes intrinsic semantic markup capabilities of a similar nature to DTBook, DTBook is no longer an alternative syntax in EPUB 3" (see http://idpf.org/epub/30/spec/epub30-changes.html#sec -removals-dtbook). In literal terms, this quotation indicates that EPUB 3's internal content structure will not incorporate DTBook because HTML5 provides all the necessary semantics for equivalent (or better) accessibility. With the addition of EPUB 3 Media Overlays, the utility of DAISY as an independent accessibility-oriented specification is radically diminished.

have any level of accessibility. The iPad is "reasonably" accessible, while the Kindle 3 qualifies as "somewhat" accessible. The software landscape is considerably better. There are quite a few software e-book readers with respectable and continually improving accessibility; for instance, K-NFB's Blio Reader, Amazon's Kindle for PC with Accessibility Plugin, and iBooks for EPUB or PDF formatted books. On the textbook side VitalSource/ CourseSmart Bookshelf and Inkling for iPad provide decent accessibility, and most recently Barnes & Noble released a new version of NookStudy, which takes significant strides toward accessibility.

Finally, though it is not always a very reliable benchmark, when considering adoption of an e-book reading technology entities should request the vendor's VPAT (voluntary product accessibility template). The VPAT benchmarks the technology's levels of accessibility against Section 508 guidelines. VPATs can be problematic because they are voluntarily produced by the vendor itself and typically not verified independently for accuracy. Nevertheless, review of a VPAT both can indicate what the vendor believes is its own level of compliance and can sometimes reveal clues about the vendor's knowledge of what accessibility means regarding a particular product.

APPROACHES FOR STAKEHOLDERS

In this final section, we want to offer some advice and possible direction for various stakeholders who have concern over e-book accessibility. Specifically, how might each stakeholder act currently and in the future to help ensure e-books are accessible to people with disabilities?

Libraries and Alternative Media Production Units

Libraries are well positioned to influence adoption of e-books and e-book readers, and they can act to effect change at many levels. As libraries are major consumers of reading technologies, they can drive change through purchasing decisions and implement internal e-book initiatives that purchase and support known-accessible platforms. To improve the visibility of accessibility issues and the availability of accessible facilities, libraries can install and maintain complementary assistive technologies on library public workstations and provide easy and obvious access to these technologies. Minimally, library workstations should have one commercial screen reader or comparable free and open source screen reader; a text-to-speech-capable screen magnifying program; a literacy software package; and an accessible e-book reading software package, preferably one that is capable of reading math content—in addition to known-accessible nondisability-specific e-book reading software. College and university libraries should also consider partnering with their campus disability services office's alternative media production unit to jointly develop best practices for creation of accessible texts, focusing on leading, mainstream formats such as PDF/UA and EPUB 3. Library e-reserves should establish policies on submission of e-reserve materials to ensure that instructors communicate what they want in e-reserves within a time window that allows for accessibility verification and remediation, if necessary, of all hosted e-reserve materials. In all of this, we believe the most important point of a partnership between disability services alternative media production units and libraries is the push for library standards for distribution and access that are universally usable. That is, the goal should not be for a partnership that merely makes certain texts accessible out of necessity—because there is a student or small group of students who require such materials—but rather that works toward institution-wide accepted production (electronic reserves and in-house conversions or publications) and purchase of e-text/e-books that serve the widest possible user base.

Publishers

First, we believe publishers should enable text-to-speech in all e-books. Such a move has long-standing and broad support. When Amazon backed off of universal text-to-speech in Kindle in 2009 and allowed publishers to set text-to-speech rights, it began its announcement with the following: Kindle's "text-to-speech feature is legal: no copy is made, no derivative work is created, and no performance is being given. Furthermore, we ourselves are a major participant in the professionally narrated audiobooks business through our subsidiaries Audible and Brilliance. We believe text-to-speech will introduce new customers to the convenience of listening to books and thereby grow the professionally narrated audiobooks business" (Stone 2009). As referenced above in the section on legal contexts, in March 2010, the Reading Rights Coalition, the Authors Guild, and the Association of American Publishers authored a joint statement that announced their belief that publishers should ensure that readers with print disabilities can access the contents of e-books "to the same extent as all other consumers" (Reading Rights Coalition 2010). Also, as we mentioned above, in May 2011, EDItEUR, the European book trade standards body, argued for enabling text-to-speech in all e-books, in its "Accessible Publishing: Best Practice Guidelines for Publishers."

One concern about allowing accessible books to be converted is that DRM, at least currently in the U.S., can be subverted. Publishers fear that having "open" accessible books in circulation will lead to piracy. But one of the reasons such conversions have to occur is that the DRM'ed book is either not accessible natively or has text-to-speech disabled. If publishers enable text-to-speech, it necessarily gives them more control over circulation, because one motivation for conversion is removed. To complete this cycle, publishers also ought to be targeting accessible formats—EPUB 3 in particular. To this end, we believe publishers should move toward standardization on accessible formats for e-book production and engage in the standards processes by participating in appropriate standards bodies. With regard to accessible formats, publishers should ensure that e-books have the following:

- Ability to adapt to user style preferences, such as enlarging text and enhanced contrast
- Navigable structure, including a hierarchically structured table of contents, an index comprised of links to locations in the document, and heading structure and other sectional elements
- Well-marked-up tables
- In-line note and source citations that link to their references in an accessible manner
- In-line pagination so that page numbering is maintained when books are "reflowed" to accommodate users increasing font size or making other style changes
- Indication of language changes, for example, using the "lang" attribute globally and also in-line on text that is in a language other than the document's main language

- Logical reading order, for example, by not interrupting the reading order by splitting a logical unit, such as a sentence or paragraph, by a sidebar, pull quote, or interruptive page break
- Alternative text for informational images and graphs; in addition, publishers should supply content providers with guidelines on how to author useful alternative text
- Encoding for math within books into MathML (or combine images plus alternative descriptions with MathML), thereby facilitating access not only for visually impaired readers and readers with various cognitive and reading disabilities but also simplifying math access for all readers

Software and Device Makers

There are some truly wonderful accessible e-book readers for Windows, Mac, and the iPad/iPhone, and as awareness increases among developers, vendors, and consumers, and the legal environment evolves toward more refined and precise understandings of what accessibility is in relation to e-books, we can expect currently accessible e-book readers to enrich their feature sets and simplify functionality, as more universally usable e-book devices and software solutions emerge. To realize this, we encourage software and device makers to integrate accessibility concerns in all stages of design—from product concept through requirements, functional and technical specifications, development, and quality assurance. The goal should be to create devices that expose all their functionality to all users, regardless of the user's ability or mode of interaction with the device. To help make sure that makers "get it right," we encourage frequent involvement of people with disabilities, in both the discovery and product testing phases. Makers should consider creating internal functionality standards, perhaps along the lines of those referenced earlier in this chapter, and shepherd these through the entire design process. Finally, we encourage makers to get involved in standards bodies and national and international standardization activities that center on software and device accessibility. IBM, Apple, Microsoft, and Google already have representatives participating in accessibility standards processes, and this should serve as inspiration to smaller and specialized makers to participate.

CONCLUSION

Though this chapter has focused on e-book use by users with disabilities, we agree with the authors of the UAAG that "all users, not just users with disabilities, should find conforming user agents to be more usable." All of us will find accessible e-books and e-book readers to be simply a better reading experience (W3C 2010B). Academics working within disability studies often point out that we are all just temporarily able-bodied and that we will, at some point in our lives, have firsthand experience with disability. But as the UAAG authors suggest, accessibility reaches beyond disability accommodation and has far-reaching benefits for people everywhere. For example, someone trying to learn another language benefits from a book that highlights the words as it reads them aloud, or a book that contains video subtitled in the reader's native language; a commuter in the car or on her bike benefits from "reading" a book by listening as it reads itself aloud; a vacationer who forgot his glasses benefits from a book that can simply increase the size and contrast of the e-reader's text; a student benefits from a book that can jump between content sections, charts, and figures. These sorts of interactions should be in all e-books—and should be commonplace and expected.

Because of cost savings for education and the need to satisfy legal and policy requirements, there is already significant pressure on e-book publishers and device makers to move toward accessibility. And as we pointed out, there are copyright protection advantages for publishers creating born-digital accessible e-books. When we add to this the advantages of accessible e-books in terms of general and broad usability, we are hopeful that the rationale overwhelms the opposition and that the reality of mainstream accessible e-books looks increasingly inevitable.

REFERENCES

Accessible Instructional Materials for Maine Students with Print Disabilities. N.d. What Is a Print Disability?", http://aim.mainecite.org/print_disability.

Advisory Commission on Accessible Instructional Materials in Postsecondary Education for Students with Disabilities. 2011. *Taskforce 1 (Best Practices), Discussion of the Definition of Print Disability,* March 31.

Association on Higher Education and Disability. 2006. "Position Statement: AHEAD's Perspective on the Issues of Textbook Access," December, http://ahead.org/resources/e-text/position-statement.

Blount, Roy, Jr. 2009. "The Kindle Swindle?" *New York Times,* February 24, www.nytimes.com/2009/02/25/opinion/25blount.html.

Cornell University. N.d. *Disability Statistics: Online Resource for U.S. Disability Statistics,* www.ilr.cornell.edu/edi/disabilitystatistics/.

DAISY Planet. 2010. "DAISY = Accessibility, Will EPUB3 = Accessibility? Part 1," *DAISY Consortium Newsletter,* November, www.daisy.org/planet-2010 -11#a2.

Department of Justice. 2010. "Justice Department Reaches Three Settlements under the Americans with Disabilities Act Regarding the Use of Electronic Book Readers," January 13, www.justice.gov/opa/pr/2010/January/10-crt -030.html.

EDItEUR. 2011. "Accessible Publishing: Best Practice Guidelines for Publishers," April, www.editeur.org/files/Collaborations/Accessibility/WIPO.html.

Engleman, Eric. 2009. "Disability Groups Demand Full Return of Kindle's Text-to-Speech." *Amazon Blog,* March 20, www.techflash.com/seattle/2009/03/ Disability_groups_demand_full_return_of_Kindles_text-to-speech_41583262 .html.

Nate the Great. 2010. MobileRead Forums, January 10, www.mobileread.com/ forums/showthread.php?t=69673.

National Center on Accessible Instructional Materials. N.d. "Accessible Instructional Materials and the Section 504 Plan," http://aim.cast.org/ learn/policy/federal/504_plan.

————. 2009. "National Federation of the Blind and American Council of the Blind File Discrimination Suit against Arizona State University," June 25, www.nfb.org/nfb/NewsBot.asp?MODE=VIEW&ID=449.

National Federation of the Blind. 2010. "Blindness Organizations and Arizona State University Resolve Litigation over Kindle," January 11, www.nfb.org/ nfb/NewsBot.asp?MODE=VIEW&ID=527.

National Library Service. 1996. "Copyright Law Amendment, 1996," www.loc .gov/nls/reference/factsheets/copyright.html.

NISO Digital Talking Books Standards Committee. 1999. "Playback Device Guidelines: Prioritized List of Features for Digital Talking Book Playback Devices." *NLS: That All May Read: NISO Working Papers: Digital Talking Book Standard,* December 30, www.loc.gov/nls/z3986/background/features.htm.

Peer Project. 1999. "Section 504, the Americans with Disabilities Act, and Education Reform," last revised March 2, 2008, www.wrightslaw.com/info/section504.ada.peer.htm.

———. 2009. "Reading Rights Coalition Urges Authors to Allow Everyone Access to E-books," March 30, www.readingrights.org/134.

Reading Rights Coalition. 2010. "Joint Statement on Access to Books by Americans with Print Disabilities," March 29, www.readingrights.org/519.

Savikas, Andrew. 2010. "O'Reilly E-book Bundles Now Include DAISY Talking Book Format." O'Reilly Radar, September 8, http://radar.oreilly.com/2010/09/oreilly-ebook-bundles-now-include-daisy-format.html.

Stone, Brad. 2009. "Amazon Backs Off Text-to-Speech Feature in Kindle." *Bits* (blog), *New York Times,* February 27, http://bits.blogs.nytimes.com/2009/02/27/amazon-backs-off-text-to-speech-feature-in-Kindle/.

U.S. Department of Education. N.d. "Advisory Commission on Accessible Instructional Materials in Postsecondary Education for Students with Disabilities: About the Commission," www2.ed.gov/about/bdscomm/list/aim/about.html.

U.S. Department of Justice and U.S. Department of Education. 2010. "Joint "Dear Colleague" Letter: Electronic Book Readers," June 29, www2.ed.gov/about/offices/list/ocr/letters/colleague-20100629.html.

W3C. 2010A. "Introduction to Understanding WCAG 2.0," www.w3.org/TR/UNDERSTANDING-WCAG20/intro.html#introduction-fourprincs-head.

———. 2010B. "User Agent Accessibility Guidelines (UAAG) 2.0: W3C Working Draft," June 17, www.w3.org/TR/UAAG20/.

Wikipedia. N.d. "National Library Service for the Blind and Physically Handicapped," http://en.wikipedia.org/wiki/National_Library_Service_for_the_Blind_and_Physically_Handicapped.

4

Making Sense of Change
E-books, Access, and the
Academic Library

LISA CARLUCCI THOMAS

E -books and mobile devices are changing the way people engage with information. The proliferation of the e-book market is revolutionizing the concept of the book—no longer defined exclusively by the physical, printed object—and is creating new concerns about access and ownership. Most books written today begin as digital manuscripts and are later printed, distributed, and marketed according to traditional routines. As consumer expectations evolve, everyone in the business of books must be flexible and ready to adapt to new demands as a common understanding of the e-book information environment evolves and is developed.

E-books have taken off in popularity in recent years, but they are not new to publishers or to libraries. The difference now is the market: the introduction of lightweight, dedicated e-readers at the right price; greater consumer familiarity and comfort with digital reading; and the increasing ubiquity of mobile devices have prompted the tipping point for e-books. As Clifford Lynch, director of the Coalition for Networked Information (CNI), points out, "[O]ne of the things that's quite striking between now and ten years ago is that e-books are no longer kind of a fringe thing for a few people who like to read electronically, they are actually a major market force" (Lynch 2011A).

At the 2011 CNI Spring Meeting, Lynch described three "prisms" of e-books in the current landscape: e-books as genres of communication, as cultural product, and as items of economic value. E-books have shifted the way readers interact with information, transitioning from print monographs to portable, digital libraries. More and more readers engage e-books on smartphones, and more publishers and authors are publishing works and revised editions of works electronically. Digital rights management (DRM) poses significant challenges, because its purpose is to limit access to e-books to select devices and users—essentially making "digital objects not behave digitally" (Neiburger 2011). E-books outside of such restrictions (i.e., DRM-free e-books) offer maximum access opportunities for libraries and consumers, as they can easily be downloaded to multiple devices, transferred, shared, and archived.

THE ACCESS DILEMMA

Libraries and publishers alike are struggling to establish effective purchasing and licensing models for digital access and ownership. Both institutions are entangled by investments and systems designed to support the print environment that now inhibit flexibility and adaptability. Librarians have demonstrated responsiveness to the e-resource environment and continue to build electronic collections as the e-resource market grows and technology allows for greater mobility and accessibility. Yet unlike e-journals, for which librarians are the predominant purchasers, "there's no player in the market with enough economic weight to serve as a counter force"; that is, to provide sufficient negotiating leverage to ensure suitable license terms for e-books in libraries (Lynch 2011A).

Eli Neiburger, associate director for IT and production at the Ann Arbor (Michigan) District Library, describes the current environment of e-books in libraries among four possible scenarios as the market continues to evolve. In each of Neiburger's four models, libraries lack control and are subject to other forces in the e-book market. He predicts that publishing can either thrive or die back and operate in a closed or open market. In the current, closed market, publishers retain control of the price point, DRM holds firm, and e-reader device exclusivity encourages proprietary formats. Libraries are required to make intermediary deals because they cannot buy digital content directly. Neiburger's second scenario proposes that if publishing flounders in the closed market, the device manufacturers will thrive, set price points, retain DRM, and—most alarmingly—work around libraries entirely. For example, the Amazon Kindle Store and Apple iBooks can already market directly to consumers. Neiburger's open-market scenarios are less bleak; he predicts that if publishing thrives, the cost of new content will diminish. He suggests that libraries would still need to maintain deals with multiple publishers; however, "publishers could let go of the 20th century worries" (Neiburger 2011). If publishing dies back and the open market thrives? "Free would be the dominant price for information." According to Neiburger, in the open market there will no longer be a need for DRM or access barriers, and type of mobile device won't matter.

MOBILE ACCESS TO E-BOOKS AT YALE

The story of e-books at the Yale University Library illustrates the challenges of Eli Neiburger's first scenario, where publishers are guardians and distributors of e-book content licensed by libraries, and e-books are restricted by DRM and device and format incompatibility. A 2009 study at the Yale University Library examined one aspect of the access dilemma: the ability of library users to successfully achieve mobile access to the library's licensed e-book collections. The study, conducted by Lisa Carlucci Thomas, was the first of its kind to explore the use of current mobile technologies in accessing the licensed e-book collections of an academic research library. Thomas inventoried the e-book collections at Yale and determined that collections increased from approximately 475,000 titles in 2005 to over one million titles by 2009. Content included e-books from ABC-CLIO, ebrary/ProQuest, Elsevier, NetLibrary, Oxford University Press, Springer, and many more. Over this same time frame, the demand for mobile access to information and e-books in particular began to grow, driven by technological developments such as the breakthrough releases of the Apple iPhone and Amazon Kindle in 2007 and by the expanding number of e-books more readily available direct to consumers.

The study, "Mobile Access to E-books at Yale," aimed to identify the percentage of Yale's e-books that could be accessed directly via mobile devices. The term *mobile devices* was defined as any lightweight, portable digital apparatus used to facilitate reading e-books, from smartphones to pocket personal computers to handheld e-book readers. Four devices were selected from the spectrum of mobile readers on the market at the time: the commercially popular Amazon Kindle 2 and Sony Reader PRS-500; the robustly featured iRex iLiad 2nd edition; and the multipurpose Apple iPod Touch (with identical firmware to the Apple iPhone). The devices themselves offered varying advantages and disadvantages.

Amazon Kindle 2

The Amazon Kindle 2 was the leading e-reader device tested in the study, with most widely popular adoption in the market. Kindle's content was displayed on an e-ink screen, and Amazon offered delivery direct purchases of e-book titles right from the Amazon store via wireless content delivery through Amazon's proprietary Whispernet cellular network. Drawbacks of the Kindle were the requirement of a personal account for e-book purchases, clunky work-arounds for downloading non-Amazon books and converting them into the required Amazon file format (AZW), and the lack of a fully functional web browser.

Sony Reader PRS-500

Like the Amazon Kindle, the Sony Reader PRS-500 was designed to be a dedicated e-reader equipped with an e-ink screen. The Sony Reader required a computer connection with specialized Sony e-book software for downloading content and did not include wireless functionality or Web browsing.

iRex iLiad, 2nd edition

The iRex iLiad 2nd edition offered similar features to the Amazon Kindle 2 and Sony Reader PRS-500, with more advanced capability. The iLiad included an e-ink touch screen, stylus annotation, and greater compatibility with many common e-book formats. The iLiad was Wi-Fi compatible but did not contain a fully functional browser.

Apple iPod Touch

The Apple iPod Touch, and its firmware equivalent, the iPhone, were increasingly popular on campus and frequently used for e-reading. Its small size, wireless access to content, mobile browser, and application store provided the convenience and opportunity to access e-books of multiple format types. In addition, this device connected seamlessly to the Yale wireless network and offered virtual private network functionality. The Apple iPod Touch is the only device with an LCD touch screen rather than e-ink screen; it is also the smallest and most lightweight of the four devices.

The inventory list of e-book packages of the Yale University Library collection served as the source document for producing the sample. Each of the four mobile devices—the Amazon Kindle 2, Sony Reader, iRex iLiad, and Apple iPod Touch—was used to attempt to access one e-book from each of the twenty-five resources in the sample:

1. History Reference Online
2. Digital Library of Classic Protestant Texts
3. Blackwell Reference Online
4. Books24x7 ITPro Collection
5. Cambridge Histories Online
6. Literature Online
7. Perseus Project
8. ebrary
9. ENGnetBASE: Engineering Handbooks Online
10. Eighteenth Century Collections Online
11. Gutenberg-e
12. ACLS Humanities E-book
13. Knovel
14. Madame Curie Bioscience Database
15. Medieval Sources Online
16. NetLibrary (OCLC)
17. SourceOECD
18. Oxford Reference Online
19. Patrologiae Graecae
20. Past Masters
21. Safari Books Online
22. Early English Books Online, 1475–1700
23. Methods in Enzymology
24. Springer Protocols
25. World Bank e-Library

The tests sought to answer four key questions to determine the percentage of e-books able to be accessed and whether an alternate method would facilitate access, what the known format type of the e-book was, and the ease by which someone could access the e-book using that particular mobile device (the "ability to access"). It was also noted whether the e-book was readable on the mobile device once accessed.

- *"Could you access e-book using device?"* This was tested by attempting to directly access Yale's e-book resources with each device and its unique features.
- *"Could you use an additional method to access Yale licensed e-books on the device (for instance: bookmark, email, download, copy, or other)?"* In the event that direct mobile access was unsuccessful, this test determined whether there were any means of providing mediated access to the Yale licensed e-book, based on an understanding of the technological functions of each individual device.
- *"What was the format type?"* This was noted to determine device compatibility.
- *"Rate ability to access using following scale:"* Ranking selected from the numbered list of options based on user's visual review of an accessed e-book.
    1. Able to access, but unreadable, unusable
    2. Able to access, may be readable, difficult to view or navigate
    3. Able to access, fairly readable, content viewable
    4. Able to access, overall readable, sized to fit screen and can navigate without difficulty
    5. Able to access, very readable, very easy to view content and navigate

The research findings indicated that 84 percent of the e-book collections of the Yale University Library could be accessed using at least one mobile device, specifically, the Apple iPod Touch. Surprisingly, the Apple iPod Touch was the only device that could directly access Yale's licensed e-books. Additionally, it had the highest-rated ability to access (64 percent), compared to the other e-reader devices tested. The tests indicated that the Amazon Kindle 2, Sony Reader PRS-500, and iRex iLiad 2nd edition could technically be used to access 24 percent of Yale's e-books but required additional methods, intermediate steps, and work-arounds, along with a computer connected to the Yale network, administrator privileges on the computer's operating system, and custom USB cable (specific to each individual device). Because the Amazon Kindle 2 required an Amazon account and charged a fee to convert downloaded files to the proprietary Amazon file format, no files were fully accessed using the Amazon Kindle 2, though the findings indicated it would be technically possible to do if in compliance with these limitations.

MAKING SENSE OF CHANGE

At the Yale University Library, the volume of e-book collections more than doubled over five years. With presently more than one million titles in the collection, the study indicated that 84 percent—or approximately 840,000 titles—could be accessed using an Apple iPod Touch or iPhone. Likewise, 24 percent—approximately 240,000 titles—could be accessed using the Sony Reader, iRex iLiad, and Amazon Kindle 2. Each of the devices tested offered unique technological strengths and weaknesses, and all the models now have updated, streamlined, and more technologically sophisticated versions on the market. New features include enhanced annotations, web browsing, integration with social media, and color screens, to name just a few. More important, there are also new competitors in the e-book market: from smartphones with competing operating systems, such as Android and Windows 7, to e-readers like the Barnes & Noble Nook, released in late 2009, to tablets like the outstandingly popular iPad, released in 2010. The Apple iBooks platform, another development of interest and potential exploration, was also released in 2010.

Each of these warrant continued investigation toward understanding and enhancing access to e-books in academic libraries. Further research should include exploring the specialized applications of the mobile devices based on the proficiencies of each device. For example, some devices may be better suited than others to provide access to course reserves, interlibrary loan, reference, and/or instruction materials. Also suggested is a consideration of alternative acquisition models to facilitate on-demand

	Apple iPod Touch	Amazon Kindle 2	Sony Reader PRS-500	iRex iLiad 2nd edition
Could you access e-book using device?	Yes: 21/25 (84%) No: 4/25 (16%)	Yes: 0/25 (0%) No: 25/25 (100%)	Yes: 0/25 (0%) No: 25/25 (100%)	Yes: 0/25 (0%) No: 25/25 (100%)
Could you use an additional method to access Yale licensed e-books on the device (for instance: bookmark, email, download, copy, or other)?	Yes: 6/25 (24%) No: 16/25 (64%) n/a: 3/25 (12%)	Yes: 6/25 (24%) No: 16/25 (64%) n/a: 3/25 (12%)	Yes: 6/25 (24%) No: 16/25 (64%) n/a: 3/25 (12%)	Yes: 6/25 (24%) No: 16/25 (64%) n/a: 3/25 (12%)
What was the format type?	HTML: 10/25 (40%) HTML/PDF: 4/25 (16%) PDF: 7/25 (28%) n/a: 4/25 (16%)	HTML: 10/25 (40%) HTML/PDF: 4/25 (16%) PDF: 7/25 (28%) n/a: 4/25 (16%)	HTML: 10/25 (40%) HTML/PDF: 4/25 (16%) PDF: 7/25 (28%) n/a: 4/25 (16%)	HTML: 10/25 (40%) HTML/PDF: 4/25 (16%) PDF: 7/25 (28%) n/a: 4/25 (16%)
Rate ability to access using following scale:				
1. Able to access, but unreadable, unusable	3/25 (12%)	0/25 (0%)	0/25 (0%)	0/25 (0%)
2. Able to access, may be readable, difficult to view or navigate	2/25 (8%)	0/25 (0%)	0/25 (0%)	0/25 (0%)
3. Able to access, fairly readable, content viewable	0/25 (0%)	0/25 (0%)	2/25 (8%)	2/25 (8%)
4. Able to access, overall readable, sized to fit screen and can navigate without difficulty	1/25 (4%)	0/25 (0%)	2/25 (8%)	2/25 (8%)
5. Able to access, very readable, very easy to view content and navigate	16/25 (64%)	0/25 (0%)	10/25 (40%)	10/25 (40%)
[Blanks], n/a	3/25 (12%)	25/25 (100%)	11/25 (44%)	11/25 (44%)

FIGURE 4.1 *Four Key Questions of the Yale Study*

downloads and circulation of e-reading devices. For these efforts to be successful, licensing terms must be negotiated to permit short- and long-term lending of e-book content, including provisions aligning with the doctrine of first-sale, interlibrary loan allowances, and permissions to own and duplicate e-book files for preservation and format migration as devices, operating systems, and formats evolve over time.

CONCLUSION

As libraries move ahead in making sense of change in the e-book environment, it is critical to remember how startlingly new this territory is for all stakeholders involved. "The book industry has never faced a disruptive technology since the days of Gutenberg, which means nobody who is alive today has lived through a disruptive moment to book publishing like we're living through right now" (Neiburger 2011). As the e-book market matures, the place and relevance of libraries will be determined by the actions and decisions taking place today. Meanwhile, as readers increasingly employ new mobile methods of accessing library collections, librarians must be informed about how these technologies operate, what potential they offer, and how they support or prohibit access to e-book collections according to hardware, software, and licensing criteria. E-books will continue to take hold as a genre of communication, particularly for scholarly works; they will be evaluated for their place in the cultural record, and they will serve as drivers of economic change for publishers, booksellers, and libraries (Lynch 2011A).

Librarians can be proactive in exploring these technologies, identifying the inherent opportunities, and developing the expertise to promote and facilitate access to burgeoning e-book collections. Studies like the one at Yale establish a critical baseline for the development of future services that will meet growing demand and new cultural expectations in the digital environment. Moreover, research findings inform and support decision-making and action plans for librarians seeking a steady voice in the rapidly evolving, industry-wide e-book conversations. Librarians expertly deliver content and services across format and function and have an important leadership role in the e-book environment. As such, to make sense of change it is essential to build knowledge locally, initiate and expand upon e-book research, and advocate for appropriate terms and services that support and maximize access to e-book collections.

REFERENCES

Lynch, Clifford. 2011A. "The Battle to Define the Future of the Book in the Digital World." *First Monday* 6.6, http://firstmonday.org/htbin/cgiwrap/bin/ojs/index.php/fm/article/view/864/773.

———. 2011B. *CNI: E-book Wars: Ten Years Later.* Video. 1:02. May 16, www.youtube.com/watch?v=1WfRBOGc4AA.

Neiburger, Eli. 2011. "E-books and Libraries in This Century." Presentation at the Connecticut Library Consortium Trendspotting Symposium: *E-books: Collections at the Crossroads,* April 5, http://vimeo.com/22577256.

Thomas, Lisa Carlucci. 2009A. "Mobile Access to E-books at Yale." Presentation at the Library and Information Technology Association (LITA) National Forum, Salt Lake City, October 2, www.slideshare.net/lisacarlucci/mobile-access-to-ebooks-at-yale.

———. 2009B. "One Million Mobile." Presentation at the Yale University Library SCOPA (Standing Committee on Professional Awareness) Forum, December 1, www.slideshare.net/lisacarlucci/one-million-mobile.

5

E-book Preservation
Business and Content Challenges

AMY KIRCHHOFF

E-books are increasingly important vehicles for scholarly research and personal enjoyment. By December 2010, e-books made up 9 to 10 percent of trade-book sales (Bosman 2010), and as seen in the statistics gathered by the Association of American Publishers and International Digital Publishing Forum, trade retail e-books sales growth increased dramatically over 2009 and 2010 and is set to continue at an exponential rate. Indeed, on May 19, 2011, Amazon "announced that since April [2011], it's sold more e-books for the Kindle than it has print books—by a ratio of 105 Kindle books to 100 print books—and that's both hardcover and softcover combined" (Knapp 2011).

In the face of this exciting proliferation, we must plan for the preservation of all these e-books. These e-books are not going onto the shelves of thousands of libraries and individuals; rather they are residing in files encumbered with digital rights management (DRM) software on proprietary appliances and on vendor-held and -maintained computers. Individuals now carry hundreds of books with them every day on their lightweight e-book readers, but the digital nature of those books still makes them fragile—and the risk of losing content is high for individuals, libraries, and society.

Digital preservation can ensure the security of e-books for use by readers of today and tomorrow. It is the series of management policies and activities necessary to ensure the enduring usability, authenticity, discoverability, and accessibility of content over the very long term. Print books were preserved for readers of today and tomorrow by their very existence on thousands of bookshelves around the world and by the dedication of a small number of libraries to preservation. While many individuals, publishers, and libraries may have copies of e-books and even backup copies of e-books, that is not sufficient long-term protection for digital content. For example, today's e-books are often tied to a specific piece of software, and even though an individual or library may own the bytes that compose the e-book, it is impossible to move those bytes from one platform to another. Thus it may be impossible to open those bytes and read the book in five or ten or fifty years. In order to preserve e-books, the intellectual content that is the book must be unpacked from its reliance on particular hardware and software, and then that intellectual content must be securely stowed away and maintained by one or more preservation agencies (such as third-party organizations dedicated to preserving digital content, national libraries, or cooperative efforts between libraries to preserve digital content). This chapter will look at the preservation requirements and challenges of e-books.

DIGITAL PRESERVATION

As described above, digital preservation is the series of management policies and activities necessary to ensure the enduring usability, authenticity, discoverability, and accessibility of content over the very long term.

The goal of long-term preservation is not just to make copies of the files that combine to form an e-book but to ensure that the e-book remains usable, authentic, discoverable, and accessible for future readers.

Usability

The file format of an e-book being read today on the current Kindle, Nook, iPad, and so on may not be the file format needed by tomorrow's appliances. "Software designed for an older operating system may not run [on] its contemporary counterpart, which in turn means that files created using the software native to these older systems might not be accessible on current computers. For example, a word processing document created in Windows 3.1 or Mac System 7.5 might not open with a modern office suite installed on Windows 7 or OSX" (Kirschenbaum et al. 2010). File formats will become obsolete—it may take a long time and the files may become more mangled in display than completely unusable, but it will happen. This process has already begun for e-books, as one of the original formats for e-books was Open eBook (OEB), which has since been supplanted by EPUB (an open e-book standard published by the International Digital Publishing Forum).

Migration and emulation are the two primary strategies used for ensuring usability in long-term preservation. Migration involves transforming digital content from its existing format to a different format that is usable and accessible with current technology. Emulation involves developing software that imitates earlier hardware and software. Migration requires a deep understanding of the content being preserved, whereas emulation is a more technology-based strategy, requiring a deep understanding of existing hardware and software.

Authenticity

Preservation agencies must prove that the current preserved objects are true to the item as originally deposited. As Hereclitus (c. 535 BC–475 BC)

Digital preservation is the series of management policies and activities necessary to ensure the enduring usability, authenticity, discoverability, and accessibility of content over the very long term. The key goals of digital preservation include:			
usability	authenticity	discoverability	accessibility
the intellectual content of the item must remain usable via the delivery mechanism of current technology	the provenance of the content must be proven and the content an authentic replica of the original as deposited	the content must have logical bibliographic metadata so that the content can be found by end users through time	the content must be available for use to the appropriate community

FIGURE 5.1 *Definition of Digital Preservation*

said, "Nothing endures but change." Changes will be made to preserved e-books: descriptive metadata will be updated, files will be migrated to new formats, corrupted files will be corrected or replaced, and so on. Preservation agencies must closely track any changes made to the original preserved content in order to ensure the current version is authentic to the original version and no damage has been done to the intellectual content of the preserved book. There are a variety of ways that this need can be met, including tracking changes through event records within the preservation metadata of the object or preserving all versions of the e-book.

Discoverability

In order to ensure the long-term preservation of an e-book, there must be sufficient descriptive (or bibliographic) metadata associated with the book to find it again. The scholarly community needs descriptive metadata for search and discovery. Just as important, the preservation agencies need descriptive metadata in order to maintain and manage a book over time so that it may be delivered to future readers. Within an archive, descriptive metadata is typically found in two places:

1. Encoded within the files that are the building blocks of the e-book being preserved. For example, a digitized book may include an XML file that contains significant bibliographic information along with the full text of the book.
2. Encoded within the archival system or preservation metadata files that provide a "wrapper" to the files that are the building blocks of the e-book being preserved. For example, the record for that same digitized book in the archival system will have a minimal amount of descriptive metadata directly associated with it (so that archival administrative queries do not need to be made against the more complex, full-text XML file).

Accessibility

We must preserve e-books for future use by readers. It is not enough for preservation agencies to simply keep the books safe and secure; the preservation agencies must be able to deliver that preserved content to users. Users and readers have high expectations for their delivery services, including stringent uptime and response time requirements, full-text search, metadata search, browsing of titles, integration with other electronic content, and integration with electronic readers. Even more important, any delivery system requires significant user support. This suite of services and skills is quite different from the skills needed to ingest content into an archival repository and preserve it for the long term, and yet it is a requirement, as the very nature of preservation is to provide access in the end. These differences between providing for long-term preservation of e-books and access to preserved e-books provide one of the significant challenges to developing a business model to support preservation.

EMERGING ORGANIZATIONAL MODELS FOR DIGITAL PRESERVATION

The most secure preservation of e-books is provided by certified preservation agencies. The primary certification option available for preservation agencies is a CRL Trustworthy Repositories Audit and Certification checklist-based assessment and certification (www.crl.edu/archiving-preservation/digital-archives/certification-and-assessment-digital-repositories). Alternatively, DRAMBORA (Digital Repository Audit Method Based on Risk Assessment, www.repositoryaudit.eu/) guides preservation agencies through a self-assessment tool kit.

A variety of organizational models are available, and three models are broadly acknowledged today for preservation of digital content:

1. *National efforts.* A number of national libraries have taken on digital preservation in support of their mission or their country's legal deposit requirements. The scope of content involved and access terms vary, but all such libraries are government funded. Examples of this type of organization are the British Library and the National Library of the Netherlands.
2. *Community-supported independent preservation archives.* These organizations may focus on a subject area or content type. Typically the costs for the preservation of this content are

shared across the participating publishers and libraries. Examples of this type of organization are Portico and the Inter-University Consortium for Political and Social Research.

3. *Cooperative efforts.* Groups of libraries have pooled their resources to share the responsibility and costs of preservation. Examples include MetaArchive, California Digital Library's Digital Preservation Repository, and HathiTrust.

PRESERVATION BUSINESS MODELING CHALLENGES

One of the challenges for developing successful business models to support preservation of e-books today is that successful access models are still under development. E-book aggregators, publishers, libraries, and individuals are still exploring a variety of business models for purchasing, licensing, and accessing e-books.

Public libraries tend to license books through a one-book, one-lend model where "a book is licensed by the library; a patron comes in and downloads that book for a set circulation period . . . [and] when the period is over, the file is no longer accessible [to that user]. Readers who want to read a popular book get into a queue and wait until the previous patron's checkout time has finished" (Kellogg 2011). Public libraries and their vendors continue to experiment and evaluate new models and license agreements. As of early 2011, HarperCollins is requiring that e-books sold to libraries "be checked out only 26 times before they expire" (Bosman 2011). Given that public libraries tend to license, not own, e-books and the restrictions being placed by publishers on library e-books, it is not clear what shape the long-term preservation of e-books for public libraries should take.

Scholarly libraries are also experimenting with e-book access models, including user-driven purchasing (or patron-driven acquisition), license or purchase by collection, license or purchase by individual title, license from aggregators, and license or purchase direct from publishers. This large variety of access business models makes it difficult to overlay preservation business models.

Individual purchasers of books may be in the most precarious of positions, as their books are often tied tightly to specific hardware and applications and are typically licensed, not owned. For example, per the Kindle end-user license agreement, "unless otherwise specified, Digital Content is licensed, not sold, to you by the Content Provider" (Amazon 2011). Indeed, there have been instances of Amazon deleting purchased e-books from readers' Kindles and simply refunding the purchase price (Pogue 2009). In addition, there are currently no models of preservation that address the individual readers whom have licensed or purchased e-books.

Just as publishers and vendors experiment with access business models, preservation agencies must experiment with preservation business models, including addressing the big questions of: who pays—and how much do they pay? Publishers, libraries, individuals, aggregators, and preservation agencies will all have a part to play in developing and implementing these business models.

Legal Issues

There are a number of legal issues surrounding the preservation of e-content, especially regarding intellectual property and media. A "primary [legal] problem is how to ensure the non-infringement of copyright, by avoiding unauthorized exercise of the authors' exclusive rights, as well as determining what content is protected by copyright, to facilitate access to content as well as consent from copyright holders. A persistent question is whether the digital content manager still has the necessary rights in the e-content" (Gathegi 2010). Another way to consider this concern is that access and preservation rights are separate. Simply because an organization has the right to provide access to an e-book does not mean that organization can preserve the e-book or has the authority to transfer the preservation rights of the e-book to a third party. The actions taken during preservation, such as migration or otherwise transforming the content, are particularly important to address with copyright holders. Aggregators, more so than original publishers, are unlikely to have preservation rights to the e-books to which they provide access.

Another particularly tricky area for all digital content is that of embedded content. Technology makes it quite simple to embed an image or multimedia element into another file (e.g., a movie may be embedded into a web page or even into a PDF file), and sometimes that embedded content has a different copyright owner than the copyright owner of the encompassing material. In addition, "some media formats are covered by rules specific to the media (e.g., sound files). Also, conversion of media from one format to another may trigger copyright infringement (e.g., conversion of text into audio formats)" (Gathegi 2010).

A number of resources on the legal issues surrounding digital preservation are available, including the digital preservation management tutorial hosted by the Interuniversity Consortium for Political and Social Research (www.icpsr.umich.edu/dpm/dpm-eng/challenges/accountability.html) and the digital preservation handbook hosted by the Digital Preservation Coalition (www.dpconline.org/advice/preservationhandbook/digital-pres ervation/preservation-issues). Legal counsel should be consulted when constructing agreements with content providers and developing terms and conditions for end users who may be accessing or depositing content.

Content Challenges

In many ways e-books are similar to other types of digital content; e-books consist of some metadata and some files.

Despite the fact that all e-content consists of just metadata and files, each category does have its own preservation challenges. A theme that runs throughout the content challenges an agency will encounter when preserving e-books is variety—variety in editions, variety in formats, variety in packaging. It is this variety that provides the challenge!

Editions, Updates, and Retractions

Some of the types of updates that can take place with published e-books have analogues in the print world. For example, identifying and tracking versions of e-books is more challenging than some other e-content types, as books have an existing, historical versioning system: the edition. However, publishing electronically also makes it considerably easier to update an e-book than it was and is to update a print book (publishers have been known to send updated pages to libraries to insert into print publications, but that is a rare and costly occurrence—whereas updating the e-book and metadata hosted only at the publisher's server is comparatively easy).

Editions

Any organization addressing the preservation of e-books will need to develop a solution to manage editions. In the print world, bookstores stop selling earlier editions when new editions are issued, whereas libraries may keep all editions. A number of similar options exist for e-books:

1. Preserve the new edition in the archive and associate that new edition with the earlier editions
2. Preserve the new edition in the archive without any formal correlation between it and the earlier editions, which remain in the archive
3. Replace the original e-book in the archive with the new edition

Many preservation agencies will follow option 1 or 2, as it is best practice to disallow deletions from a preservation archive.

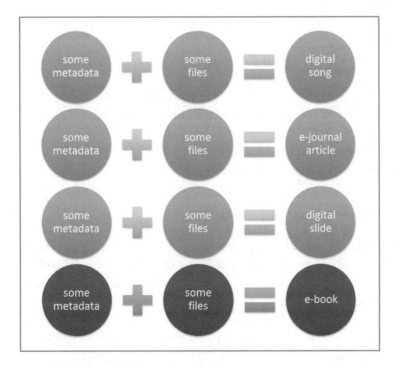

FIGURE 5.2 *Similarities in Digital Content*

Updates

In addition to releasing new editions, any given edition of an e-book may be updated by the publisher—problems in the metadata will be corrected, missing pages will be added to PDF files, misassigned figure graphics will be rearranged, and the like. Preservation agencies must develop workflows that allow them to accept updates from the original content provider and policies that describe whether the original content will be preserved or overwritten in such scenarios. In addition, preservation agencies must specify what types of updates the agency itself will perform versus what types of updates the content provider may perform, and also identify scenarios in which a third party to the agreement could (or could not) update content. For example, if a user contacts the preservation agency to report that a book is missing a page, would the preservation agency replace it on its own or go back to the original content provider for an update?

Retractions

Retractions or deletions are always a challenge for digital preservation agencies. One way of managing retractions is to leverage the concept of versions. For example, a preservation agency could keep the original, retracted article (the metadata and the content files) as one version of the preserved object (a version that may be inaccessible to the public). The agency can then create an abbreviated version that includes an explanation of the retraction in the metadata and no content files. In this way, the preservation agency can preserve the original without making it accessible to readers and offer readers an explanation.

Digital Rights Management (DRM)

DRM often complicates digital preservation. DRM is technology, often embedded in a file or a device, that enforces the rules of use defined by the provider of the content. It is particularly prevalent with e-books, where it is very common for books purchased by individuals to be tightly tied to that individual (e.g., it is often difficult to share or lend one's e-book to a friend) or to a particular device (e.g., books purchased for one appliance or application can be read only on that appliance or application). E-books sold or licensed to public and academic libraries are also wrapped in DRM, which can limit the number of times the book can be borrowed, the number of users who may borrow it at one time, or even the locations at which it can be read.

The preservation challenge is that the purpose of DRM (carefully limit access and replication) is at odds with the purpose of preservation (preserve access for the long term). In order to fully meet the definition of preservation and ensure that e-books remain accessible and usable in the future, most preservation agencies will need to strip DRM from preserved e-books. Careful definition of business models and license agreements between preservation agencies and content providers, preservation agencies and other licensors, and preservation agencies and readers may be able to mitigate the need for DRM on the preserved content. For example, one could envision a business model that would not allow a preservation agency to provide access to an e-book until such time as it was no longer being provided by the publisher; or another model that requires a license agreement between publisher and preservation agency that has the publisher providing content without DRM for preservation and the preservation agency introducing DRM on a delivery copy of the e-book (not the copy in the archive), should it need to provide access to the book in the future.

Units of Publication, Access, and Preservation

Readers tend to think of books as an entity unto themselves. In the print world, books are discrete physical objects—each has a front cover and a back cover and is filled with a series of pages. Physical books take up a set amount of space on a bookshelf, and while they may sit side by side with other books in the same series, the individual books are still discrete objects. Physical books also are not easily divided into smaller units—few people would slice chapters or pages out of books. At first glance, e-books could also be considered discrete objects. They have individual entries in readers' appliances or applications; however, the digital nature of e-books allows them to easily be merged into bigger units or sliced into smaller units. For example, many academic publishers provide access to e-books primarily at the chapter level, and on the other end of the spectrum, libraries may purchase collections of books and need to consider the collection a single, if multipart, unit.

In the face of such a variety of possible hierarchies and configurations, preservation agencies must decide how to map the supplied e-books to a preservation content model, what descriptive metadata to capture, and how to provide access to the content in the future. Inevitably, the preservation metadata and content model will provide less sophistication than the original, because the preservation agency will be preserving content

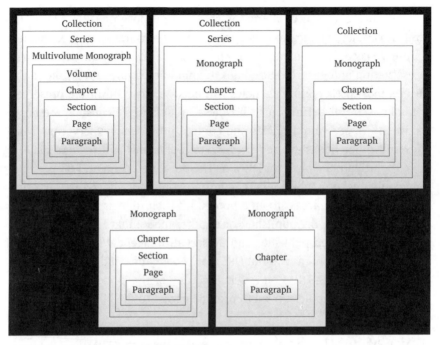

FIGURE 5.3 *Books and the Unit*

from a variety of content providers and will need to make all that variety uniform enough to manage.

For example, a scholarly publisher may have published a number of books within a single collection. Libraries purchase these books by the collection and provide their patrons with access to the e-books through a single web page representing the collection. A preservation agency, however, is likely to preserve this content book by book. If the information about the collection was not provided to the preservation agency or was not captured by the preservation agency, then when the preservation agency provides access to the content in the future, it will likely be book by book and not via the collection.

Presentation Formats

E-books are relatively new and there are a number of formats in use. Unlike the format wars between Blu-ray and HD DVD or—to go back further in time, Betamax and VHS—that arose when those formats were young, there are more than just two e-book formats currently extant and widely used:

- EPUB, which is used by most handheld e-readers
- Mobipocket
- Kindle AZW, based on Mobi and used by Amazon's Kindle
- PDF
- HTML
- National Library of Medicine/National Center for Biotechnology Information (NLM/NCBI) Book Tag Set, which is predominantly seen in the scholarly e-book market
- Proprietary XML

There are many additional formats possible—Wikipedia lists eighteen e-book formats (Wikipedia 2011). Most e-books are published in at least three formats. Several factors must be considered when selecting which formats to preserve:

1. Should all formats be preserved, or can just one be selected for preservation?
2. What tools and abilities for deriving one format from another are available to the preservation agency?
3. Is there a master format from which all other formats are derived?
4. Which format is the easiest to manage?
5. Which format will most users want?
6. Which format will sophisticated users want?

The answers to these questions will guide the development of a preservation agency's decision on what to preserve.

Packaging

The "proper" way to package and deliver e-books has yet to be defined—and if the e-journal example is followed, it may never be defined. Much like the variety of presentation formats in use, there are a large number of packaging techniques in use. In general, e-books are published as:

- a file representing the entire book (e.g., a single PDF or EPUB file),
- a file representing each chapter (e.g., one PDF per chapter),

- both bookwise and chapterwise representations of the book, or
- none of the above

In addition to the content files, there must be metadata supplied with each book (see figure 5.2, above). Sometimes there may be additional content such as a cover image, figure graphics, or media files. This variety of content is delivered to preservation agencies in all variety of manners, and the packaging of (or rather, the unpacking of) digital versions of e-books can be complicated. Some examples include:

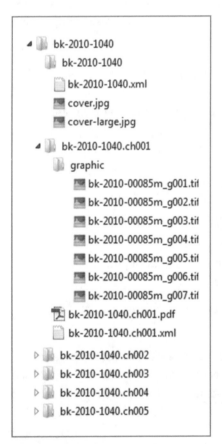

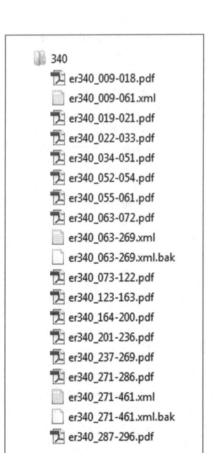

FIGURE 5.4
Book Packaging Example A

FIGURE 5.5
Book Packaging Example B

As seen in figure 5.4, "Book Packaging Example A," this package includes one directory for each book, with subdirectories for each chapter. The chapter subdirectories contain a PDF and XML file for each chapter, with another subdirectory for figure graphics from the chapter. Another top-level directory contains several cover images and an XML file that unites all the chapters into a cohesive unit.

As seen in figure 5.5, "Book Packaging Example B," another possibility is a directory with any number of books contained within it. Each book is represented by one XML and several PDFs. The PDFs cannot be associated with the proper XML file—and thus the proper book—through the file-naming convention, and each XML file must be opened to determine which PDF belongs to which article and XML file.

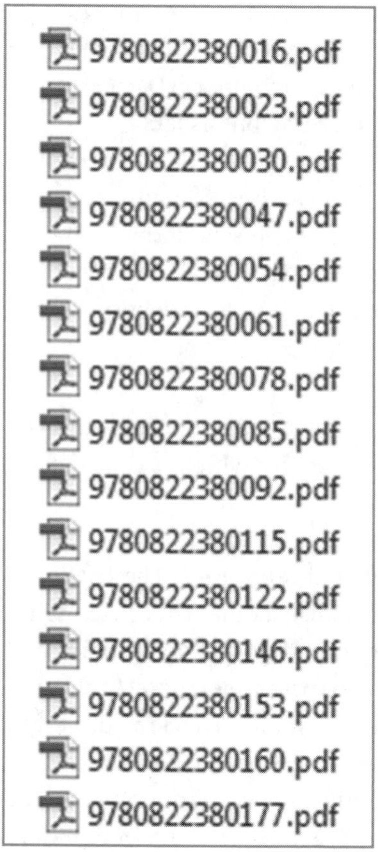

And finally in figure 5.6, "Book Packaging Example C," there is a directory full of any number of books. Each book has a single PDF file. Within that directory there is also one XML file that contains entries for each book in the directory.

The number of permutations is significant. It is time consuming to develop tools that will automatically process this variety of content. Preservation agencies should consider whether or not to require, if they are able to enforce such a requirement, that e-books arrive from content providers packaged in a particular way. They will also need to consider what the accuracy and cost implications are when they do not provide—or cannot enforce—strict packaging requirements.

9780822380016.pdf
9780822380023.pdf
9780822380030.pdf
9780822380047.pdf
9780822380054.pdf
9780822380061.pdf
9780822380078.pdf
9780822380085.pdf
9780822380092.pdf
9780822380115.pdf
9780822380122.pdf
9780822380146.pdf
9780822380153.pdf
9780822380160.pdf
9780822380177.pdf

FIGURE 5.6
Book Packaging Example C

Metadata and Metadata Formats

As librarians and publishers both know, metadata is neither simple nor straightforward—a publication does not have only an author but an author, an editor, a translator, and so on. E-books have all the traditional challenges of bibliographic or descriptive metadata and a number of unique considerations (see figure 5.3 above):

- Many e-books are delivered a chapter at a time and thus there is likely to be chapter-level bibliographic metadata provided, in addition to book bibliographic metadata.
- Many books, especially within the scholarly community, are part of a series and thus must include metadata placing them within the context of the series. The standard metadata formats available for books have varying degrees of sophistication in regard to series metadata. ONIX for Books 3.0 (a standard in common use by publishers to transmit bibliographic and cost information to booksellers; see www.editeur.org/83/Overview/) addresses many previously extant metadata problems with sets, series, and multiple-item products. However, the NLM/NCBI Book Tag Set (http://dtd.nlm.nih.gov/book/) does not yet robustly handle series metadata.

Note that it is common to receive several robust metadata files for each book, and the preservation agency should identify which it considers as primary.

A challenge faced by many preservation agencies is how to integrate varied content types into a single preservation repository. The challenge is that each preserved item should have robust, domain-specific bibliographic metadata as one of the content files and also have a diminished set of bibliographic metadata in the preservation metadata (note that this challenge can be compounded by the versioning concerns discussed earlier). The bibliographic metadata in the preservation metadata is there to provide the archive managers with a uniform way of querying across all content types in the archive and is usually encoded in the Dublin Core Metadata Element Set (Dublin Core is a community developed suite of fifteen metadata properties that can be used in describing objects; see http://dublincore.org/).

Identifiers

Books have long been identified by the International Book Number System or ISBN. Per the International ISBN Agency FAQ, "an ISBN is essentially a product identifier used by publishers, booksellers, libraries and Internet retailers and other supply chain participants for ordering, listing, sales records and stock control purposes. The ISBN identifies the registrant as well as the specific title, edition and format" (ISBN-IA 2009). ISBN assignment to e-books is particularly challenging because of historical inconsistencies and confusion in the use of ISBNs by publishers. The International ISBN Agency recommends that an individual ISBN be assigned to each file format of a book and that an individual ISBN be assigned to each version of the e-book that uses the same file format but that has different DRM or is destined for different e-readers (ISBN-IA 2010A). However, a report from the agency found that "there is presently a complete lack of consensus about which attributes define a unique product" (ISBN-IA 2010B), and presently there is a tremendous amount of discussion within the publishing, authoring, service provider, and library communities about how best to assign ISBNs to e-books. At the moment, preservation agencies can be assured neither that an ISBN represents a unique product nor that it represents the intellectual work of a single book. In addition, ISBNs can be assigned to individual chapters.

In the midst of this flux, it is advisable for a preservation agency to capture all the possible identifiers for each e-book (note that some publishers may provide over ten ISBNs for a single book). In addition, preservation agencies should assign their own unique identifier to at least each book, and advisably to each chapter and individual file, as this will allow easy retrieval and identification of these elements in the future and allow the preservation agency to define the limits and extent of the e-book. For example, the preservation agency may choose to group all versions (as discussed above in "Editions, Updates, and Retractions") of a book together as a single intellectual unit.

OTHER TYPES OF E-BOOKS AND E-BOOK PUBLISHERS

Traditional e-books are typically classified into two categories: e-books written by or for the scholarly community, and e-books written for the mass market. However, there are at least two more categories of e-books in need of preservation, and both categories include e-books that have been digitized from print counterparts.

Digitized Collections Produced for Reference Content Databases

There are a number of publishers and organizations that have digitized historical content, including books—and built products or collections with this content. For example, Gale, ProQuest, and Adam Mathew all have built substantial collections of digitized content that include books. The Google digitization work and Project Gutenberg also fall into this category of content.

In addition to the above preservation challenges associated with all e-books, this content can have additional challenges, especially in regard to rights and pure quantity of content. Obtaining preservation rights to this digitized content can be complex, because sometimes the rights are held by multiple entities (for example, they may still be held by the original publisher and not the digitization and aggregation vendor—or even shared by both entities). Rights can also be especially difficult for content that is no longer in print and yet not out of copyright (often referred to as *orphan works*). From a quantity point of view, current e-book publishers can publish anywhere from a few to tens of thousands of e-books a year, but these digitized collections can contain millions of books—which is an entirely different scale of processing and may require significantly greater hardware and/or processing time.

Digitized Collections Produced by Cultural Heritage Organizations

In addition to the large quantities of content that are present in reference content databases, many cultural heritage organizations today are digitizing their special collections or otherwise creating digital collections—collections that often contain digitized books. A 2010 survey of research libraries by OCLC showed that over 95 percent of all libraries surveyed had begun or completed digitization of one or more of their special collections.

This locally held digitized book content is in need of preservation; however, it has unique challenges due to its local nature. Often this content is not structured in such a way that the metadata and content files are

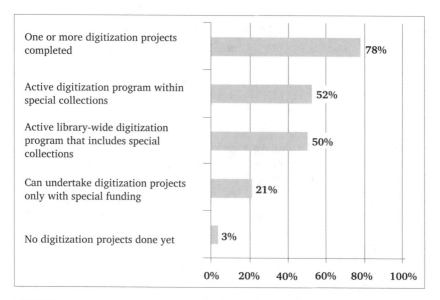

FIGURE 5.7 *OCLC Survey on Special Collections Digitization Activity (Dooley and Luce 2010)*

strongly associated to one another, which makes it difficult for a preservation agency to even receive the content. There are also significant concerns around the funding of this content's preservation, as it is not clear that the local institutions can afford preservation or that the community as a whole is willing to collaboratively support it. Further information is available in a white paper produced by Portico for the National Endowment of Humanities grant (Kirchhoff 2011).

CONCLUSION

Digital preservation of e-books is an exciting new arena with many challenges, including developing appropriate business and organizational models; legal issues around intellectual property and preservation rights; content challenges surrounding updates and retractions; DRM challenges; and challenges with the unit of publication, presentation formats, packaging, metadata, and identifiers. Preservation of e-books will require collaborative effort on the part of libraries, individuals, publishers, and preservation agencies if all are to enjoy a future that is richly equipped with access to the exponentially increasing number of e-books available today.

REFERENCES

Amazon. 2011. "Kindle License Agreement and Terms of Use." Last updated February 16, www.amazon.com/gp/help/customer/display.html/ref=hp_left_sib?ie=UTF8&nodeId=200506200.

Bosman, J. 2010. "Christmas Gifts May Help E-books Take Root." *New York Times,* December 24, www.nytimes.com/2010/12/24/books/24publishing .html?sq = ebook%20sales%20growth&st = cse&adxnnl = 1&scp = 1&adxnn lx = 1304450152-aI + T0nqS3a0m21fXCL2dKg.

———. 2011. "Publisher Limits Shelf Life for Library E-books." *New York Times,* March 15, www.nytimes.com/2011/03/15/business/media/15libraries .html.

Dooley, J. M., and K. Luce. 2010. "Taking Our Pulse: The OCLC Research Survey of Special Collections and Archives." OCLC Research, www.oclc.org/ research/publications/library/2010/2010-11.pdf.

Gathegi, J. N. 2010. *Digital Content Convergence: Intellectual Property Rights and the Problems of Preservation: A U.S. Perspective.* International Conference on Electronic Publishing, Helsinki, Finland, http://elpub.scix.net/cgi-bin/ works/Show?_id=123_elpub2010&sort=DEFAULT&search=digital%20 content%20convergence&hits=614.

ISBN-IA. 2009. "General Information about the ISBN system," www.isbn -international.org/faqs/view/5.

———. 2010A. "Guidelines for the Assignment of ISBNs to E-books and 'Apps.'" International ISBN Agency, www.myidentifiers.com/images/101118_ Guidelines_assignment_ISBNs.pdf.

———. 2010B. "Summary of Business Requirements Study on ISBNs and E-books." International ISBN Agency, www.isbn-international.org/pages/ media/ISBN%20e-books%20study%20public%20summary%20110105.pdf.

Kellogg, C. 2011. "Digital Book World: Where Do Libraries and E-books Meet?" *Jacket Copy* (blog), *Los Angeles Times,* http://latimesblogs.latimes.com/ jacketcopy/2011/01/digital-book-world-where-do-libraries-and-ebooks -meet.html.

Kirchhoff, A. 2011. "Preservation of Digitized Books and Other Digital Content Held by Cultural Heritage Organizations." Portico, www.portico.org/digital -preservation/wp-content/uploads/2010/01/NEH-IMLS-D-book-model.pdf.

Kirschenbaum, M. G., R. Ovenden, and G. Redwine, with research assistance from R. Donahue. 2010. "Digital Forensics and Born-Digital Content in Cultural Heritage Collections." Council on Library and Information Resources, www.clir.org/pubs/abstract/pub149abst.html.

Knapp, A. 2011. "What Do Amazon's E-book Sales Mean for the Future of Books?" (blog post). *Forbes,* May 19, http://blogs.forbes.com/ alexknapp/2011/05/19/what-do-amazons-e-book-sales-mean-for-the-future -of-books/.

Library of Congress. N.d. METS: Metadata Encoding and Transmission Standard, www.loc.gov/standards/mets/.

Pogue, D. 2009. "Some E-books Are More Equal Than Others." *Pogue's Posts* (blog), *New York Times,* July 17, http://pogue.blogs.nytimes .com/2009/07/17/some-e-books-are-more-equal-than-others/.

Wikipedia. 2011. "Comparison of E-book Formats," http://en.wikipedia.org/ wiki/Comparison_of_e-book_formats.

6

Weeding E-books

ALICE CROSETTO

The electronic book may be considered the ideal library resource compared to the traditional print book. No longer do librarians have to fret about torn-out pages or pencil markings throughout, cracked bindings or fallen-off spine labels, or covers ripped or soiled by the elements. Then there is the worry about the lost book, or the one eventually discovered as missing from the shelf. Once an electronic book is purchased, many of the cares and concerns that we encounter in the print world disappear—or do they?

Evaluating library collections is time consuming but definitively integral to providing optimal resources for your patrons. Part of this evaluation is an inevitable decision that some items can and need to be discarded. If this is true for print items, then shouldn't it be addressed equally for other formats such as media and electronic resources, in particular e-books? This chapter will explore the similarities and differences between weeding print books that librarians encounter as well as deciding whether or not librarians should weed e-books in library collections.

BACKGROUND

Although conferences and regional meetings are excellent venues for networking and collaborating on various initiatives and for discovering emerging technologies, librarians equally rely on the research and case studies published in their own literature. An extensive and comprehensive body of literature addressing the weeding of print resources has existed for some time. As libraries downsize their collections for space, those articles contain benchmarks and guidelines for assurance and success. However, a review of library literature for weeding e-books reveals a solitary item from 2004. A. Paula Wilson penned a short but comprehensive essay for the "Tech Talk" section of *Public Libraries*. Surprisingly, Wilson's observations and suggestions made seven years ago for the public library are as equally relevant and on target for today's libraries—all libraries, including public, academic, and K–12. Wilson reminds librarians that making users aware of these items and encouraging them to accept this new format are important contributory factors in making e-book collections valuable resources. Although time and the popularity of e-books have changed some of her accessibility concerns, Wilson does address the major issues librarians encounter or will encounter when e-books need to be evaluated for weeding. For example, criteria for evaluating the use of the e-book collection should be developed at the same time a library acquires e-books. Another concern is the initial hesitance that librarians may have for weeding e-books considering that shelving never becomes overcrowded and e-books do not physically deteriorate beyond use. E-books as well as their publishers have evolved substantially since 2004, requiring librarians to develop policies to meet the demands of individual publishers' guidelines as well as the explosion of new technologies used by patrons.

TO WEED OR NOT TO WEED

Librarians who object to weeding resources understand the concept but prefer not to employ it for a variety of reasons, such as limited staff or time. Many believe that the more resources a library has, the better the library is. Some prestigious library systems may actively collect resources—such as the Library of Congress, which according to its website currently contains over 147 million items, and the Harvard Libraries, which maintain over 17 million items in more than seventy individual libraries and collections (2011)—the majority of libraries provide only those resources that their patrons need and expect, often based on limited funds and space.

Collection development librarians who have had to address dwindling funds and disappearing space understand the important role that weeding plays in maintaining optimal resources. Regardless of the library type, K–12, special, public, or academic libraries have limited space. Off-site storage facilities do provide needed space for rarely used but desirable resources, but this typically applies to academic libraries. Public libraries that maintain collections traditionally containing popular and up-to-date resources weed to accommodate newer titles. All libraries benefit by having aesthetically pleasing shelves, not crammed-packed rows of dusty, worn, and torn tomes of long-forgotten treasures.

The recent explosion and popularity of portable devices that provide convenient venues for readers and e-books obscure the fact that utilizing the technology of computer devices to deliver the text of books can be traced to the 1940s when Vannevar Bush developed Memex, or later in the 1960s with Alan Kay's Dynabook (Herther 2008). However, the e-book format that is known today began with Project Gutenberg in 1971 (Galbraith 2011) and began appearing in library collections as early as the 1970s. E-books are long overdue in being evaluated and weeded.

SIMILARITIES WITH WEEDING PRINT

There are numerous similarities in weeding e-books and print books, such as developing an evaluation policy that considers low use and currency of content, as well as establishing a time frame for the actual weeding. The ultimate benefit of print collections, when weeded to accommodate newer materials and to encourage patron browsing along pleasing shelves, is higher circulation. This concept understandably transfers to some degree to e-book collections, although the concept of space has changed for the e-book: uncluttered virtual space replaces the overcrowded shelves.

The two traditional reasons that print items are withdrawn are their low to nonexistent use and the currency of their content. Physical items that have low use or do not circulate occupy space. Although an unused e-book is not taking up valuable real estate space on the shelves, it does occupy space in the online catalog. And while this may or may not create space issues with the integrated library system (ILS), e-books will appear during searches, possibly obscuring more appropriate and useful items. The more important of the traditional reasons for weeding is currency of content. Outdated resources occupy valuable space on the shelf and in the catalog.

Unlike low-use items, outdated resources could contain nonrelevant, misleading, even potentially harmful information, especially in the areas of natural and health sciences. Providing the most relevant resources in the areas of science, technology, engineering, and mathematics, collectively referred to as STEM, is paramount for all libraries, particularly academic and K–12. Although public libraries also maintain resources in the STEM areas, their patrons seek additional topics that demand current information, such as travel and career exploration items. Regardless of the format, unless maintained for archival or historical study, libraries usually retain items with the most relevant and current information. Whether users are browsing the shelf for physical items or going through a list of retrieved e-books in the catalog, database, or on a portable device, librarians want them to have access to the optimal resources that supplement the learning environment, support their research, and enhance personal growth and knowledge. Weeding e-books provides the opportunity to identify underrepresented topics in the collection as well as new topics of interest for public libraries and new programs and curricular needs for school libraries.

While low-use and outdated content needs to be addressed in collection development (CD) policies for both print and electronic, additional CD tenets also pertain to e-books, particularly when evaluating superseded volumes. Revised and newer editions that continually appear require a policy regarding acquisition and often the replacement of titles. Just as with their print counterparts, new or revised editions of e-book titles need to be purchased.

This is most evident with reference titles. Resources traditionally identified as reference items typically have higher costs, may contain multiple volumes, and are regularly updated, often annually. Some reference titles remained on shelves indefinitely, while others—once superseded by newer editions—were typically regulated to circulating collections, remote storage, or discarded. The same criteria used for weeding physical reference titles should be applied to reference e-books.

Many of the methods employed by librarians to weed print resources can also be used for e-books. Lists generated from the ILS (or COUNTER or SUSHI data for e-books) including the data necessary for evaluation can be exported to a spreadsheet. Titles can be sorted by last checkout or view, total circulation or downloads, purchase date, or by the specific call number system used in the library. Librarians can mark hard copies or work entirely on electronic files. Once titles are identified for weeding, the next step depends on the workflow of the individual library—where larger libraries have separate acquisitions, cataloging, and processing departments, smaller libraries are one-person operations. Regardless of the library's size, the actual action entailed in weeding an e-book from the online catalog is different than a print item; therefore, this step will be addressed in the section "Differences with Weeding Print," below.

One current topic of interest within librarianship today may already play a role in policies that outline the weeding process of library resources, both print and electronic. Should the requestor type be a factor in the weeding of items? And if the requestor is a factor, requestor types themselves need to be prioritized. For example, are patron-initiated requests not as valuable as librarian- or teacher-initiated requests? Whether the item occupies physical space or virtual space, should the requestor be as important as the number of circulations? Undoubtedly, patron-driven acquisitions will increase print and electronic titles held in libraries. Librarians may need to evaluate use statistics in relationship to the requestor especially as accountability for all resource purchases increases its importance, and senior administrative levels require justification for continued funding.

Weeding still remains one of the more sensitive activities in school libraries, especially at the academic level. Whether with their colleagues in various departments across campus or with their fellow K–12 educators, the most important way for librarians to build and strengthen the lines of collaboration is to involve all interested individuals in the evaluation process and potential withdrawing of titles. K–12 teachers, academic instructors, and researchers, who are asked to submit requests for purchasing titles, should also be included in the removal of titles. Automatic purchase and replacement policies as well as procedures for what to do with the out-dated item for e-books are equally important for e-books as they are for print.

DIFFERENCES WITH WEEDING PRINT

Often the reasons for purchasing e-books are the same factors used in policies for evaluating and weeding e-books. One of the obvious differences in any discussion of e-books is that there is no physical item. When there is no physical item, then shelves can't become crowded and items can't be damaged. Because e-books exist in the virtual space of the library, then all evaluating and weeding also exist in the virtual environment. Directly related is the second, equally important element of the weeding process of e-books: the purchasing model. The librarians need to know where the e-book resides, which then regulates how the e-book is weeded—and perhaps more important, what is meant by weeding an e-book.

Currently, libraries purchase e-books individually or in bundles. Although not as common today, publishers used to provide individual titles in a portable document format (PDF). For example, the American Psychological Association had its 2007 *APA Style Guide to Electronic References* available as a PDF. Once purchased, this title was downloaded on the library's server and made available in the online catalog to users, who could either read the text online or print out a hard copy. In this example, the process of weeding PDF e-books remained solely in-house and resembled the process of weeding print books. Purchasing e-book bundles can provide significant cost savings and appears to be the preferred purchasing model for many libraries today, particularly popular for consortia. As in the case of OhioLINK, the consortium of Ohio academic schools, purchasing bundles or collections such as titles from eBooks on EBSCOhost, Springer, Safari, Sage, and ABC-CLIO allows for downloading MARC records of individual titles into the home catalog, hence providing access for the users of member libraries. However, the e-books themselves are not downloaded on local servers. Some reside on OhioLINK servers and some on vendor servers, making the weeding process more complex. Companies have been established to facilitate the accessibility of electronic resources for libraries from various publishing companies. For example, founded in 1986 and working with thousands of publishers (representing over half a million titles), OverDrive creates and customizes individual websites for patrons of a specific individual library. Currently, OverDrive is utilized by more than 13,000 libraries, schools, and colleges worldwide. This website can be integrated with the ILS, allowing users to search for titles (OverDrive 2011). Typically, purchasing bundles or e-books from vendors such as OverDrive means that the e-books are hosted outside the library. When the books are outside of the library's purview, weeding may not be possible, as is the case with OverDrive. As of the writing of this book, they were unable to offer libraries an option to weed titles from their customized collections.

Because there is no physical item, the weeding of e-books actually represents the removal of the content from the online catalog, a publisher's customized website, or a portable reader. Therefore, it is essential for libraries to learn from each vendor and to understand the purchasing model that may govern how e-book titles can eventually be weeded or made inaccessible.

And because there are no physical shelves, the weeding process will have to be conducted using data from the ILS or vendor-supplied use data. After a review file of e-book titles is generated, all necessary data used for evaluation is exported to a spreadsheet. Regardless of where the e-book resides, the librarian still has to have essential data—such as number of times the book was accessed, searched, or downloaded, or when the item was purchased—in order to complete the evaluation. In addition, the evaluation of resources in specific discipline areas is conducted on spreadsheets, which differs from the ability to inspect the shelves in the old-fashioned hands-on method. The physical examination of the item itself always provided the opportunity to evaluate the book's physical condition (does it need mending or a new label?). In many cases, print books damaged beyond repair often became an automatic weed.

Once e-book accessibility is suspended, nothing else has to be done except deleting the record from the online catalog; weeded print items have to be placed somewhere—book sales, discard, or recycling bins—or shipped to used-book buyers like Better World Books. Two of the aforementioned options for print book disposals have traditionally been avenues for additional monies for libraries. The removal of e-books, rather than print, will eliminate these opportunities for revenue generation unless a resale market for e-books develops in the future. Furthermore, hopeful bargain hunters stalking the library book sales may come up shorthanded as fewer print books are available for resale. But library staff may appreciate not having to facilitate a book sale.

When a print book is discarded, the item is gone forever. Once the e-book title is removed from the online catalog—that is, when access ceases—the e-book is not actually gone. Rittenhouse, a distributor of science, technical, and medical titles, offers libraries the ability to create and customize a web-based database, R2Digital Library. When newer versions or editions are purchased, superseded titles are placed in an archive that, as long as libraries maintain an active R2 collection, is still accessible. For example, when the fourth edition of a title is purchased from R2Digital Library, the third edition will be held in the institution's R2Digital Library archive with a single concurrent user access at no charge. By offering this option, Rittenhouse's customized active database of e-books provides only the most current editions—understandably preferred in medical and nursing texts—as well as archiving older editions, which might be beneficial in historical and comparative research.

CONCLUSION

The question, why would you weed an e-book? might be best answered by, why not? When libraries began acquiring nonprint resources, policies that were drafted to reflect the new formats did not alter the libraries' missions, nor did they eliminate the concept of the importance of collection evaluation and possible withdrawal of items. Librarians knew that weeding nonprint items was essential in order to eliminate libraries with shelves full of 16 mm films, filmstrips, and U-matics. Therefore, regardless of format, all resources need to be evaluated.

E-books have been in libraries for a significant amount of time. E-book holdings represent a substantial number—substantial enough to be included in weeding policies, if not already addressed. However, the existence of library literature documenting the assessment and weeding of e-books has yet to appear. An examination of the literature in the future may provide answers that for today remain only hypothetical conjectures regarding weeding e-books, such as that the evaluation and weeding of resources remain a low priority for many libraries, or the philosophy that having more resources equals a better library. One possible theory for the absence of e-book weeding and any subsequent literature may reside in one of the primary differences between weeding a physical book and an e-book: the concern about disappearing physical space and the belief that virtual space is limitless. Overcrowded shelves or repurposed library space demands the removal of physical books; e-books residing outside library server space may not impact the individual library's space, but they still occupy catalog space. Virtual resources demand that librarians address issues and concerns of virtual space.

As emerging technologies and virtual resources continue to increase in importance and availability, librarians in all types of libraries will continue to uphold their professional prime directive of providing resources that meet the needs and expectations of their patron base. Embedded in this philosophy is the possession of the knowledge and ability to implement the optimal manner and method by which to accomplish this mission. As libraries increase their virtual presence, maintaining a viable online catalog becomes an even greater necessity. Providing access to outdated and unused e-books is not acceptable; the concept of weeding e-books must be embraced. As some librarians wait for the research and case studies that will document the theory and process—hence providing guidance and assurance—others may be curiously, even eagerly, waiting for the next format.

REFERENCES

Galbraith, James. 2011. "E-books on the Internet." In *No Shelf Required,* edited by Sue Polanka, 1–18. Chicago: American Library Association.

Harvard University Library. 2011. "About the Harvard Library." February 14, "About the Library."

Herther, Nancy K. 2008. "The Ebook Reader Is Not the Future of Ebooks." *Searcher* 16, no. 8: 26–40. *Library, Information Science & Technology Abstracts with Full Text.*

Library of Congress. "About the Library," February 1, www.loc.gov/about.

OverDrive. 2011. Accessed September 1, www.overdrive.com.

Wilson, A. Paula. 2004. "Weeding the E-book Collection." *Public Libraries* 43 (May/June): 158–59.

7

What Is RDA, and Why Should E-book Managers Care?

STEVE KELLEY

I n recent years, e-book managers and other librarians have posed many questions about RDA, the new cataloging code. Over the course of this chapter, we hope to answer the two-part question: what is RDA, and why should e-book managers care? RDA provides a necessary foundation for building better data structures that will change the capabilities of future cataloging systems. It is a code that was created to be compatible with digital catalogs and digital resources, as well as traditional, nondigital materials. RDA may also provide a necessary step toward integrating library resources with the much heralded Semantic Web. In short, the future of library catalogs lies with RDA. And that is why e-book managers should care about it.

WHAT IS RDA?

RDA is an abbreviation for *Resource Description and Access,* a new cataloging code designed to replace the *Anglo-American Cataloging Rules, 2nd Edition,* commonly known as AACR2. This new code should be of interest to e-book managers because it was developed in large measure to address

AACR2's shortcomings in adequately describing Internet-based resources. That RDA is intended to replace AACR2 is clearly illustrated by the fact that the JSC, the organization responsible for overseeing the cataloging rules used in the English-speaking world, has changed its full name from the Joint Steering Committee for the Revision of AACR to the Joint Steering Committee for the Development of RDA. The JSC has stopped any further revision to AACR2 and will be devoting all its efforts to developing RDA. AACR2 is, effectively, a dead code, while RDA is a growing, adaptive set of rules that can be changed over time.

RDA is a content code, which describes how information should be recorded in bibliographic records. It provides rules for how to record data, such as title information, author names, organizational names, publisher names, and the physical description of bibliographic entities. Although RDA is designed to replace AACR2, the newer code is based on the older one. RDA is intended to be compatible with AACR2, which means that databases can contain both RDA and AACR2 records without a loss of functionality. Also, RDA is intended to be used in any record format, such as MARC (machine-readable cataloging), Dublin Core, EAD (encoded archival description), MODS (metadata object description schema), and the like. RDA does not specify any changes to these formats (although they may need to be revised to accommodate the data encoding required by RDA).

Just to be clear, RDA will affect most of the content of bibliographic records but has nothing to do with subject headings and call numbers. We will continue to use LC (Library of Congress), MESH (medical subject headings), and other subject heading systems like we always have. Similarly, LC, (Library of Congress), Dewey, and SUDOC (superintendent of documents) call numbers will not change due to the new code.

WHY DOES IT SEEM TO BE TAKING SO LONG TO MOVE TO RDA?

The transition away from AACR2 toward full implementation of RDA has been, and will continue to be, a long process because there are a number of moving parts and a number of players involved. Also, quite simply, there is a lot of inertia that is slowing the process. AACR2 was adopted in 1981, in a time that not only predated the Web but a time when most libraries still relied on card catalogs. The explosion of information technology has been a boon to the functionality of modern library catalogs, but it has also created new layers of complexity. Not only must RDA be adopted broadly by libraries throughout the world, the record formats (such as MARC) must be revised to properly capture the detailed data specified by RDA, and cataloging systems must be adapted to properly display the revised record formats. Libraries are currently moving toward adopting RDA, and a few changes have been made to the MARC formats, but we are still some years away from a really full implementation of RDA, in the sense of catalogs being able to properly display all the functionality the new code promises to make possible.

The development path of RDA has already been a long one. The roots of the new code date back to the International Conference on the Principles and Future Development of AACR, held in Toronto, Canada, in 1997. Conference participants discussed AACR2's weaknesses in properly describing Internet-based resources, among other flaws. Prompted by this conference, the JSC began discussion for developing a third edition of AACR, but this was eventually abandoned for a more thoroughgoing code revision, which became RDA (Ehlert 2010). Early drafts of RDA were closely scrutinized by the cataloging community and received a fair amount of criticism, which prompted the JSC to rework the code several times. In 2010, the U.S. national libraries (the Library of Congress, the National Library of Medicine, and the National Agricultural Library) began a test of RDA, in conjunction with twenty-three other libraries throughout the U.S. (including academic, public, and special libraries), during which they created catalog records using RDA. The testing phase closed on December 31, 2010, and after a period of analysis, the three U.S. national libraries announced at the ALA Annual Conference in New Orleans that they were delaying implementation of RDA until January 2013 at the earliest. However, this decision should not be interpreted to mean that the national libraries will not eventually adopt RDA. As was mentioned earlier, the JSC has stopped further work on AACR2 and will devote all its future efforts to the development of RDA, making it the only option for a growing, changing cataloging code. The national libraries determined that the current draft of RDA did not meet several of the stated goals of the code's developers and have requested that the JSC revise RDA to meet these goals, but there is virtually no chance that they will not ultimately adopt the new code. Several libraries, including the University of Chicago, have already adopted RDA in their cataloging departments, but most libraries in the United States will likely wait to make their own decision until after the U.S. national libraries adopt RDA. The decision made by the Library of Congress will be particularly influential among U.S. libraries.

As libraries gradually adopt RDA, they will have to encode their RDA-compliant records in bibliographic formats, which will have to be revised to accommodate the new data requirements of RDA. For most libraries, this will mean the MARC formats, although Dublin Core, MODS, EAD, and other record formats will also be affected. The MARC formats are managed by the Network Development and MARC Standards Office of the Library of Congress. The MARC Standards Office has already approved several changes to the MARC formats to accommodate RDA, and more are under consideration. However, the Library of Congress has begun work on an even more fundamental change to the bibliographic record formats by beginning the process of developing a format to replace MARC. This promises to be an even larger undertaking than adopting RDA and will certainly take years to implement.

As libraries adopt RDA and record formats change to accommodate RDA, online catalogs will also have to evolve to properly display the new data encoded in the revised formats. Several catalog systems are trying to move toward RDA compliance, but both commercially available and open source systems have much work to do to fully implement RDA-style records while maintaining full functionality for older records created using AACR2. (Even after RDA is widely adopted, catalogs will have a mix of RDA and AACR2 records for many years to come, due to the fact that there are millions of AACR2 records and the retrospective conversion of these records to RDA will be an expensive, time-consuming process, if undertaken.) So, the transition to RDA is best viewed as an ongoing process that will continue for several more years as libraries, record formats, and catalog systems work toward fully implementing this new code. But why should we bother? What advantages does RDA confer on the world of online catalogs? This brings us to our next set of questions.

WHY DO WE NEED RDA? WHAT BENEFITS DOES RDA OFFER OVER AACR2?

So, why *do* we need a new cataloging code? The most fundamental issue is that AACR2 is simply out of date. Although it has been revised over the years, it was initially adopted in 1981.The code was originally designed for a world of card catalogs, when computers were not in broad general use—and that is to say nothing of the very small Internet of the time, or the not-yet-invented World Wide Web. A variety of changes and additions have been made to AACR2 over the past thirty years to bring it up to date with current information technologies, but the basic code was written for a predigital age. RDA addresses the problem of describing digital works for a digital environment by adopting the principles of FRBR, which brings us to our first sub-question:

WHAT IS FRBR?

FRBR stands for *functional requirements for bibliographic records,* a conceptual model for bibliographic entities developed by the International Federation of Library Associations and Institutions. First published in 1997, FRBR is based on entity-relationship modeling. It is not a cataloging code but rather a method for thinking about cataloging and the relationships between various bibliographic entities.

FRBR identifies the four basic tasks performed by catalog users. They use data to *find, identify, select,* and *obtain* bibliographic materials (books, e-books, journals, DVDs, etc.) (FRBR 2.2). That is, all catalog users are trying to accomplish one or more of these tasks and need the proper data to accomplish the task or tasks. Every search of a catalog is an attempt to find a work that is needed, identify a useful work, select a work from among various options, and/or obtain the work by finding its unique location (including, in some cases, directly accessing an online work through a URL).

With these four tasks recognized as essential to all uses of the catalog, FRBR then identifies four types of related bibliographic entities that are of interest to catalog users. These entities have varying levels of abstraction and are useful to different sets of user needs. The entities are, from most abstract to most particular, *works, expressions, manifestations,* and *items* (FRBR 3.1). We will attempt to explain the differences between the four types of entities by discussing the various ways we use the word *book.*

In the sentence "Leo Tolstoy is the author of the book *War and Peace,*" we are using the word *book* to refer to a work. That is, we are talking about *War and Peace* as an intellectual creation in its most abstract sense. We have even abstracted it from its original language, because Tolstoy wrote it in Russian, with the title "Voina i mir." In the example sentence we are referring to a novel by Tolstoy about a set of characters in nineteenth-century Russia, regardless of the language or format in which it is captured. No matter how *War and Peace* is rendered, Tolstoy is the author of the work.

In the sentence "Millions of copies of the German version of the last Harry Potter book were sold in all formats," we are using the word *book* to refer to an expression. Now obviously we are talking about a work when we refer to the last Harry Potter book, but we are looking at just the German translation of this work, which is one of several possible expressions of the same work. An expression is the realization of a work in text, sound, image, or other representational forms (FRBR 3.2.2). When talking about a book as an expression, we are referring, in an abstract sense, to a textual arrangement of certain words in a certain order. The German text of the last Harry Potter book consists of some thousands of German words arranged in a particular order. Whether these words are arranged inside a hardback book, a paperback, or on an e-reader, they constitute a single expression of the work.

In the sentence "The latest John Grisham book is the number one hardback best seller in the U.S.," we are using the word *book* to refer to a manifestation. The Grisham book is, of course, a work, and the English-language version is a particular expression of the book, but we are also talking about the hardback edition, which is a particular manifestation of the book. A manifestation is the physical embodiment of an expression of a work (FRBR 3.2.3). In terms of books, a manifestation generally corresponds with an edition. The manifestation is the first of the four entities described by FRBR to be tied to a physical presence. Both work and expression are inherently abstract concepts. The different manifestations of a book may be the hardback edition, the paperback edition, the Kindle version, the Nook version, and so on.

Finally, in the sentence "Please place the James Herriot book on the shelf," we are using the word *book* to refer to an item, a specific physical copy of a particular book. An item is a single exemplar of a manifestation (FRBR 3.2.4), and it is also the most concrete and conceptually easy to grasp of the four FRBR entities. An item is a physical object that you can put your hands or eyes on. The item is a single copy of a manifestation, which embodies an expression of a work.

Figure 7.1 illustrates how the four FRBR bibliographic entities relate to a specific book. At the *work* level, we have "Voina i mir," which is *War and Peace* as conceived by Leo Tolstoy. It could be in Russian or translated into any other language, but it will always be the intellectual creation of Tolstoy. Next, at the *expression* level, we have an English translation of *War and Peace,* which captures the ideas of Tolstoy's work into a specific sequence of English words. These words can be printed in a paperback book or published in an e-book. The physical carrier does not matter; what matters is the intellectual content of the expression. Next, at the *manifestation* level, we have the Oxford University Press edition published in 1983. This refers to a group of thousands of books that all look the same, and all have the same expression of the work on their pages. And finally, at the *item* level, we have the copy of this edition held at Z. Smith Reynolds Library.

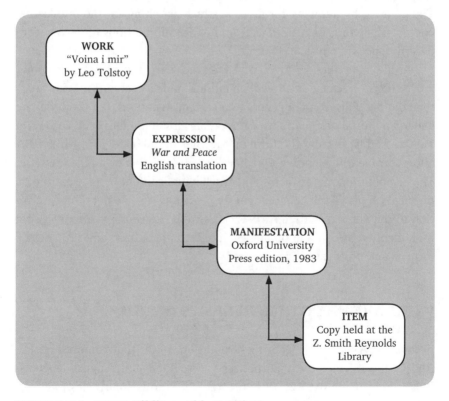

FIGURE 7.1 *FRBR Bibliographic Entities*

Now, you may be wondering, what does all this mean? Well, RDA is based on the ideas of FRBR and the four types of bibliographic entities. This means that, by using RDA, catalogers can create records that have varying levels of specificity to meet different user needs. Although AACR2 does not use FRBR terminology, the rules of AACR2 require catalogers to work at a manifestation level (in FRBR terms), referring to the particular physical forms of bibliographic works. But by using RDA, catalogers can create more abstract work and expression level records. This will be particularly useful for e-books. With e-books, the user is not tied to any one delivery device or physical format. Someone could search a catalog looking for *The Adventures of Huckleberry Finn* and with the more abstract expression level record find all versions of the English text of the book. The user may not care whether the text is available as a loan to her Nook, or by borrowing a Kindle from a library, or by downloading a file to her laptop. Or she may be willing to go to the library to retrieve a print copy of the book. The point is, by allowing for more abstract searching for the intellectual content of a work, RDA frees us from AACR2's limitations requiring us to describe specific physical objects.

At the same time, RDA will make faceted searching by material format more robust, because it allows for more detailed description of formats than did the old system of general material designations. For example, the general material designation *videorecording* was applied to both DVDs and videocassettes, putting the formats together in one category, while RDA allows for clearly encoding whether an item is a DVD or a videocassette. The combination of abstracting the intellectual content of a work from its physical carrier, while simultaneously providing a more detailed description of the carrier, will allow users to search the catalog to more easily find, identify, select, and obtain the intellectual content they seek, across formats and physical carriers.

WHAT ARE THE OTHER BENEFITS OF RDA?

Because RDA was built from the ground up rather than simply revising AACR2, the JSC took the opportunity to try to remove the English-language bias inherent in AACR2, which, after all, stands for *Anglo-American Cataloging Rules, 2nd Edition.* The bias toward English is apparent in the very name. The JSC recognized that translated versions of AACR2 are used in various countries, with varying degrees of difficulty arising from the English-centered nature of the rules; therefore, they drafted RDA with an eye toward making the code linguistically neutral.

Another structural problem of AACR2 that RDA addresses is the fact that AACR2 was initially written over thirty years ago to be used with card catalogs. The RDA rules were designed to be used with electronic online catalogs and provide for detailed, rich description of electronic resources. AACR2 provides rules for describing electronic resources, but these rules were adapted from rules for print books and can sometimes be difficult to use (the saying "trying to fit a square peg in a round hole" springs to mind). By beginning with a clean slate, RDA provides for better description of born-digital materials, as well as allowing for better and easier description of the electronic versions of print books.

Because RDA is a product of the digital age, it also explicitly addresses the role that catalog records can play in the direct access of library materials. With nondigital resources, the catalog provides bibliographic information that allows the user to locate materials; but with digital resources, the URL in the catalog record is often the means of accessing the materials. The point at which a work is found in the catalog can also be the point where the work is accessed. RDA acknowledges this important development (which is apparent in the name of the code, Resource Description and Access).

Another important benefit of RDA is that it allows for a richer description of the relationships between multiple creators, between multiple works, and between creators and works. RDA does a better job than AACR2 of describing relationships between multiple creators by providing for more accurate, detailed descriptions of the roles of various creators. This description can be so precise as to use terms like *recording engineer* or *lithographer*. This level of detail in describing the precise role played by a creator can be helpful.

RDA also provides for better description of the relationships between various works, such as derivative works, which are works based on other works. For example, the novel *Gone with the Wind* has a number of derivative works. There is a sequel novel called *Scarlett,* a parody novel called *The Wind Done Gone,* and a film version, also called *Gone with the Wind.* A book about the film called *The Filming of Gone with the Wind* is a derivative work of the film, so we would want to record that relationship. However, we would not want to have the film study directly related to the novel (see figure 7.2). RDA allows for the clear recording of these types of relationships between works, helping patrons find the works they need.

Regarding relationships between creators and works, AACR2 limited catalog records to contain access points for the names of no more than three creators of a given work (a legacy of the card catalog), but RDA does away with this "rule of three." Using RDA rules, a cataloger can decide to provide an access point for every person involved with creating a work. This means, for example, that if a user tries to search for all the works of a given author, under RDA rules the retrieval set will include a work where the author is the fourth contributor listed. This would not be possible under the AACR2 rule of three (Oliver 2010).

In addition to allowing for more detailed relationships between entities in bibliographic records, RDA also simplifies the rules for recording data in records. AACR2 required the use of many abbreviations for common

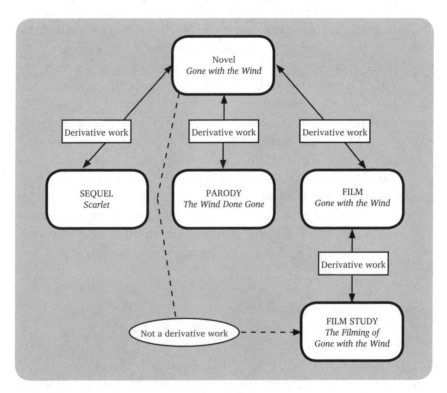

FIGURE 7.2 *Examples of Derivative Works*

terms such as *pages, volumes,* and *department.* By getting rid of these required abbreviations (another legacy of the card catalog), RDA moves toward recording data as it appears in bibliographic materials (which is also apparent in the demise of the rule of three). RDA further simplifies records by dispensing with the Latinisms that peppered records under AACR2, such as *et al., sic, i.e.,* and others. These changes not only make it easier for catalogers to catalog materials quickly, because they do not have to remember particular abbreviations or Latin terms and when to use them, but they also make the records easier for users to read and understand.

The "take it as you find it" philosophy of RDA is expected to make the cataloging rules simpler in the long run. This should result in quicker and cheaper cataloging, while also providing for richer description (in terms of relationships and electronic resources), which should result in better-quality cataloging. Of course, all these benefits are long term. In the short term, there will be some growing pains as the cataloging world transitions to RDA.

CONCLUSION: WHAT DOES RDA MEAN FOR LIBRARIES AND E-BOOK MANAGERS?

To be honest, RDA does not mean much for e-book managers in the short term. Yes, a few records may pop up that have new MARC fields, and at libraries that have in-house cataloging, the catalog librarians may be quite occupied over the next year or two learning about RDA and planning for its adoption locally. But, in truth, much of the work of implementing RDA still needs to be done. Libraries need to adopt the code, record formats need to be further changed to accommodate the code, and online catalogs need to be updated to handle the new data requirements brought about by RDA. Also, many thousands of RDA records need to be created before catalog users routinely encounter RDA records while searching.

However, RDA will help change library catalogs considerably over time. It is a foundation upon which will be built the bibliographic data structures of the future. AACR2 is simply not adequate for the digital age. RDA may not be perfect—and it definitely has its critics—but it is a code that is designed to be compatible with digital catalogs and digital resources, while AACR2 was designed for an age of card catalogs and print materials. As our bibliographic resources change, our cataloging code must adapt to these changes. RDA will allow for more precise searching for specific intellectual content, without the physical format barriers imposed by AACR2 records. RDA will also allow for richer use of faceted searches and will provide better details regarding the relationships between works. This type of information will be of enormous importance when searching for e-books especially, because they can be more difficult to browse than physical materials. We want our catalog records to be as detailed as possible to ensure a successful search, saving the patron from downloading an e-book that is not useful.

Perhaps most exciting, RDA may allow for bibliographic data structures to be integrated into the emerging Semantic Web. The Semantic Web will enable computers to process the meaning of information on the World Wide Web and may facilitate such developments as natural language searching. Data on the Semantic Web will have to be finely granulated and rigidly organized to allow computers to categorize and classify information in meaningful ways to answer the queries of human users. The more finely detailed, or granulated, data required by RDA may make our bibliographic records a functioning part of the Semantic Web. This could open the door to catalogs that respond to natural language queries, which would be quite a change from our current system of searching on precise terms or the somewhat scattershot approach of using key words.

So, in summary, RDA offers the possibility of revolutionizing the data structures that underlie our catalog systems and, by extension, the entire process of resource discovery. As was stated at the beginning of this chapter, the future of library catalogs lies with RDA. And that is why e-book managers should care about it.

REFERENCES

Ehlert, Mark K. 2010. "RDA: Why New Cataloging Rules?" *Technicalities* 30 (May/June): 19–20.

Functional Requirements for Bibliographic Records (FRBR). 2007. http://archive .ifla.org/VII/s13/frbr/frbr_current_toc.htm.

Oliver, Chris. 2010. *Introducing RDA: A Guide to the Basics.* Chicago: American Library Association.

8

Enhanced E-books
How Books Are Coming Alive in the Digital Environment

SYLVIA K. MILLER

The book publishing world is beginning to recognize the exciting possibilities offered by new technologies, but producing and consuming e-books with enhanced features is complicated. A confusing array of incompatible processes, devices, and software offers a combination of frustrating barriers and tantalizing possibilities to publishers, individual consumers, and libraries. This chapter provides an overview of the current enhanced e-book landscape—with an emphasis on the humanities and social sciences—and ventures to describe a future in which enhanced formats might become the norm.

WHAT IS AN "ENHANCED E-BOOK"?

Tools for both internal navigation and outbound linking have been integral to books since long before the digital era. Some of the most standard, commonly understood tools for navigation within a book are tables of contents, running heads, folios, cross-references, and indexes. Others almost as ubiquitous in scholarly books are in-text figure references and parenthetical citations that refer to a bibliography list. Outbound linking is represented in print by footnotes and bibliographies that refer to other sources, recommend further reading, and lead the reader on paths to further research. Often the source notes that accompany illustrations, figures, and tables also represent outbound links because by referencing sources, they recommend the sources as valuable for further research. If the illustration is a primary source such as a photograph or letter from an archive, the illustration might be said to represent the entire archive, a resource that might as a whole be of interest to the reader. Taking a phrase from science publishing, the archive of primary-source materials that was perused by a historian preparatory to the writing of an interpretive narrative might be called the historian's *data set.*

Looking back now at the predigital world of books, we recognize that all these navigational tools and outbound paths were prototypes for hyperlinks, only we did not know it. In addition, sidebars, extended captions, narrative endnotes, appendixes, and other content external to the main text—intended to contextualize or enrich it in various ways—created a multilayered reading experience potentially ideal for digital presentation. E-book formats bring these aspects of books alive, allowing them to be activated by a click or touch of the finger. Any e-book with such functionality might be considered enhanced.

Accustomed to the physical form of the book, the reader might at first be confused by the quick linking action and the jumping around in the digital environment. Handed a physical book, the reader does not have to ask what the running heads mean or where the table of contents is located. In e-books and collections of e-books, we are presented with a dizzying array of formats and functional capabilities because navigational standards have not yet been agreed upon. Nevertheless, when the electronic format works well and the reader becomes used to it, the user experience is akin to magic.

The baseline of e-book functionality is continually rising, along with reader expectations. Most e-books now have some level of internal linking—from the table of contents to the first page of the chapter, for example. The logical next step is more magic: books in which the pictures move and speak, music on the page can be heard, and references to places and sources are really paths that take us, virtually, to other spaces, collections, and publications.

The type of publication that over the last couple of years has come to be known as the *enhanced e-book* is an e-book that has this additional bit of magic in it, in the form of audio or video content attached to a central written narrative; it might also be called a *multimedia e-book.*

THE ENHANCED E-BOOK'S BEGINNINGS

Good ideas tend to have many proponents and early prototypes, making it challenging, if not foolhardy, to attempt to pinpoint the very first enhanced e-book in the social sciences and the humanities. In the 1990s, digital encyclopedias (first on CD, then online) such as *Grove Art* began to include outbound links to museums and other sites, as well as audio examples. Alexander Street Press included multimedia materials in thematic aggregations of content that serve libraries as reference sources.

It took the advent of the iPhone to inspire a proliferation of multimedia books designed to be purchased one title at a time by the consumer. With its colorful touch screen, multimedia capabilities, and invitation to users to become entrepreneurs by submitting software programs, the iPhone prompted creation of many homegrown e-books with multimedia and interactive features. Soon publishers joined in by venturing to invest in some iPhone publishing experiments, specially commissioned from software developers at significant cost.

Some were audiobooks linked to the text so that the user could toggle back and forth between listening and reading. The reader could read on the subway, for example, then switch to audio when arriving at the train station and walking to the gym; the book "knew" where in the narrative to begin streaming the audio file. One publisher experimented with creating short films that would enhance the reader's experience of a novel. Another turned a young adult novel, *Cathy's Book,* into a sort of game, prompting some observers to wonder whether the end of the book as we have known it was near. Readers were presented with a mystery to solve via a fictional young woman's handwritten journal; the book took advantage of iPhone capabilities by responding to touching, turning, and shaking. Scribbled doodles were hyperlinked, and readers listened to the protagonist's telephone messages. The form of the book itself seemed to be on the verge of exploding and becoming something different and new (Stewart and Weisman 2009).*

At the close of 2009, the number of iPhone software applications (popularly known as *apps*) that consisted of e-books with special features was already growing so rapidly that it was eclipsing the number of games; many of these special book apps contained video (Petway 2009). The larger iPad screen inspired additional individual experiments; for example, a scientist created a beautiful illustrated reference to the periodic table of elements in which each element was illustrated by an object such as a rock or a tool; at a touch, the pictured objects rotated gently 360 degrees (Gray and Mann 2009).† Although it was an original, unique project, this stunning publication was still recognizable as a book and, perhaps ironically, ushered in a rush to standardize enhanced e-books. It also began to demonstrate that such enhancements might be suitable for scholarly content and education.

THE WORLD OF SERIALS: THE E-BOOK'S CRYSTAL BALL

Observing developments in the science, technology, engineering, and mathematics (STEM) journal publishing fields and serials in general is instructive, because these publications tend to run technologically ahead of books in the humanities and social sciences by several years. For example, the bibliographies of most STEM journals in large journal databases are populated with digital object identifiers (DOIs), invented in the 1990s to cross publisher boundaries and link bibliography entries to full-text online

---

* The original hardcover of *Cathy's Book* was published in 2006. There are several YouTube videos about the book, including one that resembles a movie trailer. You can see a demonstration of the enhanced features here: www.youtube.com/watch?v = h50x8cmhmVU.

† The enhanced e-book for iPad was prepared prior to the release of the iPad in early 2010 and made available immediately thereafter, according to Gray on one of the YouTube videos about the book (www.popsci.com/gadgets/article/2010-04/exclusive-making-elements-one-ipads-most-magical-apps).

In an effort to expand on his experience with *The Elements* and standardize its successful format, Gray started Touch Press, which collaborated with the University of Chicago Press and the Field Museum in 2011 to publish *Gems and Gemstones: Timeless Natural Beauty of the Mineral World* by Lance Grande and Allison Augustyn. Like *The Elements*, it is a stunning iPad app, with rotating images that allow 360-degree examination of objects whose reverse side is not normally visible in a museum case. For a demo, see www.youtube.com/watch?v = 6LX2Bz6xC4s.

publications. DOIs have moved into the humanities and social sciences but are still used mostly in journals and have just begun to be used in e-books.

Looking at a few examples of established multimedia journals might be like looking into a crystal ball to see the future of scholarly book publishing:

- The *Journal of Visualized Experiments* (www.jove.com) is a peer-reviewed medical journal in which each article includes a video expressly created for the publication. The videos illustrate procedures that are opaque when presented in prose, in many cases eliminating the necessity of expensive travel and time-consuming apprenticeships and preventing much costly trial and error in scientific experiments.
- *Southern Spaces* (www.southernspaces.org) is an online journal published at the Emory University Libraries about the culture and landscapes of the southeastern U.S. Each issue presents multimedia content; for example, to learn about a poet, the reader clicks a link and is greeted by a film recording of the poet herself, who performs one of her poems while walking in a meadow, part of the landscape that is meaningful in her work.
- *In media res* (mediacommons.futureofthebook.org/imr) is an online journal in the field of media studies, published at the New York Universities Libraries. The content of each weekly "issue" is centered around a short video. Authors may post in text or video format, putting the medium under discussion on an equal footing with the text format of the traditional journal.

One can easily imagine scholarly books with these same attributes. An intriguing example related to the third item above is *Learning from YouTube,* a 2011 experimental book from MIT Press in which text and video are integrated to create a new kind of content module. (See http://vectors.usc.edu/projects/learningfromyoutube.) However, current experiments are based on proprietary software that is not used in the same form elsewhere; the resources to replicate this type of publication in book publishing and the standards to support such books are in their infancy.

THE ROAD TO STANDARDIZATION

Amazon's Kindle application is now available for PC, iPhone, and iPad as well as the Kindle. When the University of North Carolina Press published *Give My Poor Heart Ease: Voices of the Mississippi Blues* by William Ferris in enhanced e-book format in 2010, it was one of the first enhanced e-books available via the Kindle application. In print, the book included a CD and a DVD in an envelope glued inside the back cover (typically a challenge for libraries to catalog and track); in enhanced e-book format, the audio and video recordings of the blues musicians can be accessed within the text. Although most of the 248 enhanced e-books listed in the Amazon store as recently as March 2011 were nonscholarly how-to books (*Yoga in Bed* was a typical example), only six months later the number of enhanced e-books had jumped to 1,848, with more classic literature and science textbooks in the mix. Clearly, there will continue to be more and more enhanced e-books available in all categories, with *Give My Poor Heart Ease* demonstrating the usefulness of multimedia enhancements in humanities scholarship. Somewhat confusingly, the audio and video in *Give My Poor Heart Ease* cannot yet be viewed on the Kindle for PC platform; although the PC is a multimedia-enabled device, the software has not yet been developed to allow the audio and video in a Kindle enhanced e-book to work on a PC. Nor is this multimedia content accessible on the Kindle device, because it is not a multimedia-enabled device. The content is, however, accessible via the Kindle software for iPhone and iPad. The enhanced e-book is also being developed for the Nook, the reading device from Barnes & Noble. The book may eventually become available in the Apple bookstore as well, but UNC Press is still attempting to negotiate with Apple over the Apple bookstore contract, which apparently was not devised with small, scholarly publishers in mind. These complexities confuse and frustrate publishers and customers alike. Nevertheless, the mere existence of standards such as Kindle, Apple, and Nook is an important advance.

BEHIND THE SCENES: PRICING AND VERSIONS

Publishers must contend with myriad technical requirements for e-books from both new and established vendors from Kindle to EBSCOhost. Each tends to require a different version of the electronic file for the book and the metadata. In some cases, the vendor will give the publisher a head start by offering to convert the electronic file to their proprietary format free of charge; however, delays ensue, preventing the publisher from achieving the goal of simultaneous print and electronic publication desired by publishers, consumers, and libraries. Another issue for the publisher is that these converted files belong to the vendor, not the publisher; to publish the e-book through another vendor, another conversion must be done. Fortunately, a standard called EPUB is emerging that may eventually simplify the process, but for now publishers must manage a complex matrix of file conversions and metadata preparation for multiple outputs. One can imagine that in the near future, at least, the addition of multimedia aspects to some but not all available platforms and devices will compound the challenges surrounding e-book publication.

An additional challenge for publishers is the cost of third-party copyright permissions. Museums, archives, and other publishers and copyright holders often charge higher fees for the reprinting of their content in e-books than in print books, even when the author is responsible for paying or the publisher is a nonprofit. The reason is twofold, an interesting tension between ambition and fear: (1) In the 1990s the dot-com boom appeared to generate an anticipation among some of these content owners that revenues and profits from any kind of online business would be astronomical, and it was only fair for them to share in the general good fortune; such permission-fee schedules, once established, do not tend to change. (2) Anticipating widespread online plagiarism and piracy that might erode their control over the content, copyright owners considered limited access and high fees prudent.

Obtaining permission to include multimedia content in an e-book usually adds to the permission fees associated with publishing that book. Permission fees, together with the cost of staff time to negotiate and obtain the permissions, often explain why some illustrations, examples, or other content that appear in the print book are omitted from the e-book. In collections of content licensed to libraries, it frustrates librarians and publishers alike that the extent to which the print book and the e-book versions diverge will tend to vary from one title to another. This problem of inconsistent incompleteness will only worsen with enhanced e-books. There are no full solutions in sight.

The costs associated with multiple file formats and permissions only add to the cost of content acquisition, editing, design, proofreading, marketing, and publicity; printing fewer copies makes printing more expensive, and overall the cost of the publishing process from content origination to output in multiple formats in increasing. This explains why publishers do not price e-books lower than print books. As one might expect, enhanced e-books are no exception, although prices are variable at this time. Generally, the price hovers at around the same as for the print book, or slightly more; if there is a hardcover edition, the enhanced e-book price is closer to that price than to the lower paperback price. Publishers are testing the market to see whether the enhanced content will be seen by customers as having an intrinsic, additional value. It is possible, though, that in the future enhanced content will be ubiquitous and assumed to have been included when available, without variable pricing for it or multiple versions of the publication being offered in the marketplace. Look at the current market in movie DVDs, which routinely contain behind-the-scenes interviews, footage from the first cut, and so forth; the cost is built into the retail price, and there is often no cheaper, less enhanced version available for purchase from the publisher. (Pirated versions are another story, however.)

TWO BASIC WAYS TO ENHANCE E-BOOKS

Even as the available technologies continue to change rapidly, it is possible to identify two basic ways that e-books are currently being enhanced, to consider the advantages and disadvantages of each, and to wonder what the implications will be if one becomes more prevalent than the other. The two ways are (1) embed the multimedia files in the e-book and sell the resulting combination as a package, or (2) include live links in the e-book to multimedia content that is hosted separately.

Embedded files are convenient for the reader because they appear quickly—at a click—whereas access to linked content depends upon the technology at the host site as well as the accessibility and speed of the reader's Internet connection. Embedded files might be more permanent, because links can go bad unless they are regularly checked and updated; on the other hand, file formats, software, and devices have a history of rapid obsolescence, too. (It is worth pointing out here that publishers who make a perpetual-access commitment to library customers are taking on enormous new costs and responsibilities; after all, in the not-too-distant past, it used to be libraries that archived books for perpetual access, not publishers!)

A disadvantage of embedded files is that currently audio and especially video files tend to be large; for example, the multimedia features of *Cathy's Book* made the e-book file so large that the book had to be released in installments. For a library, a collection of such books could demand a great deal of costly server space. Presumably, in the future this problem could diminish as the efficiency of software and the capacity of devices continue to improve. Linked files, on the other hand, are already hosted elsewhere, where storage capacity has already been addressed and an access interface established; linking rather than duplicating takes up less server space on the customer side.

In the Long Civil Rights Movement Project at the University of North Carolina, the experimental publishing platform allows registered users to contribute comments at the paragraph level and embed links in the comments. Scholars, students, and archivists have contributed annotations containing links to oral histories, photographs, and handwritten documents. The individual items sit within larger collections that might also be of interest to the reader; having clicked a link to access a particular item, the reader is able to observe the context in which that item lives—the Southern Oral History Program archive at UNC, for example, or the Lowcountry Digital Library at the College of Charleston—and explore the collection. In this way the reader is introduced to new resources for research, while archives increase the discoverability of their collections. Via this commenting feature, links can continue to be added as more archival materials are digitized and made available online so that the books are dynamically enhanced over time. It remains to be seen whether this type of enhancement will become commonplace in the e-book market, but it is likely that enhancements will become dynamic in some way. Perhaps e-books will become like other software in our computers, regularly checking back with their publishers online and automatically updating themselves. For libraries, books now regarded as static monographs might become mini serials within larger collections sold by license. The purchase of e-books is already morphing into a license, via variations on the simultaneous user–access contract. Future expansion of the number of enhanced e-books available—and the possible dynamism of those books—will confirm that change in the purchase model.

SCHOLARLY AUTHORS AND ENHANCED E-BOOKS

Scholarly work in history, folklore, music, literature, and media studies is routinely intertwined with multimedia content. Until recently, scholarly presses did not have the means to publish a book that included or linked to this material; authors might ask their editors whether they wanted their interview tapes, for example, submitted with the manuscript, and the answer had to be no. Now the possibilities online have become apparent, via an advance guard of innovative journals and enhanced e-books, and a small but growing number of authors have begun to push more strongly for inclusion of multimedia content in their books. Publishers will need to respond in order to compete for authors in the future.

As described above, these enhanced e-books could have multimedia files embedded within them, they might link to multimedia hosted elsewhere, or both. For content that is not yet hosted elsewhere, it might be appropriate to partner with a special collections library in the early planning stages of publication. In parallel, the library would acquire, digitize, and make available to the public the author's oral histories, while the publisher would shepherd the manuscript through the traditional peer-review, editing, and production process, including in the finished book contextual links to the newly archived primary-source material.*

In the near future, authors who envision their books from the beginning as multimedia productions will be few. However, once there are more such books available, they will be recognized as valuable in both scholarly discourse and teaching. Historians who attended focus groups at UNC Press during the last two years were enthusiastic about the possibility of linking monographs to primary sources because they recognized the potential for teaching students where historical narratives come from, demonstrating concretely and conveniently how historians begin with voices and documents from the past and write interpretive narratives based on them.

---

* At UNC Press, we have two to three book projects in the early planning stages that may demonstrate this model; our partner is the UNC Special Collections Library.

Textbooks may develop into enhanced e-books before enhanced monographs become widespread. Examples that move and demonstrate concepts, news clips, examples of performing arts performances—the possibilities are limitless and follow naturally from the current form of textbooks, with their numerous sidebars, definitions, review questions, and other pedagogical apparatus often available on separate CDs and websites. It may seem surprising that more textbooks are not electronic even now, but e-textbooks are waiting not only for the just-right device and software but also the right business model and the right integration with course-management software (such as Blackboard, Sakai, or Moodle). One challenge for publishers is the potential loss of revenue if an adoption textbook is made available to multiple simultaneous users via a library. One solution might be to include the textbooks in student fees, enhancing the library budget so that the library would purchase the access license; then the campus course-management software system would integrate the textbook with its own pedagogical apparatus as well as the rest of the course materials and communications.

CONCLUSION

Enhanced e-books are in their infancy; even the language used to describe them is developing and fluid.* However, it is clear that the possibilities are exciting for every type of book, including scholarly works in the humanities and social sciences, which are underrepresented in the current enhanced e-book landscape. It seems reasonable to expect that eventually the confusing differences and restrictions that we now experience will be erased by the demands of both the consumer and the library markets. The baseline functionality that all e-book devices and software platforms are expected to deliver will become established and recognizably consistent, and it will include multimedia accessibility. Then authors and publishers will be able to return their focus to their greatest interest and expertise, the development of worthwhile content.

Other technology that is still peripheral in the current landscape might blossom and become more important, like commenting features that allow

---

* For example, a content segment in Learning from YouTube is called a *texteo*. While the Long Civil Rights Movement Project investigated whether marginal additions were more appropriately termed *comments* or *annotations*, the author of *Dangerous Citizens* dubbed hers *parerga*. (See http://dangerouscitizens.columbia .edu). Even the definition of *enhanced e-book* is fluid, hence my delimiting of the term at the start of this chapter.

discussions in the margins of books and encourage communities to form around them, or ways of linking related content to books that are automated, based on the reader's already established interests and the pattern of the text on the page.* Even now there are so many experiments with annotation being conducted† that the Mellon Foundation has funded a project to help standardize annotation systems and make them communicate with one another (the Open Annotation Collaboration, www.openannotation .org). One might expect, and perhaps fear, the advent of a chaotic confluence of information in which books disappear—or all books become one book—but the human mind appreciates a story, a filter, a guide through the growing web of interconnected content. This is one of many reasons to develop and preserve the long-form narrative as a genre of publication.

Added to multimedia content that is contextually integrated within the book, we will see links to related primary and secondary sources and, in bibliographies, DOIs linking to the full text of secondary sources—all bringing alive the outbound navigation that was always implied in the print medium and reminding us that a scholarly book is really, in the words of Tim O'Reilly, "an interface to a body of information" (Adobe XD 2009).

REFERENCES

Adobe XD. 2009. "Tim O'Reilly and Michael Gough on the Future of Publishing." Video, Oct. 20, 30:21, https://xd.adobe.com/#/videos/video/436.

Gray, Theodore, and Nick Mann. 2009. *The Elements: A Visual Exploration of Every Known Atom in the Universe.* New York: Black Dog & Leventhal.

Petway, Randy. 2009. "E-book Standards." Charleston E-book Preconference, November 4, www.libraries.wright.edu/noshelfrequired/wp-content/uploads/2009/11/petway.pdf.

Stewart, Sean, and Jordan Weisman. 2009. *Cathy's Book: If Found Call 650–266–8233.* Philadelphia: Running Press.

---

* In its September 13, 2010, issue, *Publishers Weekly* reported on an iPhone app called Icandy Mobile, which can transform the pattern of text on a page into an unobtrusive link that will activate video and audio content, suggesting that the formats and ways in which books are connected to multimedia content will continue to develop and change.

† For an experiment in annotation, see *Candide: A Networked Edition of Voltaire's 1759 classic* (http://candide.nypl.org/text/), based on CommentPress, software created by the Institute for the Future of the Book (www.futureofthebook.org). CommentPress has also been used in experiments at New York University and Yale University Press. A future version of CommentPress will work on EPUB files. See also the Long Civil Rights Movement Project, https://lcrm.lib.unc.edu/voice/works, and *Dangerous Citizens,* referenced above.

9

E-book Sea Change in Public Libraries
Lending, Devices, Training, and Budgets

MICHAEL PORTER, MATT WEAVER,
AND BOBBI NEWMAN

After Christmas it hit like a storm.

Lori Reed (2011)

The situation for e-books in public libraries changed radically at the beginning of
2011. For many gift givers, the e-reader was simply the cool gift to give
and to receive. It was a fresh, new kind of gift for many, and with its wide
market penetration and media buzz it became an easy choice for those
who could afford to give it in the 2010 holiday season. In the last week of
December 2010 alone, some three to five million e-readers were activated
(Minzesheimer and Memmott 2011), and as a direct result public libraries
experienced a substantial jump in e-book use.

Understandably, libraries like the Charlotte Mecklenburg Library
reported new patron use of OverDrive rose 160 percent from the previous
year, while at the same time digital content circulations increased 399
percent and holds on digital content spiked up 178 percent (Reed 2011).

The Stark County District Library in Ohio experienced similar changes,
reporting that in the first nine weeks of 2011, 1,050 e-books were borrowed. This is almost as much as the entire total for all of 2009. E-book
checkouts there are now expected to exceed 6,000, which is a more than
a 100 percent increase from 2010 (Biliczky 2011). While this is a new

jump in e-book and e-reader activity, in the coming years and decades these numbers are expected to continue to rise at startling rates across nearly all the communities that libraries serve, raising a host of challenges, opportunities, and new realities.

So while libraries clearly find themselves in the wake of an explosion in e-book use, there are significant challenges. Libraries share parts of an industry that has seen multiple format and standards changes and adjustments, marketing campaigns galore, a Borders bankruptcy, the imposition of lending restrictions on e-books by HarperCollins (see the spotlight essay by Michael Porter following this chapter for more information on the HarperCollins lending restrictions), and even the announcement that the Kindle will be able to use OverDrive e-books. Considering the trends and all the significant changes that abound, it becomes clear that new lending paradigms and solutions are needed for libraries. And while some changes have been announced and implemented, libraries must become more and more informed and engaged when it comes to e-books. The solutions that are being developed in this turbulent era for libraries and e-book access must include the understanding and expertise of libraries and library staff, and the ultimate solutions must result in furthering the mission of public libraries both in the short and long term.

With new entrants in the library e-book sector and major advances from current players, assessing what is on the market can be a challenge on its own. This chapter will help public libraries make decisions about e-book services by exploring these key areas: new developments in e-book services to libraries, e-readers in libraries, training, budgets, and the HarperCollins/ OverDrive situation.

E-BOOK PROVIDERS: NEW PLAYERS, MAJOR DEVELOPMENTS

Over the past few months, the sector has changed rapidly, and further changes are likely in the near future. As markets and players in those markets shake out, being familiar with the myriad issues will help libraries uncover, find, and even create better deals and systems for e-book and e-reader use. There have been a number of developments in 2011 of interest to public libraries.

Currently, OverDrive remains the strongest player in the public library e-book market, having made many technological advances in recent months, including launching mobile apps for Apple's iOS, Droid, Windows Mobile, and BlackBerry. While those apps have added functionality and reduce the reliance on Adobe Content Server, the company's biggest advance was a deal that will allow Amazon's Kindle e-reader, and Kindle apps, to use OverDrive e-books. A major gap in OverDrive's services was the ability to provide e-books to the most popular e-reader on the market. What's more, the deal will not require the library to allocate additional dollars for yet another e-book format or to add the Kindle to their offerings (Estrovich 2011). That is not to say the addition of the Kindle will not represent increased costs: when the service goes live, a new group of e-book readers will draw on collections that have the restrictions of OverDrive's one-user/one-checkout e-book lending model. With that will come further pressure to acquire more copies of e-book titles.

Another development at OverDrive is its work on an e-reader certification program, which was a recommendation of the Chief Officers of State Library Agencies (COSLA) report on e-books (2010). COSLA wanted the company to indicate which devices were compatible with library e-book services. According to David Burleigh, OverDrive's director of marketing, the company developed specifications for e-readers after consulting libraries with a view to designing and manufacturing devices that libraries would acquire and lend. OverDrive took the specifications to devices manufacturers in China. But the certification program has been delayed by a couple of changes in the technologies involved in delivering e-books to patrons. First, a new version of Adobe Content Server (ACS)—the system that handles the digital rights management for e-books in OverDrive's system—is pending. ACS, long criticized by users and librarians alike for the complications it adds to the e-book lending process, is expected to undergo improvements that will benefit libraries and their patrons. Second, OverDrive's own apps have significantly increased device compatability with library e-books. The program is still developing, but when it is announced it may not reflect the original goal. The company's main objective is to improve user experience.

Plans to launch a cloud-based e-book lending system were announced by 3M Library Systems at the ALA Annual Conference in June 2011. The service includes touch screen devices for within libraries, special e-reader apps for mobile devices, and its own e-readers (Toor 2011).

The e-book collections of NetLibrary, acquired by EBSCO in 2010, were migrated into the EBSCOhost database platform in 2011 so that e-books could be searched along with other content. The some 300,000 e-books and audiobooks will be expanded as EBSCO adds the EPUB format later in 2011 (Kelley 2011).

OCLC and Ingram have partnered to offer e-books that will feature short-term loans made through the latter's MyiLibrary e-book collection. The loan term under this new service will be a maximum of nine days. WorldCat Resource Sharing interlibrary loan fee management will handle the fee, which will amount to 15 percent of Ingram's price. Users will have immediate access to titles when they request them (OCLC 2011).

Academic e-book specialist ebrary's offerings have evolved with the launch of short-term loans that are initiated by use. This program—separate from but combinable with its patron-driven acquisition program—will have loan terms of either one day or one week. Depending on agreements between ebrary and publishers, the cost to the library of such a loan will range from 10 to 30 percent of the cost of the title (Rapp 2011B).

After three of these short-term loans, the library will be required to acquire the title for further use. In addition to its long-standing presence in the academic market, ebrary has broadened into the public library market (Hadro 2010; Rapp 2011B). Ebrary's public library offerings include a simultaneous access offering in stark contrast to the one-copy/one-user model offered by OverDrive.

Another new approach to e-book lending in public libraries has been launched by the Internet Archive. Like the Sony Reader program, the Internet Archive's e-book program is restricted to a select number of participants. The program will offer some 85,000 e-books that had been digitized and donated by libraries for in-library loans as part of its Open Library service. Initially, only libraries who contributed e-books to Open Library will have access to the collections (Rapp 2011A).

The Open Library project will include donated content from indie publishers like Smashwords, Cursor, and OR Books, according to Internet Archive founder Brewster Kahle and director Peter Brantley (Kahle 2011). Titles will be license free. Patrons will be able to download up to five titles at once, which they can have for a maximum of two weeks. Books can be read outside the library after they have been checked out. These collections can be downloaded as PDF or EPUB e-books, or viewed in a browser-based reader called BookReader developed by Internet Archive. Included in the Open Library project e-books are titles that are out of print but otherwise still subject to copyright.

E-READERS IN PUBLIC LIBRARIES

E-reader lending programs in public libraries have had a slow and cautious start. A survey of public libraries by *Library Journal* in 2010 found that only 5 percent of public libraries were lending e-readers, but 24 percent were considering it (*Library Journal* 2010). Examining what libraries are currently doing when it comes to e-reader lending gives insight into the nature of the market and the ways e-reader and e-book lending seem to be evolving. It also provides a useful backdrop for working for more cohesive, library-centric systems that increase efficiency and efficacy of e-book technologies while creating a substantial connection across libraries. So, how have public libraries responded to the popularity of e-books and e-readers? Some libraries offer downloadable e-books through an aggregator like OverDrive or eBooks on EBSCOhost. This allows the opportunity for patrons to download books to their personal devices but does not require the library to invest in e-readers. A second option is to acquire e-readers, load them with e-books, and loan them directly to patrons. In this context the e-reader constitutes a service, a collection, and a tool for technological instruction, with particular considerations in each aspect. A third option is to offer a "gadget zoo" or "petting zoo." In this example a variety of devices and other current technological gadgets are placed on display for patrons to sample. These items may not be available for borrowing but rather as an educational opportunity. Often libraries bring in staff from a local electronics store who can demonstrate multiple devices of a given type.

LEGAL ISSUES

Perhaps one of the reasons for the low number of e-reader lending programs in libraries is the legality of offering the service. Looking at the terms of use of both the Barnes & Noble Nook and the Amazon Kindle, nowhere is library use addressed. So the legality of lending e-readers is simply unclear. Libraries that choose to circulate e-readers enter uncertain territory. E-reader lending is not mentioned in the terms of service for the Kindle either, and differing responses from Amazon employees have been noted. An Amazon staff member told the Howe Library in Hanover, New Hampshire, that lending Kindles was permitted, but Amazon spokesman Drew Herdener has stated to *Library Journal* that it is not permitted (Odor 2009).

Peter Hirtle argues that based on Amazon's terms of use for the Kindle, which says that the software on the Kindle cannot be lent, libraries cannot and must be wary of pursuing such a service. He recommends that any such lending program be done with the input of an attorney (Hirtle 2010).

To this point, none of the producers of e-readers have endorsed or prohibited lending of their devices and e-book content by libraries. Publishers, whose content is being lent on these devices, have been silent on the specific nature of e-reader lending in libraries.

While BYU decided to scrap an e-reader lending program when they could not get the company's assent in writing (Haddock 2009), other libraries are taking the risk in order to best serve their patrons.

NOOK E-READER LENDING AT MENTOR PUBLIC LIBRARY

The Mentor Public Library (MPL) began circulating Nook e-readers in 2010. The collection began with four readers gradually increasing to twelve due to popularity. According to David Newyear, adult information services manager at MPL, initial demand was significant, with each Nook having twenty to thirty holds at one time. Once the library increased the number of Nooks to twelve, they found one or two available on the shelf at any given time. In the first year of the program, the Nooks circulated a total of 214 times.

PLANNING THE E-READER COLLECTION

When MPL began considering developing an e-reader lending service, there were many decisions to make, not least which e-reader to offer.

They considered the Nook and the Kindle, based on consumer reviews recommending the devices highly. Several factors led them to choose the Nook, including:

- *Licensing.* Nooks allow one copy of a book to exist on six Nooks at a time, versus one copy per Kindle at that point in time. Currently, there can be up to six Kindles associated with the e-book titles on one account (Amazon n.d.). The ability to share a $9.99 title across six readers is a cost savings for libraries.
- *Legality.* At the time, Amazon was facing a potential lawsuit over the text-to-speech functionality from publishers.
- *Partnership.* MPL tries to build partnerships whenever possible. The local Barnes & Noble bookstore, with whom they had an established relationship, provided them access to staff members' expertise with the devices.

MPL did not consult with an attorney, as Hirtle suggests, but dealt directly with Barnes & Noble (and Amazon, when it was considering the Kindle) staff, making clear their intent to lend the devices to patrons. Representatives from Barnes & Noble aided in training library staff on the Nooks. Having received no prohibitions from either company, and after looking closely at the policies of other libraries that were loaning e-readers, MPL moved forward with the program.

Despite the partnership with the local Barnes & Noble, MPL was not able to get a discount for buying multiple units. At Amazon for a discount to kick in, they would have had to buy fifty units.

After deciding on the device, MPL needed to set policies and determine how the e-reader collection would fit in the library's workflow. An important consideration in the development of the service was the intent to make managing this collection as easy on frontline staff as possible. Equally important was protecting these expensive devices throughout their journeys from library to home and back again. Library staff looked at other libraries that were circulating e-readers in order to learn the best approach, as well as those libraries' policies. Ultimately, they decided to put the same fifty titles, mostly best-selling fiction and nonfiction, on their Nooks.

HOUSING THE COLLECTION

The MPL Nooks are on display behind the circulation desk, keeping them safe from theft, where they are electronically charged upon return. This arrangement requires as little management of the devices by staff as possible.

When a patron takes out a Nook, she receives the e-reader, a quick-start reference guide, and a charger. To protect the device, MPL found that a plastic case designed to store handguns was the perfect fit and offered excellent protection. That said, a "no-brainer policy" was that the devices cannot be returned in the drop box.

POLICIES

The MPL policies for the collection needed to protect the devices and their content. The exact prices of the items in the package are itemized so the patron knows precisely what they are responsible for, including the warranty for the device, the cost of the charger, the case, and so on. Devices are locked down: patrons can neither add nor remove e-books.

Every Nook transaction requires the patron to go through a simple checklist to ensure that the device leaves and returns in working order and in its complete package. At checkout, the patron must complete an electronic device agreement, which states, "I agree to accept full responsibility for the Electronic Device while it is checked out to me." Specific terms are spelled out, such as:

- I will not tamper with the Electronic Device, accessories, and digital books, attempt to load digital books, or attach any equipment not designed for use with the Electronic Device.
- I agree to pay all costs associated with damage to, loss of, or theft of the Electronic Device while it is checked out to me ($333.85 plus accrued late return fees for the Nook e-reader).
- I agree the library may use any appropriate means to collect the amount owed for fees, damage, loss, or theft of the Electronic Device and that my record will be submitted to collections within 30 days.

The process of checkout/return takes between two and three minutes. It was designed to be as short as possible, yet to make sure that the device transitions between institution and patron and back with a clear understanding of responsibility. Forms were designed to be simple to fill out, while clearly communicating the patron's responsibility for the device when it is in his possession.

Newyear said that the Nooks generated a good return on investment. At the time of the interview, MPL did not offer OverDrive e-books but will have added them in May 2011.

Because of the Nook collection, at least some of the library's customers and staff members will have gained some expertise with e-readers.

THE SONY READER LIBRARY PROGRAM

In 2010, Sony launched the Reader Library Program in order to ensure that library staff would be well trained in the use of its line of Readers and be capable in assisting library patrons. The program is available to libraries who offer OverDrive e-books, but they must fill out an application on the program's website to enroll. The program includes, as of the latest application, a two- to three-hour training session led by Sony staff, three Readers for use and display, a floor stand, access to online web training and materials, and brochures and bookmarks.

The Mark & Emily Turner Public Library (M&E) in Presque Isle, Maine, was among the first group of participating libraries that was announced in September 2010. They received four e-readers—two Pocket and two Touch models—and stands on which they can display one of each type of e-reader.

Two of the e-readers are tethered to the library's Sony. Two others, while not bar-coded like other library materials that circulate, can be checked out the same way that noncirculation reference materials can be checked out for special loans. The focus for these circulations of e-readers is educational so patrons can learn how the devices work, particularly those who are considering buying one.

The quality of the training that Sony provides is high, according to Lisa Neal Shaw, a reference librarian at the M&E library, as it offered staff the opportunity to "test-drive" Sony Readers and learn everything they needed to know. This experience with the devices has made troubleshooting device questions for patrons, either in person or over the phone, substantially easier. The company has kept in touch. Shaw said, "They didn't just send us some Readers and then disappear; they really seemed to want to make the program work for library patrons" (personal communication, 2011).

Shaw said that the program "has truly exceeded [her] expectations" and that Sony's representatives were genuinely interested not only in her library but the direction of libraries in general. As a result, there was a strong sense of commitment to the library's mission.

TRY BEFORE YOU BUY

At both MPL and M&E, having e-readers in the library were of benefit to patrons because they could familiarize themselves with the technology before acquiring it. MPL has several Nooks; M&E also has a Kindle and a NookColor that patrons can check out as special items, like the Sony Readers. At both libraries, patrons have access to the iPad tablet.

Lending e-readers specifically so patrons can experiment and learn—rather than for access to content—is a service that has value for patrons who intend to acquire their own devices. A full-fledged e-reader lending program provides some increased access to materials for those who cannot afford an e-reader, in addition to do-it-yourself, hands-on training.

Some independent publishers and authors have gone e-book only, like mass romance publisher Dorchester Publishing, which no longer mass publishes its books but prints on demand to augment its e-book model (Milliot 2010). With more content available only to readers who have e-readers, a lending program that provides only limited titles on those devices cannot provide broad access to those who cannot afford them. A lending program that allows the patron to borrow an e-reader and select the titles to upload would be a major advance in this area.

TRAINING STAFF AND PATRONS ON E-BOOKS AND E-READERS

As we have seen, the deluge of e-readers as holiday gifts created a lot of interest and opportunity for libraries in early 2011. In addition to challenges with increasing collections came the challenge of instruction and learning. Many library patrons received their e-reader as a holiday gift whose giver was assured by a well-meaning store clerk that the e-reader model did work with library books. Unfortunately, these assurances didn't come with any instructions, and as a result patrons turned to their local library staff for answers.

Some libraries were fortunate to have the staff, funding, and foresight to prepare for the holiday boom by rolling out training in the form of videos, handouts, and glossaries, as well as being able to provide a "genius bar"–type, hands-on experience for library patrons (Circle 2010). This multifaceted training approach for both staff and patrons is a best-case scenario and surmounts the challenges that many other libraries face.

CHALLENGES TO TRAINING

Many library systems found themselves unable to prepare for the holiday e-reader onslaught due to challenges out of their hands. The most common challenges are:

- *Staffing.* In the current economic climate many library systems are short staffed, which means just making the time for training can be a challenge.
- *Access to devices.* Many libraries do not have the ability to buy all the e-readers on the market. Even in situations where a library was able to get one or two devices, not all brands or models could be purchased. There is also the stress of knowing that the device(s) you choose will most likely be replaced by a newer model in a year.

Not having access to the devices provides the unique challenge of learning to use a device you have never seen. Fortunately, many libraries and library groups, like the Westlake Porter Public Library (www.westlakelibrary.org/?q=taxonomy/term/571) and Maryland's Digital Library eLibrary Consortium (maryland.lib.OverDrive.com/4C8B0D69-EEDC-4A0B-94A9-2D95A8DF4194/10/336/en/Help.htm and www.youtube.com/user/alleganycountylibrar) are producing pages, FAQs, and even videos on how library users can use e-readers and get e-books from the library. Many libraries are going so far as to produce web pages and multimedia to address the common "what e-reader should I buy?" question. Others take patrons step-by-step through the process of downloading e-books onto e-readers or tablets, from installing Adobe Digital Editions or other software, to deleting e-books from devices after the borrowing period has expired. In the case of libraries' OverDrive services, which include an interface that can be customized for the library, library-specific instructions eliminate the need for patrons to interpret generalized instructions.

Many library systems do not have a dedicated trainer on board. In many situations it is still common that e-reader and e-book training falls on the young or tech-savvy staff members who in truth may not be all that familiar with e-readers. Even in systems with a dedicated training department, the staff may not be familiar with e-book and e-reader technology.

In any case, even though knowing where to start can be daunting, progress is being made. In interviews with trainers about the e-book and e-reader training programs at their libraries, several themes, methods, and efficiencies stood out. The following interviews give a solid sense for the practical realities of training staff and patrons how to use e-books and e-readers as part of their library work and use. From confusion to resentment of technological, logistical, time, and cost issues, these trainers are representative of the current reality in e-reader and e-book training in public libraries today.

A LIBRARY SYSTEM WITH A DEDICATED TRAINER

Beth Tribe, IT instructor and specialist at Howard County (Maryland) Library System, is responsible for training staff on e-books and e-readers, but she aims to get more staff to participate in training customers. Training on Nooks, which the library circulates, began with customer service supervisors and "tech squads" at the system's branches. These squads are comprised of tech-savvy and customer service staff. In subsequent rounds of training the rest of the staff received training. Tribe is working on a training program for all staff that will cover all the e-readers that they have in their stable: Nook, NookColor, Kindle, Kobo, Sony Reader, iPad, Android tablet, and Pandigital. Until the library acquired its own Nooks, staff—despite having taken OverDrive's training—had not had direct experience with e-readers.

Tribe has conducted training classes for the public that taught the differences between dedicated e-readers and e-reader apps on tablets, smartphones, and the like and a series of device-specific classes called "Are You Ready?" The next phase of the training is to create screencasts of OverDrive-related classes and short videos of the particular e-readers that will be available via the library's website.

According to Tribe, e-book/e-reader training is no different from any other, in that the largest obstacle in getting staff trained is managing employees' schedules. Despite the staff's interest in these technologies, getting people to free up time to learn is always hard. To make sure training is most effective, focus on these key areas:

- *Devices.* Having a stable of devices is a great resource for a library, but not everyone has the money for that. The Howard County Library System got money from some e-readers from a state grant and paid for others from its budget. If your library can only acquire a few, buy the most popular ones: the Nook, the Kindle, and the iPad. Tribe says the Kobo is also popular among patrons. Libraries cannot be expected to know every device.
- *Vendor offerings.* If a library cannot acquire devices, focus training initiatives on content from vendors like OverDrive, or free sources of e-books like Project Gutenberg and the free offerings from Google Books.
- *Best practices.* Training should explain the easiest way to accomplish tasks, and file formats. The differences between EPUB and PDF formats, for instance, are nuanced in some cases: OverDrive EPUB e-books can be returned early by patrons, while PDF e-books cannot.

TRAINING WITHOUT A DEDICATED TRAINER

In the absence of a dedicated trainer, Daniel Messer, circulation supervisor for the Queen Creek (Arizona) Library, a branch of the Maricopa County

(Phoenix) Library District, said that various staff have stepped up to help out with e-books and e-readers at his library. Brianna King, at the North Valley Regional Branch, produced handouts on each of the major e-readers designed to facilitate their use with the library's digital collection (http://maricopa.lib.OverDrive.com/). Messer himself, a renowned computer "geek," takes troubleshooting and assistance calls "from customers all over the Valley of the Sun."

All staff have had the chance to get trained on e-books and e-readers, but not all have done so. King did a demonstration at the library's staff training day that included a breakout session on the Nook featuring a Barnes & Noble representative. At his branch, Messer estimates that more than half of the staff have received some training on e-readers. Many staff, who otherwise are well versed in e-book services, will defer to those with more expertise with the devices if an e-reader "just doesn't work." Messer says that at this point "select staff" have received training but elaborates that training is available to everyone because "we're all going to deal with these devices more and more as time goes on."

For Messer, the goal of training is to foster familiarity with the devices, not make people into experts. Staff training has largely been done in classes led by Messer and King. Messer has also conducted one-on-one training sessions with staff. Of great benefit was the e-book conference seminar at the Arizona State Library, where every attendee received an e-reader bundle to keep and take back to their library. Messer's branch received an iPad, a Kindle, and a Kobo, and other libraries received Nooks and other devices. The bundles were comprised of devices and gift cards so branches could buy e-books and apps for their devices.

Messer says a major variable in a training program's success is the individual's attitude toward technology. Those who are excited about new technologies are eager to explore not only the device but how it can help the library. Others acknowledge the arrival of e-readers as part of the library of today, but they don't own one or see a need for it. Some reject the very concept of the e-reader. Some negative attitudes have been tempered by the massive success of e-readers. Working with these attitudes is important. Messer says, "You may not change their mind about what the device means, but you're certainly going to have to teach them what the device is."

Another variable is the staff members' capability or comfort with technology. At the library, there is a wide range of skills, from "geek" to novice. Other challenges lie in a person's technological abilities. Some staff may have a great attitude toward learning new technologies but lack fundamental knowledge for even basic operation of devices.

Access to devices and distance between branches are other major challenges in training staff. Having to troubleshoot patrons' device-specific problems over the phone is problematic because libraries don't have access to every device on the market. Not having the device in his hands, Messer says, makes such customer service interactions very challenging.

As for distance, where branches are up to two-hour drives apart, "sometimes, the biggest problem is just finding a day when someone can cut six hours from their workday (two hours driving there, two hours of training, two hours driving back) so they can learn."

MONEY AND CHANGE

Unfortunately, the increased demand for e-books and e-readers comes to institutions that are more often than not operating under the tightest of budgets, with little or no room for new expenditures. In the face of critical, traditional library services, the money to pay for these new resources and their support is difficult, if not impossible, to come by. According to a report on library spending priorities, "37% of public libraries increased their budgets in 2010 and 30% expect an increase in fiscal 2011. Conversely, while 43% reported budget decreases between 2009 and 2010, the number anticipating a decrease is projected to decline to 32% for fiscal 2011" (McKendrick 2011, 5). The report also notes that "increases are coming on the heels of years of soft budgets, and the increases being reported are not necessarily enough to keep the libraries operating at levels constant with inflation" (3). Some libraries have found money to expand their e-book collections, but this is not the rule, and most e-reader purchases often come at the expense of other library services or resources. As a result, holds lists for e-book titles have grown, sometimes dramatically.

This is complicated by the fact that we are in a time when our library patrons have quite high expectations. These expectations are driven by both our excellent past performance and the quality of service many (who can afford it) have come to expect from commercial e-book and e-reader services. Given these factors it is easy to see how the increased delay in access to library content threatens to undermine libraries' efforts to remain relevant in the e-book era. This does not yet touch on the challenges many users face in accessing e-book content once the library has built e-books into the collection.

Regardless of how the details in the e-book and e-reader market shift, several things are clear to libraries. First, the market, service providers, and products are in a state of rapid flux and rapid growth. Second, libraries are doing all they can to respond appropriately given their budgetary restraints. Third, as library users migrate to electronic format(s), libraries will need to be vigilant, thoughtful, and bold in adopting new solutions, ideas, and methods of service provision. With great change comes the difficulty of changing. Priorities and resource allocations will likely need to shift, potentially in very significant ways. We can see that libraries are responding and doing their best to serve their communities in a world where e-books are a relevant service offering.

After looking at the landscape and the response of those working in libraries, the largest questions now seem to be: How far will this all go? What role will libraries serve in the "new normal" of massive e-book circulation? And how will we fund this evolution in libraries and content consumption while still fulfilling our mission as community institutions? Libraries must grapple with these questions and their solutions in order to find their place in this dynamic e-book environment.

REFERENCES

Amazon.com. N.d. "How Many Kindles Can I Use to Access Titles in My Library?" www.amazon.com/gp/help/customer/display.html/ref=hp_kip _faq_num?nodeId=200298470&#howmany.

Biliczky, Carol. 2011. "Prospects Wide Open for Future of E-books." *Ohio Beacon Journal,* March 19, www.ohio.com/news/118286559.html.

Chief Officers of State Library Agencies. 2010. "COSLA: E-book Feasibility Study for Public Libraries." June 30, www.cosla.org/documents/COSLA2270_ Report_Final1.pdf.

Estrovich, Karen. 2011. "Kindle Library Lending and OverDrive—What It Means for Libraries and Schools." *Digital Library Blog,* OverDrive, April 20, http:// OverDriveblogs.com/library/2011/04/20/Kindle-library-lending-and -OverDrive-what-it-means-for-libraries-and-schools/.

Haddock, Marc. 2009. "BYU suspends Kindle Program over Legal Concerns." *Deseret News*, June 21, www.deseretnews.com/article/705310939/BYU -suspends-Kindleprogram-over-legal-concerns.html.

Hadro, Josh. 2010. "Ebrary Launching into Public Library Market with New Collection." *Library Journal,* May 24, www.libraryjournal.com/article/ CA6729088.html.

Hirtle, Peter. 2010. "May a Library Lend E-book Readers?" *LibraryLaw Blog,* June 20, http://blog.librarylaw.com/librarylaw/2010/06/may-a-library-lend-e -book-readers.html.

Kahle, Brewster. 2011. "Internet Archive and Library Partners Develop Joint Collection of 80,000 + E-books to Extend Traditional In-Library Lending Model." February 22, www.archive.org/post/349420/in-library-e-book -lending-program-launched.

Kelley, Michael. 2011. "EBSCO Previews Remodeled Platform Integrating NetLibrary Ebooks." *Library Journal,* March 23, www.libraryjournal.com/ lj/newslettersnewsletterbucketacademicnewswire/889816-440/ebsco_ previews_remodeled_platform_integrating.html.csp.

Konrath, Jon. 2011. "E-books and Self-publishing—A Dialog Between Authors Barry Eilser and Jon Konrath." *A Newbie's Guide to Publishing* (blog), March 19, http://jakonrath.blogspot.com/2011/03/ebooks-and-self-publishing -dialog.html.

Library Journal. 2010. "Survey of Ebook Penetration in U.S. Libraries." www .libraryjournal.com/csp/cms/sites/LJ/info/Reportpurchase.csp.

McKendrick, J. 2011. *Funding and Priorities: The Library Resource Guide Benchmark Study on 2011 Library Spending Plans.* Unisphere Research, www .libraryresource.com/Downloads/Download.ashx?IssueID=2585.

Milliot, Jim. 2010. "Dorchester Drops Mass Market Publishing for E-book/POD Model." *Publishers Weekly,* August 6, www.publishersweekly.com/pw/by -topic/industry-news/publisher-news/article/44085-dorchester-drops-mass -market-publishing-for-e-book-pod-model.html.

Minzesheimer, Bob, and Carol Memmott. 2011. "Week after Holidays, E-book Sales Outdo Print. " *USAToday,* January 5, www.usatoday.com/life/books/ news/2011-01-05-1Aebooksales05_ST_N.htm.

OCLC. 2011. "OCLC and Ingram to Offer New Option for Access to E-books," last modified April 11, www.oclc.org/news/releases/2011/201116.htm.

Oder, Norman. 2009. "Mixed Answers to 'Is It OK for a Library to Lend a Kindle?'" *Library Journal,* April 7, www.libraryjournal.com/article/ CA6649814.html.

Rapp, John. 2011A. "Internet Archive Tests New E-book Lending Waters: In-Library, and License-Free." *Library Journal,* March 2, www.libraryjournal.com/lj/home/889508-264/internet_archive_tests_new_ebook.html.csp.

———. 2011B. "Ebrary's New Short-Term E-book Loan Service Triggered by Use." *Library Journal,* May 9, www.libraryjournal.com/lj/home/890534-264/ebrarys_new_short-term_ebook_loan.html.csp.

Reed, Lori. 2011. "E-readers, Libraries, and Training . . . Oh My!" *Learning Round Table of the American Library Association* (blog), February 18, http://alalearning.org/2011/02/18/e-readers-libraries-and-training-oh-my/.

Toor, Amar. 2011. "3M Announces Cloud Library E-book Lending Service for '21st Century' Libraries." *Engadget,* last modified May 20, www.engadget.com/2011/05/20/3m-announces-cloud-library-e-book-lending-service-for-21st-cent/.

HarperCollins, OverDrive, and the ALA: Reactions to Limits on E-Book Access

MICHAEL PORTER

I f OverDrive's Kindle deal could be overshadowed by anything, it came in the form of an e-mail from Steve Potash to "OverDrive Library Partners" sent February 24, 2011. Tucked a few screens down, wrapped in language that seemed carefully designed to soften the impending blow and shield the company from negative backlash, was a warning about major coming changes to e-book circulation in libraries from a major publisher and OverDrive partners:

> The past several months have brought about dramatic changes for the print and eBook publishing and retail industries. Digital book sales are now a significant percentage of all publisher and author revenue. As a result several trade publishers are re-evaluating eBook licensing terms for library lending services. Publishers are expressing concern and debating their digital future where a single eBook license to a library may never expire, never wear out, and never need replacement.
>
> OverDrive is advocating on behalf of your readers to have access to the widest catalog of the best copyrighted, premium materials, and lending options. To provide you with the best options, we have been required to accept and accommodate new terms for eBook lending as established by certain publishers. Next week, OverDrive will communicate a licensing change from a publisher that, while still operating under the one-copy/one-user model, will include a checkout limit for each eBook licensed. Under this publisher's requirement, for every new eBook licensed, the library (and the OverDrive platform) will make the eBook available to one customer at a time until the total number of permitted checkouts is reached. This eBook lending condition will be required of all eBook vendors or distributors offering this publisher's titles for library lending (not just OverDrive) (Potash 2011).

Just days later, as warned, OverDrive announced that the publisher HarperCollins would be limiting library circulations on the e-books they publish and sell access to. The new rules for libraries boiled down to this: after twenty-six circulations of an e-book, the item would simply disappear from the library's digital collection. If the library wanted or needed to circulate the item again they would have to repurchase the right to do so for another twenty-six circulations.*

The reaction to the HarperCollins announcement caused shock waves, not just in the library industry but for many dedicated library users as well. Hundreds of blog posts, newspaper and magazine articles, and radio and television spots all talked about the issue. Clearly this did not paint a favorable picture of HarperCollins in many people's minds. Yet at the same time it served as a teachable moment for libraries. As many people associated e-books with the Kindle in recent years, libraries were also clearly in people's minds when it came to e-books. After watching the spectacle of the HarperCollins/Overdrive announcement (referred to as #hcod on Twitter) unfold, it became very clear that people want to borrow e-books from libraries—and they want to make sure their libraries can permanently access them at an affordable price.

When considering #hcod, though, there certainly are many factors at play. At the root of the problem is that libraries and publishers have different priorities. Libraries are critical to the health of a community because they provide ongoing access to materials. Particularly in this economy, budgets are tight; libraries can't afford to purchase the same e-book twice. Publishers, in turn, are concerned about revenues and ensuring their business remains liquid. These issues come at a time when, for example, the music publishing industry is reeling and shifting in massive ways, with major players simply going out of business. So it is understandable that things will get shaken up and evolve in the coming years. It is also reasonable to expect that as this happens, publishers will experiment with business models as they struggle to ensure their business remains liquid. Libraries must remain vigilant during this time, protecting their investments and access to digital content.

To a majority of observers—particularly the vocal observers—the decision to limit circulations of e-books and then require additional purchases was seen as unnecessary. To some it even seemed to display a lack

---

* We will touch on the backlash to this announcement next, but in writing this chapter it was discovered that some blog posts announcing these changes on both the OverDrive and the HarperCollins *Library Love Fest* blog appear to have been removed. At the time of this writing, the twenty-six-circulations rule for e-books from HarperCollins still exists, but some of the initial announcements via these respective blogs—posts that contained a massive amount of outcry and negative response—no longer appear to be available on their respective blog sites.

of understanding and care for libraries and library services. To others still it simply read as greedy.

Many in the library world, most often privately, were calling for calm. The argument was made in some circles that because some of the major publishing houses in the United States did not currently allow libraries to access and circulate their titles in e-book format, we should not lash out, even as individuals, against these changes by HarperCollins. "Dare we alienate a major publisher by taking them to task for something that an individual had personally perceived as shortsighted or worse? Can libraries afford to lose the ability to circulate e-books from major publishers given the trends in increasing e-book purchases?" In the wake of #hcod, these questions were asked in many quiet meetings and conversations around the country between library leaders and staff alike in the spring of 2011.

Wherever the observer found themselves on the issues, it was clear to most folks in Libraryland that what had become known to many as "#hcod" was a scandal that had captured imaginations and the attention of the profession and the national media alike. ■

HarperCollins *Library Love Fest* Blog

March 1, 2011, post
http://harperlibrary.typepad.com/my_weblog/2011/03/open-letter-to-librarians.html
135 comments on May 24, 2011

We are striving to find the best model for all parties. Guiding our decisions is our goal to make sure that all of our sales channels, in both print and digital formats, remain viable, not just today but in the future. Ensuring broad distribution through booksellers and libraries provides the greatest choice for readers and the greatest opportunity for authors' books to be discovered.

Our prior e-book policy for libraries dates back almost 10 years to a time when the number of e-readers was too small to measure. It is projected that the installed base of e-reading devices domestically will reach nearly 40 million this year. We have serious concerns that our previous e-book policy, selling e-books to libraries in perpetuity, if left unchanged, would undermine the emerging e-book eco-system, hurt the growing e-book channel, place additional pressure on physical bookstores, and in the end lead to a decrease in book sales and royalties paid to authors. We are looking to balance the mission and needs of libraries and their patrons with those of authors and booksellers, so that the library channel can thrive alongside the growing e-book retail channel.

We spent many months examining the issues before making this change. We talked to agents and distributors, had discussions with librarians, and participated in the Library Journal e-book Summit and other conferences. Twenty-six circulations can provide a year of availability for titles with the highest demand, and much longer for other titles and core backlist. If a library decides to repurchase an e-book later in the book's life, the price will be significantly lower as it will be pegged to a paperback price point. Our hope is to make the cost per circulation for e-books less than that of the corresponding physical book. In fact, the digital list price is generally 20% lower than the print version, and sold to distributors at a discount.

We invite libraries and library distributors to partner with us as we move forward with these new policies. We look forward to ongoing discussions about changes in this space and will continue to look to collaborate on mutually beneficial opportunities.

To continue the discussion please email library.ebook@HarperCollins.com.

Sincerely,

Josh Marwell
President of Sales
HarperCollinsPublishers
(Marwell 2011)

Actions from Libraryland in Response to #hcod

As the issue began to unfold in the library press and commercial media, many looked to the American Library Association for a statement and leadership. To some the response of the organization was slower than they wanted or expected. To explain this, ALA President Roberta Stevens released a letter to the membership, saying:

> First and foremost, I want to thank you for your patience. I held back on a public statement on the recent decision by HarperCollins to restrict the lending of e-books until the Equitable Access to Electronic Informa-

tion Task Force (EQUACC) met last week. Please know that I heard your voices of concern about the impact of additional costs on your libraries and ability to meet the needs of the communities you serve . . .

As an outgrowth of EQUACC's working retreat, a website will be launched within the next week. The site will allow you to provide your comments and ideas. The site's availability will be announced using the many ways we have within the association to "get the word out." (Price 2011)

This statement certainly generated interest in ALA's fledgling Task Force on Equitable Access to Electronic Information (EQUACC), which conveniently happened to be meeting for their first retreat at the Washington, D.C., offices of ALA the week following the break of the #hcod story. Given that this meeting had been in the planning stages for months and the task force members announced only in December 2010, there certainly was much work to be done. Issues related to #hcod were high on the group's list of conversations before, during, and following the retreat.

EQUACC also set up a website with a blog and forums about #hcod and any issues related to electronic content access and the future of libraries. These measured and more traditional approaches, however, did not satisfy some, who looked to ALA for a different kind of leadership on the issue. And this reaction resulted in several interesting, organized responses.

Among the hundreds of bloggers posting about #hcod, a petition started by librarian Andy Woodworth saw massive participation. By late May 2011 the petition had roughly 70,000 signatures and had garnered further national and international attention on the specific HarperCollins decision as well as larger issues around e-book circulation and access for and through libraries. The points made in the text of the petition clearly strike a chord with many. Regardless of the position a person takes on the issues, it is a worthwhile read:

On March 7, 2011, the publisher HarperCollins instituted an expiration policy on eBooks that are licensed to libraries. Under this new arrangement, eBooks would "self-destruct" after being checked out 26 times. This would require libraries to re-purchase the eBook if they wanted to continue to make it available. Libraries across the country are boycotting future purchases of HarperCollins eBooks, but our voices alone will not change their policy. **We need your help.**

As Cory Doctorow wrote, "the durability of eBook is a feature, not a bug." To place a cap on the circulation of eBooks in order to "simulate" the wear and tear of a physical book is not only insulting to readers, but this video shows how easily it can be proven wrong with physical books.

The significant advantage of eBooks for libraries is that it allows people to borrow books from home and read them on their computer or e-reader. When the book is due to be "returned" to the library, the file is rendered inert and the next library user can check out the eBook. Limiting a book to 26 total checkouts means that it could be there one day and gone the next, leaving that 27th borrower in limbo as the library assesses whether to re-purchase the eBook. **If left in place, this policy would threaten public access to eBooks by making them disappear from the virtual shelf.**

Please join us in voicing your opposition to this policy of self-destructing eBooks.

To see if libraries are still boycotting HarperCollins, you can visit the website Boycott HarperCollins (Woodworth 2011).

Interestingly, the Boycott HarperCollins web page (http://boycott harpercollins.com/) referenced at the end of the petition contains a link to a *Library Journal* article that actually names dozens of libraries who took action in response to #hcod. Some of these responses were quite strong, moving the idea of a boycott from an individual statement to a more substantial, actionable decision. Hundreds of libraries from Kansas to New York, Iowa to Texas, Missouri, and Illinois all took formal steps to refrain from purchasing any new e-book content from HarperCollins as long as these new restrictions were being applied. While most were refusing to purchase HarperCollins e-books, others went so far as to refuse to continue purchasing audiobooks and in some occasions even print books from the publisher (Kelley 2011).

Many speculate that this has meant a cut into the business not just of HarperCollins but to OverDrive as well. This may be a logical conclusion, for at the time of the announced change, OverDrive had secured its place as the major behind-the-scenes provider of circulating e-books in libraries. OverDrive's work with publishers (certainly including HarperCollins), device creators, and libraries ensures that the company remains at the center of the e-book consumption market, so many now conclude that #hcod could not have been especially good for business. (This would also partly explain the nature of their February e-mail to customers, preparing them for significant impending e-book access fees and changes impending from HarperCollins.)

To add further fuel to the #hcod fire, several well-known authors added their frustration to the discussion, garnering further attention to the issue. Best-selling HarperCollins author Neil Gaimin led this charge, saying simply, "I think it's incredibly disappointing" (Scott 2011).

In another unexpected chapter to the #hcod story, on April 5, 2011, Josh Marwell, president of sales for HarperCollins, was quoted responding to the main #hcod issue in *Library Journal,* saying,

> Is 26 set in stone? No. It's our number for now, but we want to hear back. Immediately. Honestly, it doesn't make sense that one size fits all. We consider it a work in progress. But this is the number that we have now. I invite you to test the water. Use it. Give us feedback. We're in the water. We want to be here. . . . We try to be intelligent about our policy . . . and when we landed on 26, the information that we had was that most books don't circulate 26 times. In terms of the long tail, this particular number probably works for a different part of the collection. We realize it doesn't work for the best sellers. (Kelley 2011)

In this same interview, though, Marwell added that when it comes to selling e-books with continual open circulation and access to libraries, there are grave concerns "about the overall ecosystem. That is at the heart of the issue" (Kelley 2011).

Looking to the Future

At the 2010 ALA Annual Conference, the EQUACC Task Force presented its final report and recommendations to the ALA Council for approval (see http://connect.ala.org/node/151800). These were accepted and passed by the council and then passed on to ALA leadership so that action could continue. At the heart of the task force's recommendation: ALA must allocate resources for e-content issues. These issues must have a solid home base within the organization. ALA had to take more organized strategic action in relation to e-content.

ALA responded to this recommendation by forming a Blue Ribbon Working Group in their organizational structure who can advise the core association on e-content and other digital matters. The group will consider key studies and reports, economic analyses, and other policy documents to shape their recommendations. As ALA executive director Keith Michael Fiels points out, "ALA's ability to negotiate or 'broker' industry-wide agreements is strictly limited by anti-trust law, as is the abiity of the publishers themselves to enter into any joint agreements" (e-mail communication, 2011). But the working group is a step toward increasing awareness for libraries' needs and helping shape policy while publishers explore new models for digital alternatives.

Fiels also stated, "Our goal is to help shape the legal and policy environment so that libraries can continue to provide equitable access in a digital environment, and that libraries have the information, training and inspiration that they need to develop vibrant digital services going forward" (e-mail communication, 2011).

While the drama of this story is still unfolding, the underlying issues for public libraries are the same as they have always been. Libraries must be able to offer people the books they need and want, regardless of format. As ALA President Roberta Stevens aptly said, "The transition to the e-book format should not result in less availability." If #hcod teaches us anything, it is that librarians, library staff, and library supporters must remain informed, vigilant, and engaged with these issues if we are to ensure e-books take their necessary place in library collections.

REFERENCES

American Library Association. 2011. "Restrictions on Library E-book Lending Threaten Access to Information," March 14, http://ala.org/ala/newspresscenter/news/pr.cfm?id = 6517.

Kelley, Michael. 2011. "HarperCollins Executive Calls Circulation Cap a 'Work in Progress.'" *Library Journal,* April 5, www.libraryjournal.com/lj/home/890077-264/harpercollins_executive_calls_circulation_cap.html.csp.

Marwell, Josh. 2011. "Open Letter to Librarians." *Library Love Fest* (blog), March 1, http://harperlibrary.typepad.com/my_weblog/2011/03/open-letter-to -librarians.html.

Potash, Steve. 2011. "Improved User Experience, New E-book Lending Terms, Direct Access and Integration with Your ILS, OPAC and Discovery Services" (e-mail), February 24, http://librarianinblack.net/librarianinblack/wp -content/uploads/2011/02/OverDrive-Library-Partner-Update-from-Steve -Potash-2-24-2011.pdf.

Price, Gary. 2011. "ALA President Roberta Stevens Sends Letter to Membership about E-books/Libraries/HarperCollins." *InfoDocket,* March 15, http:// infodocket.com/2011/03/15/ala-president-roberta-stevens-sends-letter-to -membership-about-e-bookslibrariesharpercollins/.

Scott, Carol. 2011. "Best Selling Authors Criticize HarperCollins E-book Policy." Change.org, May 11, http://news.change.org/stories/best-selling-authors -criticize-harpercollins-e-book-policy.

Woodworth, Andy. 2011. "Tell HarperCollins: Limited Checkouts on E-books Is Wrong for Libraries." Change.org, April 11, www.change.org/petitions/tell -harpercollins-limited-checkouts-on-ebooks-is-wrong-for-libraries.

10

Libraries as Zones for Content Creation, Indie Publishing, and Print on Demand

THOMAS A. PETERS

E veryone knows that libraries serve readers, but libraries support authors and other content creators, too. As the e-reading revolution sails beyond the relatively safe harbors of gadget envy, battery lust for life, and format wrangling into the much more interesting, uncharted waters of what we all are going to do, individually and collectively, during the e-reading era, librarians are planning strategically how libraries can and will support the culture of reading, where reading probably will involve much more than interacting with alphanumeric characters printed on paper. While it's not uncommon for librarians to become distracted by the challenges presented by publishers, vendors, and content distributors, as well as internal processes, policies, and procedures, librarians ultimately are drawn to how libraries can serve and add value to the activities, needs, desires, and experiences of readers and authors.

For several decades there have been periodic reports and predictions that libraries are poised to become major content creators themselves, far beyond the usual types of content—metadata, reports, and overdue notices—that libraries traditionally have created. For instance, in June 2010 the Chief Officers of State Library Agencies (COSLA) issued a report about the future of public libraries in light of e-reading. The report contained seven areas of needed action. (This chapter will expand upon the fifth action item from the COSLA report.)

1. **Consolidate and leverage the purchasing power of public libraries.** Library consortia and state library agencies have been doing this for decades, but it is time to take this activity to the next level, which may be some sort of national purchasing consortium. While the idea of a national purchasing system creates its own set of concerns and challenges, such a system does not obviate the need for quality control, awareness of local information needs, and local measures of benefits and impact. As the COSLA report (2010, 19) notes, "A national consortium would also need to quell concerns about collection quality and continually measure benefit at the local level."

2. **Develop a consolidated access point for e-books from public libraries.** Library-supplied e-book collections need to get to a critical mass (e.g., at least one million titles, with ten million titles not a far-fetched idea), and they need to be much more easily and quickly discoverable by members of the reading public.

3. **Develop a device certification process.** Libraries and library users need devices that are accessible to everyone, including individuals who are vision or hearing impaired or have other physical challenges. We need reading appliances that allow flexibility regarding file formats, DRM systems (including no DRM), modes of interaction (taking, sharing, and incorporating notes and comments; highlighting, rating, reviewing, etc.), and modes of access (including visual, auditory, and tactile reading). A library device certification process would assure library users and librarians that a cluster of certified devices are good for library-related e-reading experiences.

4. **Document how public library use contributes to a culture of reading—and to the buying of books.** Many publishers and booksellers seem to hold the opinion that libraries and library use hurt their businesses. We need to make a concerted, ongoing research and public awareness effort to take a long

view of how libraries and library use actually support a culture of reading in our society and benefit all the stakeholder groups, including publishers and booksellers.

5. **Help local authors and support self-publishing efforts.** The field of self-publishing is growing rapidly and appears to have an even brighter future. The market share of the Big Six publishers almost certainly has peaked and will be in decline in the coming years and decades. Libraries need help in identifying and selecting indie and self-published works, and indie publishers and authors need help producing and promoting their works.

6. **Exhibit more leadership about the future of reading.** While item 4 is a step in the right direction, we will need strong, persistent leadership from librarians to carry forward our message about the social, economic, and cultural value of libraries in the e-reading era, including all the attendant issues and challenges, such as the future of copyright, ownership, right of first sale, and fair use.

7. **Experiment with public library laboratories for new reading experiences.** Many if not most of these new reading experiences will be communal in nature to an extent that will make the traditional book discussion group seem quaint. New forms of communal reading experiences may be online, in the cloud, in real time while one is reading. The implications for how the individual reader experiences, interprets, and applies a text are enormous.

There are many stakeholder groups involved and interested in the e-reading revolution, including authors, publishers, other rights holders, booksellers, technology companies, libraries, library vendors, educators, and readers. Librarians need to work with all these stakeholder groups. We can think of authors and readers as two anchors for this chain. That libraries serve readers is generally accepted by the general public, but how can libraries serve authors, especially as the e-reading (and e-writing) revolutions continue to unfold? The ability to engage in significant content creation—texts of all types and lengths, still and moving images, sounds and music—has never been as easy, inexpensive, and broadly diffused as it is today. "Digitization makes possible a world in which anyone can claim to be a publisher and anyone can call him- or herself an author" (Epstein 2010). This chapter will focus on how libraries can serve authors and other content creators through support for emerging authors; support for authors who self-publish, print on demand, and use other distribution and archiving services; and even by becoming content creators in their own right.

LIBRARIES SUPPORT AUTHORS AND OTHER CONTENT CREATORS

Libraries always have cultivated authors and the culture of reading. Visits to libraries often are recalled by authors as seminal experiences of their childhoods that instilled in them the inspiration necessary to envision their adult lives as authors. Libraries also support authors by providing the information sources and services that help them with the processes of writing.

Libraries can support authors by helping them find and communicate with their readership. Ranganthan's law, "Every book its reader," sounds so simple that it glosses over the fact that every instance of a good book connecting with a good reader is a minor miracle and cause for celebration, not only by that happy reader but by the entire society, comprehending all of librarianship.

As the ability to create content and access millions of books and other digital objects becomes easily accessible by all, we may experience a diffusion of expertise out from universities and other organizations back into the general population. As Peters (2007) speculates, digital libraries can support the rustication of expertise. "Works of genius will emerge from parts of the world where books have barely penetrated before, as such works after Gutenberg emerged unbidden from the dark and silent corners of Europe" (Epstein 2010). Authors and other content creators who do not have institutional support for their creative activities may look to libraries to provide a basic support structure and a nurturing community.

While author readings and book signings at local libraries may continue into the foreseeable future, with the continued expansion and adoption of online networks and communities of interest, specific libraries can gain international reputations and users by supporting specific fictional genres and nonfiction topics.

Lankes (2011) asserts that the mission of librarians is to improve society through facilitating knowledge creation in their communities. Librarians can achieve this mission by providing the infrastructure, which may or may not include a print-on-demand (POD) service, that enables member of the communities they serve to create knowledge. To be effective and beneficial to society as a whole, created knowledge must be disseminated in some way, and the usual way to disseminate knowledge is through some utterance.

Lankes (2011, 67) sees librarianship on the verge of a sea change, from primarily purchasing and handling publications to their actual production:

> I foresee the day in the near future when librarians spend the majority of their time working with community members and community organizations making their content accessible: where acquisition is a matter of production, not purchasing. The future of libraries (and librarians) is in becoming publishers of the community.
>
> If libraries do refocus their mission somewhat to become "zones" for content creators, content creation, and content curation, will these zones be primarily physical spaces or online communal spaces? It probably will be a mixture of both, but the key point here is to let the community work out its preferences and work style. The library should not be prescriptive here. Each community of content creators will create its own style and preferences.

For instance, Lankes (2011, 68) describes how a group of writers use the Free Library of Philadelphia as a content creation zone. A POD service was available to print member works, but Lankes observes that the truly remarkable aspect of the content creation zone was not in production but in the area of editorial control. The writers in this particular local community wanted none. "The writers wanted no filters or selection process. If a member wrote it, it was in."

Lankes goes on to report that other communities of content creators in the same geographic area and using the same library as a content creation zone had a different attitude toward editorial control. A group of musicians wanted to include in their local repository only scores and works that had been performed. The community itself selected and appointed a curator who would select which works were performed.

The point here is that even individual libraries that get into the "content creation zone" service area—not all libraries will, if there is no pressing need for such a zone within their community—need to be very flexible about how the content creation zone is configured and managed. Ultimately, each individual community of content creators will need to configure and manage the library zone to meet their particular needs and preferences. This will be a new wrinkle in the old concept of community standards.

LIBRARIES SUPPORT SELF-PUBLISHING

While libraries can and do support authors in many ways, one specific and increasingly important area is self-publishing. Self-publishing is growing by leaps and bounds, overcoming the vanity publishing stigma it has held for decades and going mainstream, with both established and new authors going the self-publishing route. The COSLA report (2010), based on data from Bowker, notes, "The cultural production represented by self-publishing is now more than twice that of mainstream publishing." Bradley (2011) observes, "The traditional control that the publisher has is falling away, and the author is in a much better [position] to circumvent them."

The self-publishing revolution offers both a challenge and an opportunity for the collection development activities of libraries, both individually and collectively. Most collection development activities in libraries now center around published book reviews and publisher announcements. Yet, as the COSLA report (2010) notes, self-published works can be difficult to find, are less frequently reviewed than published works, and often have inadequate descriptive metadata attached to them. Current collection development practices in most libraries are not well positioned to easily and efficiently beef up the number of self-published titles in local collections. But that may be exactly where collection development needs to head in the coming years.

In the keynote address at ILEADU in 2010, Eli Neiburger of the Ann Arbor Public Library briefly outlined a new direction for collection development activities, one that leads away from serving as a conduit for national best-selling authors to curators and champions of local and regional self-published authors. In a YouTube recording of another version of this basic talk, Neiburger notes that the original purpose of libraries was not to serve as a conduit for commercial content purchased for the community but to store and organize the content of the community. Neiburger suggests that in the e-reading era, libraries need to return to this earlier sense of purpose and behavior.

For most collection development and management programs in libraries, this new challenge will require major retooling. Rather than read mainstream reviews and make purchase selections based on them, library collection developers will need to cultivate and curate locally created content, both fiction and nonfiction. As noted in the COSLA report (2010), Jana Bradley, a professor of library and information science at the University of Arizona, "feels it's time to return to traditional selection that reflects the flavor of the community. Self-published materials are an untapped source of readable, relevant materials. They just need a librarian's touch: someone to discover them, describe them, and make them easier to find."

Even in the portable e-reading era, traditional author events at brick-and-mortar libraries will continue to be popular. Libraries could form loose collaboratives to develop author tours for local and regional authors who have chosen to go the routes of self-publishing and small press publishing rather than with an imprint of the Big Six publishers. As the COSLA report (2010) notes, "This idea caters to interest in 'indie' culture and art—forms of expression that are less processed and closer to the source."

If libraries revamp the way they undertake collection development and serve the authors in their communities, the most competition may come not from the Big Six publishers but from local booksellers, if any local booksellers survive this initial phase of the long e-reading revolution. Epstein (2009) notes, "Some booksellers have already become publishers in their own right of regional authors and self published titles, a vigorous new industry even at this early stage of development and one that echoes the early development of Gutenberg technology."

The COSLA report (2010) also suggests that libraries may want to collaborate to create a public library press. This press would provide services such as editorial assistance and advance review copies, provide the seeds of word-of-mouth marketing, and aid in the discovery of unsung authors. Those who agreed to have their works published by the public library press would agree to donate free electronic versions of their books to all the public libraries who were members of the press.

The Poet's House in New York City could serve as a micro model for this type of tighter relationship between authors and libraries. As one person interviewed for the COSLA report (2010) noted, "Today's well-run libraries are all about genre fiction and midlist writers, not to mention local or regional authors."

In a world in which most content is available in one or more digital forms, what will be the value of printed versions? Epstein (2009) notes that "the codex will remain the most efficient, durable and economical format for textual content worth saving."

Bradley (2011) sees so many potentially fruitful and mutually beneficial collaborations between authors and libraries that authors may come to vie with readers as the core clientele of some libraries:

> I can see authors, and potential authors, asking librarians for advice on publishing. In fact, it's quite possible that a library could get directly involved with the publishing process and produce their own imprint. Universities have university publishers—why shouldn't libraries? Indeed, a library imprint would be a mark of authority in its own right. Furthermore, with self publishing of the physical item via publishers such as Lulu libraries could print physical copies if they were needed, and if necessary or if considered desirable, sell them.

As Carr (2010) notes, the advent of movable type printing in Europe in the fifteenth century resulted in a rapid increase in the number of book volumes: "A virtuous cycle had been set in motion. The growing availability of books fired the public's desire for literacy, and the expansion of literacy further stimulated the demand for books. The printing industry boomed. By the end of the fifteenth century, nearly 250 towns in Europe had print shops, and some twelve million volumes had already come off their presses." At the dawn of the e-reading era, with the rapid expansion of self-publishing, are we witnessing something similar? If so, what does this foretell for the growth and evolution of libraries and library services?

LIBRARIES SUPPORT PRINT ON DEMAND

The e-reading revolution—on personal, portable devices that may eventually enable widespread reading in the cloud—seems to be well under way now and unstoppable. This revolution causes many people to wonder about and discuss the future of the printed book, both as a way to have a reading experience (either as an individual or as part of a group) and as a storage medium for the long-term preservation of texts. While printing via movable, composable type has been common in Europe for over 500 years, the technologies underpinning movable type printing have evolved enormously. One recent development is print on demand (POD). POD diminishes the size of a print run to one. It also enables printing to be done at many locations, such as libraries and bookstores. POD enables printing to occur close to the point of need, measured both temporally and geospatially.

While POD makes printing easier and more convenient, questions remain: What will be the demand for library or bookstore vended POD services in, say, ten years? Will the generations that appreciated and sought out printed books be passing away? Or will new generations find new uses and appreciation for the printed book? By analogy, currently people still appreciate, purchase, and use candles and horses, even though those have long ceased as a primary means of lighting and moving about.

One interesting entrant onto the POD scene is the Espresso Book Machine (EBM) from On Demand Books. An EBM takes a digital book file and produces a paperbound, trimmed, printed version in a few minutes. Geitgey (2011) reports that the realistic page range for POD books printed using an EBM version 1.5 machine is roughly 60 to 450 pages. On Demand Books claims that the cost of the consumables used to create POD books is approximately a penny per page, which includes the paper, cover stock, toner, ink, and glue (On Demand Books n.d. [B]). Covers can be printed in four colors, but evidently the text block is strictly black and white, with no possibility for color illustrations.

The EBM software, called EspressNet, connects each EBM machine to a network of content. On Demand Books has content agreements with both the Open Content Alliance and Google to print books in the public domain, as well as a strategic alliance with Lightning Source, a subsidiary of Ingram Book Group. Geitgey (2011, 53) notes that using book files retrieved through ExpressNet reduces local print and preparation time. "Fortunately, books printed from ODB's recently-released EspressNet catalog have the advantage of pre-made book blocks and covers, so there is no manual file prep work involved in printing an EspressNet title."

Epstein (2010) notes, "The cost of entry for future publishers will be minimal, requiring only the upkeep of the editorial group and its immediate support services but without the expense of traditional distribution facilities and multilayered management." This may prove to be a huge challenge for libraries, because they are not known for convening, nurturing, and sustaining small groups of creative people for tasks such as content creation and editorial handiwork. Also, it is not self-evident that libraries are an optimal location for EBM machines. Of the forty-six EBM locations worldwide listed by On Demand Books, approximately one-third are located in libraries (On Demand Books n.d. [A]). That percentage may fall in the coming months and years, because in May 2011 the American Booksellers Association and On Demand Books announced a joint marketing agreement with a goal to get more EBM machines deployed in ABA member bookstores (On Demand Books 2011).

The EBM has been deployed in academic and public libraries, in retail and college bookstores, and in other locations throughout the U.S. and abroad. "With the Espresso Book Machine, enterprising retail booksellers may become publishers themselves, like their eighteenth-century forebears" (Epstein 2010). Dinger (2011) describes the experiences with POD by Third Place Books in Lake Forest Park, Washington, which has had an EBM since November 2009.

POD also may have a role to play in the preservation of content. "Digital content is fragile. The secure retention, therefore, of physical books safe from electronic meddlers, predators, and the hazards of electronic storage is essential" (Epstein 2010).

The cost of the basic EBM two-module unit is approximately $100,000, which includes the EspressNet software system and the full-color cover printer, plus the cost of the printer, which ranges from approximately $4,000 for the slower printer to approximately $25,000 for a faster one. Freight, installation, and training will cost approximately $10,000. EBM support and maintenance cost $600 per month.

Clearly, the start-up costs for a library wanting to become a serious POD provider are not insignificant. Kenning (2011, 63) notes, "The chief disadvantages of the EBM are initial cost and complexity. . . . New technology always comes with a high price tag, and over time those costs diminish." Geitgey (2011, 52) reports that the University of Michigan Library relied on donor support to purchase an EBM. They have priced their POD books to try to recover the basic production and operating costs.

The quality and durability of the final product also are areas of concern. Brantley (2007) notes that "Google's [mass digitization] effort is focused on the indexing of the texts to power discovery, and a marred display image is an acceptable compromise to make in order to reach the magnitudes of digitization necessary to make the operation—an industrial one in scale—sustainable." The problem with this approach is that using this huge collection of scanned books to fuel a POD service may result in unattractive if not downright unusable books. POD allows some production flexibility in meeting either an immediate, onetime need or long-term archival interests. Geitgey (2011) reports that their EBM has been used both to create archival POD books printed on high-quality, acid-free paper and to print inexpensive books using regular 20-pound paper used on photocopiers and printers.

Pricing of locally created PDF book files and payment processing for all EBM productions are left up to the local organization. Geitgey (2011, 55) reports that the EBM machine itself cannot accept and process any form of payment. He also observes that, for various reasons, it is better to collect payment from the purchaser after the POD book has been produced, not before. The notion of having a library sell large quantities of POD books moves the library toward being a bookseller, which may cause some consternation in the library profession (not to mention among traditional booksellers), even if the sale price is geared only toward recovering costs. Kenning (2011, 65) sees this situation as a good challenge: "Selling books moves libraries away from their traditional missions, . . . but the profound effect of disruptive technologies requires a reconsideration of mission."

An EBM in a library setting need not be used exclusively to sell POD copies to individual library users who desire a printed copy. Both Geitgey (2011) and the University of Michigan Library FAQ (2010) list several applications of POD copies, including:

- Replacement copies for books lost, stolen, or damaged
- Customized books for very specific interests or audiences
- Interlibrary loan borrowing institutions could be given the option of getting a POD copy that need not be returned and would thus be owned by the "borrowing" institution

- Rapid updating of textbooks from semester to semester, based on feedback from students and instructors about prior POD editions
- Collaborative publishing ventures with local independent presses, regional publishing consortia, and self-publishing authors

How POD alters the way books are published, distributed, and used remains to be seen. One interesting and potential high-use POD service focuses on rare and antique books. Geitgey (2011, 52) states that the EBM "provides the perfect mechanism for tapping into the Long Tail concept of selling few copies of many obscure books, rather than many copies of a limited number of popular titles." One can imagine an entire crop of online communities emerging that are centered around reading the works of authors from the mid-twentieth century back in time in POD facsimiles of the original versions. Such readers may relish the printed version, even if the same image of the antique text can be presented on a tablet computer.

The future of print on demand remains unknown. The start-up, ongoing, and replacement costs for a POD machine and related services are not cheap, and the prospects for timely recovery of costs are not blazingly bright, because there are so many unknown variables concerning future demand. The cost of the technology almost certainly will decline, but the demand for POD editions may increase or decline. Many people, including Epstein (2009), see printed editions as a fail-safe hedge against some major electrical change or long-term outage. Many scholars still prefer either web-based searchable databases of scholarly books and other content and/or printed versions over scholarly content that is accessed and interacted with an electronic device. If cloud computing takes off and results in large-scale cloud e-reading by many readers, the benefits of web-based databases and portable e-reading may conflate, thus decreasing the demand for printed editions. Kenning (2011, 65) notes, "While some readers still prefer the feel of a paper book in their hands, generational change will undoubtedly see an increase in those who prefer digital renditions. What this pressure means to permanent book collections in academic libraries is unclear, but a gradual reduction in size is almost certain."

A study and survey conducted in early 2010 by the American Council of Learned Societies and published in August 2010 summarizes the tripartite conundrum many scholars current face. "HEB's initial findings in this study indicate that titles formatted for existing handheld devices are not yet adequate for scholarly use in terms of replicating either the benefits of online collections—cross-searchability, archiving, multifarious interactive components—nor certain aspects of print editions that users reported missing, such as being able to mark up and rapidly skim text" (ACLS 2010, 6).

LIBRARIES AS CONTENT CREATORS AND PUBLISHERS

Libraries also can support authors and other content creators by becoming content creators themselves. Shapiro (2010) thinks that content creation zones in libraries will pull libraries out of their current fiscal crisis and position them to ride the crest of the coming wave of the second renaissance. He suggests that librarians "start using the library space as a collaborative space to make things: books, music CDs, instructional videotapes, screencasts, art, inventions, software, and so on. And then you start selling those creative things to fund the library's operations."

Bradley (2011) says that libraries are in a much better position than both publishers and booksellers to move into the future of publishing, because libraries always have focused on the knowledge, information, and ideas contained in bookish containers rather than on the production, sale, and distribution of the containers themselves.

Although writers and readers are the traditional power base of libraries, Shapiro (2010) thinks that content creation zones in libraries can and should support a wide variety of types of content: "Writers, composers, filmmakers, choreographers, artists, inventors, and other creative types could all get their start working on collaborative projects for their own neighborhood library."

If some libraries plan to become significant content creators and publishers in their own right, they will need to bring new skill sets and organizational structures to bear. While the systems and services focus on helping users find and apply information—as long as the processing, organization, and retention of materials gained from others will not decline—larger libraries may need to develop entirely new divisions or work groups to address the content creation needs.

CONCLUSION

Even as the era of e-reading dawns, it is clear that the days of reading printed materials are not numbered. Libraries will need to remain involved on all fronts, offering content and services in a wide variety of platforms that support many formats and ways to experience information.

It may be too soon to relegate printed books to the sidelines as the e-reading revolution gathers momentum. The heretofore radical differentiation between reading a printed page and reading a screen may blend and blur. For example, quick response (QR) codes embedded in printed books and journals may make it very easy to jump or toggle between reading printed material and accessing related information online. For instance, beginning with its February 2011 issue, the *Journal of Bone & Joint Surgery* has included QR codes (Anderson 2011). POD and QR codes may breathe some life in the production and use of printed information.

In the modern era—which we can tentatively define as the era from the introduction of movable type printing into Europe by Gutenberg and Furst to the end of the twentieth century—the expansion of readers far outpaced the expansion of authors. Libraries grew and developed primarily to serve readers, as well as all the texts and text-bearing devices that were developed and distributed to serve readers. In the near future, however, we may experience a situation where authors and other content creators actually begin to catch up to the sheer number of readers and others who experience information content that teaches and delights. Over the course of the twenty-first century, libraries may need to redirect their resources and sense of mission, not entirely away from services to readers but rather to achieve a better balance between content creation, content ingestion, and content curation.

To expand and improve their support for authors and other content creators in the ways outlined in this chapter, as well as in other ways, libraries will need to collaborate with other stakeholder groups, including publishers and content aggregators. As Brantley (2007) observes, "[T]here are interesting potential co-service offerings between library information vendors and publishing distributors." To serve authors well, the wellspring of all reading, libraries will need to collaborate to a greater and more complex extent, both within and beyond the profession. Although this chapter has not focused on internal changes in libraries—goals, staffing, organization, processes, procedures—that such a realignment of the library's purpose would entail, such changes may be substantial.

Regardless of the form a book takes—printed or digital; visual, auditory, or tactile—libraries help authors and readers connect through textual experiences. To do this, libraries need to ramp up activities and services that were largely handled by publishers and booksellers during the print era. The glory days of both the Big Six publishers and the major brick-and-mortar booksellers have passed. As Bradley (2011) succinctly states, "[L]ibraries can become publishers and booksellers. Publishers and booksellers cannot become libraries." If a fair number of libraries decide to move in this direction in this century, there will be considerable tossing and turning, both within and beyond libraries. Some librarians may become seasick and born-again landlubbers, perhaps kissing the terra firma of museums and archives. If such a storm of change is in the offing, we can draw comfort, direction, and strength by recalling that authors and readers are the twin anchors of the ship of librarianship, one fore and one aft, that steady libraries in both calm waters and rough seas.

REFERENCES

American Council of Learned Societies. 2010. "Handheld E-book Readers and Scholarship: Report and Reader Survey." ACLS Humanities E-Book White Paper #3. New York: ACLS Humanities E-Book Project, www .humanitiesebook.org/HEBWhitePaper3.pdf.

Anderson, Kent. 2011. "QR Codes in a Journal—Printing Little Computer Programs for Mobile Integration." *The Scholarly Kitchen* [blog]. January 31, http://scholarlykitchen.sspnet.org/2011/01/31/qr-codes-in-a-journal-printing-little-computer-programs-for-mobile-integrations/.

Bradley, Phil. 2011. "Librarians in the Publishing Role." *Phil Bradley's Weblog,* April 9, http://philbradley.typepad.com/phil_bradleys_weblog/2011/04/librarians-in-the-publishing-role.html.

Brantley, Peter. 2007. "Print on Demand and Digitization." January 11, http://blogs.lib.berkeley.edu/shimenawa.php/2007/01/11/print_on_demand_and_digitization.

Carr, Nicholas. 2010. *The Shallows: What the Internet Is Doing to Our Brains.* New York: W. W. Norton.

Chief Officers of State Library Agencies. 2010. *COSLA: E-book Feasibility Study for Public Libraries.* Portland, OR: Pinpoint Logic, www.cosla.org/documents/COSLA2270_Report_Final1.pdf.

Curtis, Richard. 2011. "Are POD's E-books?" *E-reads* [blog], January 30, http://ereads.com/2011/01/are-pods-e-books.html.

Dinger, Frances. 2011. "'Espresso Book Machine' Changing Publishing Game." The *Spectator* at Seattle University, March 9, www.su-spectator.com/entertainment/espresso-book-machine-changing-publishing-game-1.2085760.

Epstein, Jason. 2009. "Technology and Human Nature: Speech Given by Jason Epstein at the 2009 O'Reilly Tools of Change for Publishing Conference." www.ondemandbooks.com/docs/TOC%202009%20Speech.pdf and http://assets.en.oreilly.com/1/event/19/Technology%20and%20Human%20Nature%20Paper.pdf.

———. 2010. "Publishing: The Revolutionary Future." *New York Review of Books,* March 11, www.nybooks.com/articles/archives/2010/mar/11/publishing-the-revolutionary-future/.

Geitgey, Terri. 2011. "The University of Michigan Library Espresso Book Machine Experience." *Library Hi Tech* 29 (1): 51–61.

Kenning, Arlitsch. 2011. "The Espresso Book Machine: A Change Agent for Libraries." *Library Hi Tech* 29 (1): 62–72.

Lankes, R. David. 2011. *The Atlas of Librarianship.* Cambridge, MA: MIT Press.

Neiburger, Eli. 2010. "LJ/SLJ E-book Summit: Libraries Are Screwed, Unless . . . Part 2." YouTube Video, 8:39, www.youtube.com/watch?v = bd0lIKVstJg.

On Demand Books. 2011. "American Booksellers Association and On Demand Books Form Partnership," May 12, www.ondemandbooks.com/docs/ABA-Espresso-Release.pdf.

———. N.d. (A). "EBM locations," www.ondemandbooks.com/ebm_locations.php.

———. N.d. (B). "The Espresso Book Machine Hardware," www.ondemandbooks.com/ebm_hardware.php.

Peters, Tom. 2007. "The Rustication of Expertise." *ALA TechSource* [blog], January 11, www.alatechsource.org/blog/2007/01/the-rustication-of-expertise.html.

Shapiro, Phil. 2010. "It's Time for Public Libraries to Get Creative." *PC World,* April 26, www.pcworld.com/article/194960/its_time_for_public_libraries_to_get_creative.html.

University of Michigan Library. 2010. "The Espresso Book Machine at the University of Michigan Library: Questions and Answers," www.lib.umich.edu/espresso-book-machine/espresso-book-machine-university-michigan-library-questions-and-answers.

11

Getting Control, Staying Relevant

How Libraries Can Push the E-book Envelope to Their Advantage

JOSEPH SANCHEZ

The Internet was widely hailed as the harbinger of library doom. For was it not a faster, more fluid replication of a library's core services? Even though the first decade of the digital age did not bring about the demise of libraries, the argument and question persists. As the horse-drawn carriage eventually rendered horses mere luxury items, there are reasons to believe that libraries, and even printed books, will become irrelevant niceties to be enjoyed on a Sunday afternoon, but certainly not Monday through Friday necessities. In the discipline, we would like to think this cannot or will not happen, but history tells us that irrelevance is a natural occurrence that affects every aspect of human society. Libraries would not be the first institution to fade into obscurity as a result of new developments and technological progress. The digital revolution has already succeeded in creating an environment of doubt and insecurity across the field, as libraries have lost their roles as information gatekeepers. The advent of e-books has only exacerbated the problem, because publishers and vendors want to control content, placing libraries in an increasingly marginalized role. The literature is replete with complaints and manifestos. Clearly, librarians recognize the problem, but to date no working solution has been offered. This is because the problem has so many components and variables—it's like trying to hit a moving target in the dark while riding a merry-go-round. One thing seems clear: libraries need to take advantage of the digital revolution and develop their own content management systems rather than continue to outsource. Our budgets cannot sustain a continued outsourcing trend. Just as libraries are beginning to develop their own ILS systems, they need to bypass OverDrive and Adobe to create software packages from within the discipline that put libraries back in control. Once these are developed, libraries can leverage their long history with first sale doctrine and fair use doctrine to purchase and control their own e-content.

At this point in history, it seems safe to conclude that if libraries fade into obscurity, it will not be the Internet that is to blame. For the Internet never really threatened the core identity and services of libraries. Some floor space for DVD shelving and computer pods for the Internet may be delegated, but the vast majority of resources are still dedicated to books—for libraries are ultimately about books. So when the nature of the book is challenged and redefined, so too is the very nature and essence of *library*. When Amazon introduced a functional and user-friendly e-reader, it was a direct challenge to libraries: adapt or become irrelevant. Many in the discipline thought this was an overreaction five years ago. E-readers had been around for years, and so had e-books. But none of them offers the ease of use and immediate satisfaction the Kindle offers. Kindles did for e-readers and e-books what iPods did for MP3 players and digital music, and librarians can expect the change in the book market to be as complete and final as the change in the music market has been. Today, it is difficult to imagine anyone in the discipline not realizing how serious the e-book issue is, as digital book sales surpassed paperback books sales for the first time in February 2011 (Association of American Publishers 2011).

Unfortunately, libraries have watched all this from the sidelines. Some of this was simple willful ignorance combined with the inability of large organizations to adapt and manage the rapid evolution of technology. But there are deeper roots. When information was first digitized, libraries settled for a business model based on subscription packages, little realizing that this would come back to haunt us a few decades later. In the early nineties, it made sense to subscribe to database packages from EBSCO, Gale, and ProQuest rather than think long term about the implications of such a new (for libraries) content management system. This was a quick and easy solution for the sudden tidal wave of information suddenly available. It was less about copyright and security issues, because this model developed before Napster highlighted the vulnerability of digital information. Rather, libraries lacked both the human and fiscal capital necessary to manage the massive amounts of content suddenly available. So we outsourced the work and responsibility, willing to pay a yearly subscription to give our patrons access to content they could not afford as individuals. Libraries were suddenly capable of offering their patrons far more information than ever before, and that information was not available on the Internet.

Twenty years later we are now in the opposite situation, because we did not anticipate the repercussions of not taking a more active role in the legal and business evolution of digital content. Now we are unable to purchase a ten-dollar e-book our patrons can download instantly as private citizens. Instead of continuing to offer more content, we are in the unenviable position of offering less, even as the expectation and awareness arises that there is so much more available. Our budgets were designed for a predigital age when libraries could take advantage of first sale doctrine to pay cover price for an item and circulate it to all patrons within their geographic environs. First sale even helped us with interlibrary loans. First sale limited a publisher's control of a published work to the first sale of that work, establishing a firm right for consumers and libraries to control lawfully purchased property (Pike 2010). But its application in the digital realm has been hotly contested due to two unique and seemingly contradictory characteristics of digital content. First, digital files are *vulnerable,* because they can be so easily copied and duplicated. Second, digital files are *permanent,* because they can be so easily copied and duplicated. This odd paradox came to a head in 2000 when Napster was sued for copyright infringement (*A&M Records v. Napster* 2001). The digitization of information could have been an unprecedented opportunity to create limitless collections, where libraries simply configure more server space rather than weed their collections. Eventually even small libraries could have offered their patrons previously undreamt amounts of resources. But Napster highlighted the vulnerability and permanence of digital content from a negative perspective, scaring businesses and legislatures. One can only imagine how different the situation would be if it had been libraries instead of Napster bringing vulnerability and permanence to public consciousness. Combined with libraries' early acceptance of the subscription-based business model, the Napster lawsuit set a course for what the library community now recognizes as an untenable situation.

Libraries cannot afford a subscription-based e-content model, as most libraries would be rapidly priced out of the market and would lack the local control of their collections that has been so valuable and useful to their patrons. OverDrive is a wonderful product because it has e-content where and when our patrons want it, but it is expensive and the content is extremely limited. Whereas libraries have a legal right to purchase, own, and manage any physical item, they are forced to approach the digital industry as second-class citizens begging for a few crumbs—and paying five-star prices for those crumbs. Libraries do not have a seat at the bargaining table, and their collective budgets are not big enough to attract the attention of multibillion-dollar international companies like Apple and Amazon. Moreover, while digitization questioned the relevance of libraries, the digitization of books brings the relevance of publishers and vendors into question as well, because publishers no longer need to calculate print runs and figure out distribution models with e-content. One book file can be duplicated and transferred on demand at the point of need. Do authors need publishers anymore? Or do they simply need a website with good marketing and high traffic? The question is certainly driving many of the actions in the industry, like HarperCollins' arbitrary and outrageous twenty-six-loan cap on e-books (Hadro and Kelley 2011).

Publishers and vendors saw how digitization has ravaged the revenues of the music industry and is trying to duplicate the movie industry's success at protecting content and, ultimately, profit. The problem is that e-book files are nowhere near as complicated as video, which makes digital rights management (DRM) more challenging. E-book files, like music files, are easier to pirate, which makes publishers understandably skittish. DRM is beyond the scope of this article, but suffice it to say that DRM is the Gordian knot that grew out of the legal/business environment's response to Napster. Obviously, first sale doctrine and fair use was and is given less weight because of the historical circumstances that have driven the argument. As latecomers to the party, libraries are at a serious disadvantage but not entirely powerless. Moreover, as will be demonstrated later, libraries may be able to leverage their advantages to make themselves competitive in the information market again.

EXPLORING THE POSSIBILITIES:
AN E-READER EXPERIMENT

In 2007, Red Rocks Community College library in Lakewood, Colorado, received permission from its dean to begin "experimenting" with e-readers. This was a very different experiment than the highly publicized pilot study done at seven major universities across the U.S. using Kindle DXs (Univ. of WA 2009). First, it was library centered and managed. Second, the focus was not on students' use and perceptions of the e-reader but rather on ways that libraries can utilize and leverage the devices (and consequently e-books). Third, the scope was more comprehensive. Before a device was adopted, a handful of Kindles and Sony e-readers were purchased and distributed to a group of beta testers from the college's population. The group was specifically selected to represent all age groups, technical skill levels, and reading interests. Users had items of interest purchased and preloaded for them. They were informed that the only requirements were to provide open-ended feedback on their experience. Loan periods varied from as short as a week to as long as a month, depending on the user's preference. Feedback was both fascinating and unpredictable. Almost the entire beta test group still utilizes the service. Many of the older book lovers have communicated a slow and grudging appreciation of the devices almost against their will; one of them even purchased one in the spring of 2011. Kindles were overwhelmingly more popular than Sony, so about a dozen Kindles were purchased. They were bar-coded and placed into circulation after the library determined that sensitive information like credit card data was protected. The ultimate goal was to begin developing long-term data and information that was necessary to developing useful strategic plans for e-books (and ultimately e-content) rather than the abstract and theoretical discussions that currently dominate the discipline.

In addition to circulating e-readers as if they were books (same circulation parameters, etc.), the staff determined to implement a unique patron-driven acquisition model that outsourced all the collection development for their Kindle book collection to the patrons. This decision was both deliberate and accidental. It was based on a couple of early unique experiences with the Kindle. Like most small libraries, Red Rocks has a very limited collection and often cannot fulfill the book needs of its professors and patrons. But a chance encounter between the director and a student looking for a book recommended by a certain professor suggested that e-books offered a brand-new collection development model. The student requested a title that was unavailable, and instead of suggesting an ILL or using the regional book lending program available through the local public library, the director looked up the title of the book on the Kindle while talking to the student, found it, and downloaded it in less time than it took to check out the Kindle to the student. Based on the student's overwhelmingly positive reaction at that moment and upon returning the Kindle, library staff recognized that e-books offered them an opportunity to compete with Google and larger academic libraries by purchasing from the Kindle cloud on an as-needed basis. Moreover, the decision was made to outsource collection development to the patrons themselves by setting up a policy of one title per patron per month. Patrons were informed that they could access the Kindle store from the device at any time and purchase a title without approval of library staff, provided they limit their purchases to one title per month. This radical choice made sense for our smaller patron base (and staff) and was far less intimidating than it sounds because Amazon sends e-mail invoices immediately upon purchase of a title. As the account administrators, any staff member could immediately cancel a remote patron order. This has never been done, but it is possible.

This crowd-sourced collection development has evolved over the years and continues to be one of the most popular and successful services at the library. It has also taught us a great deal about patron behavior, expectations, and needs. Initial fears about cost have been completely wrong, as the nature of social networking quickly established a core collection of titles that met the vast majority of patron needs. Purchasing follows growth curves depending on new course content and new faculty. Once a core body of titles is purchased, purchasing slows down and returns to a slower rate of growth. Fiction and pleasure reading have longer and steeper growth curves but seem equally predictable and less costly than anticipated. Informal interviews and questioning of patrons revealed that many patrons forget to purchase their intended title, as they became distracted and engaged with the number of titles already available in the archived cloud. Like shelf browsing, patrons discovered a less organized but still engaging set of titles they had not anticipated.

The success of the Kindle project was used as a foundation to purchase iPads when they were launched. The library collaborated with the physician's assistant program to manage and embed iPads on a long-term basis with the program's sixty students. The library would manage content, both apps and books, while the program would advise the library on the purchasing of relevant material and apps. The library realized early on that iPads were a quantum leap forward and replicated more than simple book lending but could in fact manage and duplicate multiple needs for the library and its patrons. The revolutionary nature of the iPad is at the heart of this video (http://vimeo.com/12678227) produced by the library as a way of viscerally illustrating the radical challenge e-books and multifunction tablets represent not only to libraries but to all academia.

FUTURE STEPS AND SOLUTIONS

As mentioned earlier, the Internet did not challenge the core identity of libraries. But the advent of e-books has. Books have been the core of library services and identity, and any change in books inherently means a change in libraries. At this point, it does not seem likely that e-books will fade into obscurity, indicating that libraries need to do some deep soul-searching and thinking about the future. There are two possible outcomes. First, e-books may replace books as the primary and dominant information medium. Print books will be an expensive luxury and hobby of a dedicated group of devotees, but they will be expensive due to the cost of limited print runs, and interest or desire will be passed down to future generations like horses or classic cars. But future patrons may end up having no knowledge of or desire for print books. Yes, there are studies and surveys that suggest students still prefer print (*Publisher's Weekly* 2011), but when their responses are examined the issue is more function than form. As e-books evolve like MP3 players, it is equally possible to expect an iPod moment when book culture shifts just like music culture did. That moment already happened when the Kindle was introduced. The second foreseeable option is that e-books and print books exist more symbiotically, side by side, serving disparate needs. This is a very attractive option when one considers that e-books are rapidly evolving and may soon resemble a portable website rather than a printed book. Like a website they will be nonlinear and contain multimedia. Obviously, fiction will still be read in a linear fashion rather than searched, but even fiction may evolve so much with eye-tracking software and embedded sound/video effects that print fiction may survive to serve a large niche market.

However, it is clear that the long-held tradition of a building filled with bookshelves needs to be reexamined, as books get stored on servers and delivered wirelessly rather than with bookmobiles and circulation desks. This change has to be carefully managed by local staff—who are best situated to understand their demographic and avoid making the transition too rapidly. But the plan needs to be set in place now rather than later. Likewise, the role and job duties of librarians need to be reevaluated as well. In short, the core identity and nature of *library* needs to be reevaluated. Regardless of the details, it should be evident that the essence of libraries needs to be assessed in light of the digital nature of e-books.

Red Rocks' experience with e-readers and iPads stimulated some very revolutionary ideas and plans. The library has already created a contingency plan where the print book collection will be heavily reduced—by 50 percent or more—and the extra floor space dedicated to content creation. The library has absorbed the main computer lab on campus as well as computer tutoring and installed a digitization studio complete with a fully functional recording studio for producing and cataloging original content. Previously, this type of service could only be found at large academic institutions, central public libraries, or specialized libraries, but the staff at Red Rocks have recognized a need among students, staff, and the local community for a collaborative content creation environment.

Technical Solutions

More important, library staff began experimenting with models for bypassing OverDrive and the subscription-based model for e-content. In September 2010, the Apple software development kit for iOS was downloaded to a local Mac laptop, and a student employee was tasked with developing an app that would authenticate users on a one-to-one basis for accessing a library of digital files stored on a server. Hopes were high that in a few months a working model could be developed that would demonstrate the feasibility of creating a software package that replicates the functionality of OverDrive but whose content would be determined and controlled by the library. The idea was to take advantage of the core legal rationale behind first sale and fair use doctrine that allowed libraries to circulate one item per user. The idea is that such a software platform would allow libraries to advantageously leverage their long legal history, relieve budgets, and place libraries back in control of their content. The reason OverDrive is so expensive is not because it authenticates one local user at a time but because OverDrive does that all across the country with the same *content,* thereby incurring massive licensing costs from the copyright owners. Netflix faces the same high costs but offsets those costs across millions of subscribers individually. Libraries and consequently OverDrive cannot offset costs this way, leaving libraries holding the bill.

Why not return to the old model where each library purchases their own material and manages it locally, like they always have? All that is needed is a working mechanism that can assure DRM and a one-patron-per-item lending model. To be sure, the permanence of digital content is a legitimate concern for vendors and producers, because libraries could theoretically create unlimited collections over the years and never need to weed again, which is obviously a new issue to consider. But libraries could leverage this situation to argue that libraries are the perfect nonprofit, nonpartisan entity for archiving the massive amounts of information and data currently being produced. Our argument should be, who better to manage and store the data our society is currently creating than libraries? Moreover, we should be able to use our massive amounts of organized statistics to create a more equitable pricing model than the reactionary and arbitrary lending limits like the HarperCollins one. Libraries need to dust off their shelf life and circulation stats in order to deliver hard data to legislators, judges, publishers, and vendors when these negotiations take place.

Because the new content management model is possible *now.* Prior to attempting to develop an Apple app, Red Rocks had determined that Adobe Content Server could manage the lending of institution-owned and locally stored e-books but found the cost prohibitive. At the same time, staff decided to begin ripping the entire music collection in preparation for the day when the actual CD will be taken off the shelf and stored while the digital file will be uploaded and loaned. Even though the legal questions are far from settled, staff hope to see a day when all e-content can be loaned in this fashion and are preparing for that day. Moreover, the question of permanence in the music industry has already been settled (seemingly), as there are no legal obstacles to private citizens ripping their music and creating a permanent backup.

To the surprise of all involved, Red Rocks' student employee had a working model of an app running in the app emulator within two months. It was crude and simple, but it was able to authenticate users from a database and stream a file to one user while blocking another user. This should not have been much of a surprise, because this type of functionality is fairly standard. While a fully developed product will be an entirely different challenge than the crude early model that has by now been abandoned, it is definitely possible to create a product that will bypass OverDrive and allow libraries to control and own their own e-content. All that remains is the legal battle.

Political and Legal Solutions

Libraries must become involved in the power struggle over DRM, fair use, and first sale doctrine. But we cannot limit ourselves to theoretical arguments. First sale and fair use need functional software support in order to remain advantageous for libraries. Our best advantage to date seems to be developing a software suite that will be a combination of OverDrive and Adobe Content Server but allow libraries local control, because publishers' and vendors' concerns about security and the potential permanence of digital files are legitimate. Resolving the security issue is the natural first step, because it removes the most serious and obvious roadblock to an argument based on first sale and fair use. Once that is done, use stats and shelf life can be utilized to establish equitable and reasonable purchasing agreements. Such a scenario offers a number of advantages. It creates a reasonable foundation for maintaining the interpretations of first sale and fair use that are most friendly to libraries. It also alleviates publishers' fears and links new agreements to past history, which is both reasonable and fair. Finally, the ALA should be prepared to take the argument to the highest level of judicial and legal recourse, as even an argument based on such comfortable and familiar terms is still filled with unknown variables, because technology evolves so fast and in such unanticipated ways. At the very least, such an argument creates a firm legal foundation for proceeding forward based on a century's worth of precedent and equitable business practice.

Immediate Solutions

In the meantime we can bypass the industry and begin working more locally, and in the realm of public domain books. ALA and the entire library community need to create formal alliances with Project Gutenberg and other free e-content providers rather than watching Sony (Albanese 2009) and others take advantage of what should be the business of libraries. Here in the state of Colorado, a library consortium (clicweb.org) created MARC records for the 500 most popular titles in Gutenberg that libraries can now download and add to their catalogs, but the time has come for a more formal and national alliance with Gutenberg, Google Books, and other content providers. Free and legal e-content is all over the Web. The difficulty for patrons is locating it. Libraries as aggregators of that content make natural sense, because that is what libraries have always done. While many libraries have had novel and colorful solutions like cataloging and linking to free content, libraries and library consortia should start looking at bigger and more comprehensive approaches that remove the constant, often redundant work involved at the local level. A formal agreement between OCLC and Gutenberg or SnagFilms is mutually beneficial to all parties, as it increases use at minimal cost and ensures standardized cataloging for all new content. Regardless, it is time for libraries to take the lead and build relationships with such partners.

For example, a series of meetings in late 2010 between leaders at Red Rocks and Douglas County libraries resulted in a plan that would put the above vision into action. Both directors discovered a shared vision and willingness to push the envelope. Under the leadership of Douglas County, a deal has been reached with the Colorado Independent Publishers Association for the purchasing and marketing of books from authors across the state. Using Adobe Content Server, Douglas County will loan the books to their patrons using the model outlined in this article. Part of the agreement and benefit for the author is that the library will embed hyperlinks to the author's online vending site from the library OPAC. The rationale is that libraries have always supported literacy and authors in a far more complementary and benign way than the publishing industry, which always has to consider profits. Building off the highly successful Amazon model where more content is only a click away, the OPAC will offer immediate access for the patron to purchase more titles and content directly from the author. Negotiations took place during the spring months, and the project went live that summer, complete with a marketing and media campaign.

The goal is to implement the vision immediately wherever possible and begin working out the larger and long-term issues as they become actionable and legal. But by demonstrating a working model that is up and running now, it seems reasonable to assume that libraries can begin developing some leverage of their own to take into the legal battle that makes owning and purchasing e-content far less scary and more profitable for all parties concerned. It is also the best possible outcome for libraries faced with decreasing budgets and less local control of their collections. While this may not answer the far bigger question as to what libraries will become, it can solve the more immediate and pressing issue of e-content access and management.

FOR FURTHER INFO

Joseph Sanchez, formerly Red Rocks Community College, currently University of Colorado Denver, Auraria Library, www.thebookmyfriend.com.

Jamie Larue, executive director, Douglas County Libraries, www.jlarue.com/.

REFERENCES

A&M Records, Inc., et al. v. Napster, Inc., 239 F.3d 1004 (2001).

Albanese, Andrew. 2009. "Sony, Google Strike Public Domain Deal." *Library Journal,* 134(7), 17. Retrieved from ABI/INFORM Global.

Association of American Publishers. 2011. "Popularity of Books in Digital Platforms Continues to Grow, According to AAP Publishers February Sales Report." April 14, www.publishers.org/press/30/.

Hadro, J., and M. Kelley. 2011. "HarperCollins: 26-Loan Cap on Library E-books." *Library Journal,* 136(6), 16, 18. Retrieved from Library Lit & Inf Full Text database

Pike, G. (2010). Is First Sale for Digital Content at Risk? *Information Today,* 27(10), 17, 19. Retrieved from Library Lit & Inf Full Text database.

Publisher's Weekly Staff. 2011. "BISG Survey Finds Students Prefer Print." *Publisher's Weekly,* January 7, www.publishersweekly.com/pw/by-topic/industry-news/publisher-news/article/45699-bisg-survey-finds-students-prefer-print.html.

University of Washington Computer Science and Engineering. 2009. *Kindle DX Pilot Project,* www.cs.washington.edu/news/KindlePilot/.

12

The iPad Loaner Program at Oberlin College Library

JESSICA GRIM AND ALLISON GALLAHER ·

I n the spring of 2010, Oberlin College Library ran a pilot project to loan iPads to students from the circulation desk in its main library. In fall 2010 a full iPad loan program was introduced, which has been extremely popular among library users from the first day.

By the fall of 2009 the library had been following developments in mobile readers for some time, with the thought to purchase a stable of e-readers to loan so that the library's rich e-book collections could be accessed as freely as any print book—from a completely portable, easy to transport device. The library was also looking for a way to test and evaluate mobile apps for general library utility.

With new evidence in the literature indicating that e-book readability on the iPod was quite good, and with the imminent appearance of the iPad, the library decided in early 2010 that the time was right to initiate an iPad loaner program. This chapter describes the planning, implementation, current status, and future plans for Oberlin College Library's iPad loaner program.

Oberlin is a residential liberal arts college with a student body of about 2,800 including students in both the College of Arts and Sciences and the

Conservatory of Music. The Oberlin College Library is composed of a main library, a science library, an art library, and a conservatory library. The iPad loaner program described in this article is based in the main library.

By early 2011 a number of academic libraries had mobile device loaning programs in place, and some of those programs focused on the iPad. One notable difference in how Oberlin chose to implement its program is in the decision not to lock down the iPads in terms of content addition, discussed in "Moving toward the Pilot Launch," below.

WHY LOAN PORTABLE READING DEVICES?

Since 2001 Oberlin College Library has run a very successful laptop loaner program from its circulation desk and, in part based on the success of that program, had been considering for some time providing a similar service loaning portable reading devices (PRDs). While the function and uses of the laptops and uses of PRDs would have some level of overlap (Web browsing, e-mail, etc.), what particularly excited us about the idea of loaning out PRDs was the capability to read e-books on a fully portable device.

Oberlin, like most academic libraries today, makes available to its users an extensive and rich array of e-book content, representing significant investment in both monetary and staff terms over the last ten or more years. Providing an avenue for Oberlin's users to access that content in as convenient a fashion as possible—in as portable a form, for example, as a print book—seemed like good sense.

In addition to providing portable platforms on which patrons could access library e-book content, mobile readers would also provide a platform on which the library could evaluate mobile apps for general library utility.

Yet in 2008 when the library first considered the idea of purchasing a PRD that might serve the vision of a "walking e-book collection," the PRDs on the market clearly did not have the necessary functionality. The Kindle, followed by the Nook, with their proprietary restrictions, were "dead-end" devices as far as accessing the library's e-book content. Thus the planning for loaning out PRDs was set on the back burner.

TIMING AND CHOICE OF DEVICE

When in the fall of 2009 Lisa Carlucci Thomas's report "Mobile Access to E-books at Yale" (Thomas 2009) appeared, it was clear that the time was right for the library to revive the discussion about loaning PRDs. The beauty of Thomas's report was that the testing that had been conducted at Yale used a list of library-purchased e-book resources nearly identical to the resources Oberlin was eager to start making available on PRDs (including e-book content from ebrary, Eighteenth Century Collections Online, Early English Books Online, Organisation for Economic Cooperation and Development, and the American Council of Learned Societies Humanities e-book).

Thomas's report compared several mobile readers with respect to usability of the library's purchased e-book content and found that 84 percent of that content was easily accessible and readable on the iPod—compared with significantly smaller figures for other e-readers. Given these findings, and the then-imminent appearance of the iPad—providing the same level of accessibility as the iPod, with a significantly larger reading screen—the library made the decision to initiate its loaner program using iPads, which were slated to hit the market in April 2010.

In March 2010 a document was drafted, "Portable Readers for Loan at OCL," which outlined the basic thinking behind and strategy for a loaner program. This document was shared both among library staff and with staff from Oberlin's Center for Information Technology (CIT), which broadly supports software and hardware in use across campus.

PILOT PROJECT—SPRING 2010

Why Do a Pilot? And Initial Logistics

The decision to start with a pilot project loaning iPads was logical, given the many unknowns involved: Could a reasonable way to manage the program (syncing of iPads, purchase of apps, battery life, loan policies, etc.) be arrived at? Would students use and appreciate the iPad loans? Was this a reasonable use of library funds and staff energy?

The library director supported the general idea of circulating PRDs and agreed to purchase two iPads for use in the iPad loaner pilot.

A pre-pilot period, during which the iPads were loaned to selected library student staff, was used to determine whether any major issues would arise relating to the technology or support needed before the pilot was launched. Several students borrowed iPads for a week each during this phase, and feedback was solicited from users after each loan. In April 2010 the iPad was brand new—neither staff nor users had experience with them, and although much of the functionality mirrored that of other Apple products, they were untested in many respects. Happily none of the pre-pilot experiences resulted in red flags, and the pilot phase moved ahead.

Moving toward the Pilot Launch

After having had the opportunity to work with the iPads, library staff better understood some of the trade-offs involved in running the loaner program envisioned. It was important to the library for users to have easy access on the iPad dock to apps and links the library particularly wanted them to encounter—such as the library's e-book content—but it was also desirable to allow users to explore the iPad's functionality as fully as possible. For this reason the decision was made not to restrict functionality on the iPads but instead to allow users to add apps, reorganize the screens, and possibly even sync the iPads to other iTunes libraries. This meant users would have the capacity to wipe out the library setup or delete library-selected apps. The decision not to lock down iPad content and screens appears to be a distinctive feature of Oberlin's program; the program at Briar Cliff University, for example, outlined in the April 2011 issue of *C&RL News* (Thompson 2011), has many similarities to Oberlin's program but differs notably in regard to this central question of user access to full iPad functionality.

It was also important to keep the iPads in circulation as much as possible, so the choice was made not to re-sync the iPads between each user. This meant that in the time between syncing, the iPads would likely drift far from the original setup. Of particular interest was whether this level of unpredictability would prove a problem for users, or if they would be willing to accept it as the flip side of the freedom that allowed them to manipulate the iPad.

During this pilot planning phase, the library was taken somewhat by surprise by a request from Oberlin's CIT staff that the launch of the pilot be delayed, which was agreed to (the initial launch date was April 19 and was delayed to May 5). The CIT's concern was that the iPads were brand new on campus, and CIT staff had not had an opportunity to work with them enough to feel fully prepared to provide support for any software or hardware issues that users might have. The library was in close touch with CIT staff during the pre-pilot loans and in fact requested that the students using the iPads during the pre-pilot report directly to the CIT any questions or problems they were having with the iPads. No tech problems arose during the pre-pilot, nor have they, to the library's knowledge, in the many months since.

To get user feedback, a brief survey was created and distributed in paper form to all iPad borrowers during the pilot. The survey asked for general feedback on what worked for borrowers, what didn't work, and whether iPad loans from the library seemed like a good idea.

A low-key approach to publicity for the pilot was adopted, as there were just two iPads in circulation, and avoiding potential user aggravation resulting from turn-aways was desired. An announcement was posted on the library blog, and flyers were placed at strategic points within the library. Beyond that, word of mouth did the work.

The first iPad was loaned out on May 5, 2010. The iPads circulated for three hours, with overnight circulation starting three hours before closing each night. The decision to circulate on a three-hour loan was based on the goal to have as many students use the iPads as possible during the pilot yet provide each borrower with adequate time to explore the iPad's functionality and potential uses.

The iPad loaner pilot ran for the month of May, which included Oberlin's finals week, senior week, and commencement weekend. The two iPads circulated a total of 211 times during the pilot month. Eighty-six completed user surveys were received.

What We Learned from the Pilot Surveys

The majority of the eighty-six respondents (fifty-four) indicated that they thought that loaning iPads from the library was a good idea, and many were quite enthusiastic about the service. Borrowers particularly liked the convenience of the iPad, the ease of web surfing and e-mail functionality, and the ease of reading text on the iPad. Oberlin's course-management

Mudd iPad Loaner
Pilot Project, May 2010

As the borrower of a Mudd iPad loaner you are part of a grand test. We're especially interested in how the iPads work as readers for our vast array of ebooks. Your input (↓) will help us shape the service which we plan to officially launch in the Fall.

We ask that you:

1. Have fun
2. Try stuff
3. Let us know how it went

Tip: if you're having trouble launching things it may be because you haven't authenticated on the network; open Safari to make sure you're authenticated.

PLEASE FILL OUT & RETURN WHEN YOU RETURN THE IPAD:
What worked well for you (details great!)?

What did not work well (details great!)?

Do you think loaning iPads from the Library is a good idea?

Why/Why not?

Other comments/suggestions (use back if nec):

NAME *(optional)* _____

Contact jessica.grim@oberlin.edu if you have more input or questions.
Contact client.services@oberlin.edu if you have technical issues or feedback.

THANK YOU!

FIGURE 12.1 *iPad Loaner Pilot Survey*

system, Blackboard, has an app that a number of respondents found particularly useful. Borrowers were generally unimpressed with the keyboard function on the iPad, and some borrowers felt the iPads offered limited applications in an academic setting.

FULL LOANER PROGRAM—FALL 2010

Planning for the Full Program

Based on the pilot survey feedback, and the agreement among staff involved that the Pilot had gone well, planning started for a full-scale rollout of the iPad loaner program at the beginning of the fall term.

The library director agreed to the purchase of an additional thirteen iPads for the program, bringing to fifteen the number of iPads available for circulation. Although this represented a significant expense, discretionary funds were used; thus the purchase did not put pressure on regular library budgetary lines.

An overview of the iPad loaner program was developed and linked on the library's web pages, as well as bookmarked on each iPad. The overview included tech hints, borrowing policy, and an FAQ (http://www.oberlin .edu/library/circ/iPads.html).

Did you know:

That OBIS contains links to hundreds of thousands of ebooks??

Yup. Everything from encyclopedias, to early printed books, (we're talking 15th & 16th centuries here), to tech manuals of all kinds, to scholarly books on almost any subject imaginable.

You can read them on your desktop or laptop computers of course, as well as on some of the portable devices you may own…

OR

You can read them on an iPad, checked out from the Circulation Desk!!

We kid you not.

PILOT PROJECT STARTING MAY 5.

FIGURE 12.2 *Promotional Ad for the iPad Loaner Pilot Project*

Several logistical and technical issues needed to be settled before the start of the full loaner program. These issues included the creation of an iTunes account for the library (for the pilot, a staff member had been willing to use her own account), deciding under what circumstances the library would pay for apps for the iPads, and settling on a circulation period that would work well considering the increased number of iPads available for loan.

It was not clear if it was possible to have a single suite of apps synced to fifteen devices. Upon trying it, it worked and proved easy to maintain. The iPads remained unlocked for users to add apps if they chose. The thinking was that (1) borrowers couldn't hurt the iPads by adding their choice of apps; in fact (2) apps added by one student borrower might well be of interest or use to another student borrower; and (3) the clutter and unpredictability of this approach had not been a problem for users during the pilot.

The decision was made to expand the loan period from a three-hour circulation to a three-day circulation. Any borrowers using the iPads for research and e-book access would need an extended loan to complete whatever work and reading they were engaged in, and with fifteen iPads in circulation, a three-day loan would still allow reasonably good availability of iPads.

The decision was also made not to recharge the iPads between each use, but instead to circulate adapters with the iPads, allowing borrowers to recharge the batteries as needed.

Publicity

To advertise the iPad loaner program, an article appeared in the library newsletter, a short article was placed in the student newspaper, an announcement was posted on the library blog, and signage was placed in the library.

Observations from the First Full Semester

Over the course of the fall 2010 semester—from September through December—there were a total of 625 iPad circulations. Of those, 583 were to students and 42 were to faculty/staff. On most days all fifteen iPads were in circulation.

The circulation staff posted "iPad now available" signs to alert potential borrowers, and circulation was on a first come, first served basis.

The library chose not to implement a reservation system as it would undoubtedly have resulted in iPads sitting on the shelf waiting for a specific user rather than in use.

Users received reminder e-mails one day before the iPads were due, and the fine rate was $10 per day. Of the 625 circulations in the first semester, only 37 were returned overdue and generated fines. There were no problems with loss or damage during the first semester, but the policy is in place to bill users $700 for the replacement cost of the iPad should it be necessary.

Perhaps the most prominent unknown was whether the decision not to lock down content on the iPads would prove problematic for the library, or in some way have an adverse effect on either the iPads or the borrowers generally. After a full semester of the program it was determined that taking this open approach had not presented problems from the staffing perspective, nor had it compromised the iPads.

Each iPad did get re-synced by library staff approximately weekly. Users are free to add apps to the iPad simply by signing in to their iTunes account; in the re-syncing process there are often apps that library staff decide to add to the library profile based on anticipated interest and use by

---

NOW AVAILABLE

Borrow an iPad

WHERE: Circulation Desk
FOR HOW LONG: 3 days
WHAT YOU NEED: Your OCID

Whatchya Waitin' For?

FIGURE 12.3 *iPad Loaner Project Announcement*

future borrowers. What was unexpected was the occasional discovery that a user had re-synced an iPad to his or her own iTunes library (easily done by connecting the iPad to a computer running iTunes), adding gigabytes of music and removing all our apps! The stored backup for each device, however, made it easy to restore the library setup during the maintenance process.

The iPad loaner program was envisioned as a service to Oberlin College students. While consideration had been given to whether iPads should be loaned to faculty and staff as well, the decision to start up the service as student-only was based largely on the knowledge that faculty and staff had other options for using iPads on campus, including a borrowing program through another office. As it happened, the other campus program was quite limited (iPads were being loaned to a small number of faculty for a semester at a time), and requests from faculty and staff to borrow the library iPads started early on in the fall semester. The decision was ultimately made to open up the iPad loaner program to Oberlin faculty and staff. While even after the policy change borrowers of iPads were overwhelmingly students (93 percent in the fall 2010 term), there were a number of faculty borrowers, and faculty clearly appreciate the access. The fact that reservations are not accepted for iPad use makes borrowing library iPads an impractical option for many faculty and staff.

Based on requests from library staff wanting to use an iPad for travel and presentation purposes, an additional iPad was purchased solely for library staff use.

User Survey

A survey sent out to a random sampling of 300 Oberlin students (about 10 percent of the student body) early in the spring 2011 semester provided a tool by which to gauge the overall impact of, and response to, the iPad loaner program.

Ninety-five students completed the survey, a response rate of 3 percent. Just over 19 percent of students responding had checked out an iPad from the library at least once. Of those who had not checked out an iPad, 72 percent indicated they had not done so because they were not interested in using an iPad, and 18 percent indicated they were not aware they could check out iPads from the library. Of those who had checked out an iPad, about half had done so only once or twice, 35 percent had done so several times a semester, and 15 percent had checked out an iPad four or more times in the semester. The most frequent use of the iPads was for web browsing, followed by e-mail and access to Oberlin's campus courseware. Seventeen percent indicated they had used the iPads to read e-books, and 18 percent indicated they used the iPads for research purposes.

OBSERVATIONS AND FUTURE OF THE PROGRAM

IPads are ideally suited as, and designed to be, personal devices for individuals; sharing iPads among a large group of people, as with the library's loaner program, by default means users are not able to take full advantage of the functionality of the iPad. The e-mail app, for example—or any other app that requires creating an account—is not a convenient option for users on an iPad that's being shared with many people.

The library adds apps to the loaner iPads based on reviews, experience, and user requests. Apps are also added based on evidence of use by library iPad borrowers. The re-syncing process assures that each iPad gets loaded with the most up-to-date list of apps. This bounty can be confusing or annoying to users trying to find a specific app of interest, however. The use of folders to help organize apps on the iPads has been quite useful, although if the folders are tampered with by users, they need to be re-created during the re-syncing process, thus adding to the iPad maintenance time for staff.

Considerations for the Future

Based on the spring 2011 survey results, it was clear that a primary driver in the library's desire to provide PRDs—the ability to easily access and read the library's purchased e-book content—is not as frequent a use of the iPads as the library hoped it would be. Part of the issue is that the majority of e-books available are still browser dependent; the expectation is that reader apps for some of the larger library collections and resources (ebrary, Early English Books Online, etc.) will be available in the near future. Strategies for highlighting e-book reading functionality also need to be considered, perhaps working with students to design publicity pieces focusing on the library's e-book content.

The random spring 2011 survey indicated that almost 20 percent of students don't know about the iPad loaner program; a continuing effort to publicize the program is clearly needed.

Another area for consideration is how the library might facilitate the addition of one-off e-books identified by users but not available as part of the existing e-book packages. At this point there are more questions than answers about how this might work, but one option could be to purchase copies to load on the iPads, then point to those titles in the OPAC by using a location of "iPad." At the present time neither the iPads themselves, nor any of the iPad apps, are cataloged.

The Library iPad loaner program was not designed to meet all potential campus needs—for example, classroom uses or uses in the field by large groups—and access to iPads through the library has highlighted some of those additional campus needs. While there are hopes for the further development of programs elsewhere on campus to address these kinds of needs, it does put pressure on the library's program in the interim.

Finally, while thus far there has not been a high level of demand for reservations of the iPads, it is clear that time-bound uses for the iPads— such as classroom presentations—will emerge, and the need to rethink the reservation policy will likely arise.

The library will continue to track the use of the iPads via user surveys, paying particular attention to trends involving research and e-books, to help library staff think about ways to draw attention to these uses. Developments and trends in the larger market of tablet devices will be followed closely, and it is possible the library will consider experimenting with additional devices if it seems they offer a significant improvement in utility.

REFERENCES

Thomas, Lisa Carlucci. 2009. "Mobile Access to E-books at Yale," www.scribd.com/doc/28984716/Mobile-Access-to-E-books-at-Yale-Lisa-Carlucci-Thomas-2009.

Thompson, Sara Q. 2011. "Setting Up a Library IPad Program: Guidelines for Success." *C&RL News* 72 (April): 212–36.

13

Leading and Learning
Technology and E-book Adoption in School Libraries

CAROLYN FOOTE

Technology use in schools should be like
"oxygen: ubiquitous, necessary and invisible."

Chris Lehmann, principal,
Science Leadership Academy

The same should be true of technology in libraries, gathering places where students go to satisfy their curiosity, conduct research, read, collaborate, and create. School libraries are at the forefront of technology use in schools, and as information specialists, librarians are ideally positioned to incorporate new technologies into their programs. The twenty-first-century library ideally has become what Springfield Township High School librarian Joyce Valenza calls a *libratory*, a place where students come to interact and experiment with ideas—stirring the pot through communication, research, collaboration, and creation of their own ideas and products (Valenza 2008).

To this end, many libraries also serve as technology hubs in their schools, providing video cameras, webcams, iPads, laptops, Kindles, Nooks, or whatever device is needed by students and, more essentially, providing general computer or laptop access for the campus. In fact, according to the American Library Association 2010's School Librarians Count survey, the average number of computers in school libraries has increased by 7 percent in the last year alone, to an average of twenty-seven computers (compared to twenty-two in 2007), and the number of computers on campuses with access to library materials has increased over 8 percent just in the last year. But libraries are far more than the "stuff" students can access. Libraries also play an obvious and critical role in literary enjoyment and information literacy instruction, as more and more student activity has shifted to an online or mobile environment. The library fits naturally into a shift described by "Grown Up Digital" author Don Tapscott: "from a traditional, broadcast model of education to one that is customized, collaborative and interactive" (Tapscott 2011). David Loertscher describes the model of a library that reaches beyond library walls as a virtual learning commons, "a giant school-wide conversation where students, classroom teachers, teacher librarians, teacher technologists, administrators, other school specialists, and parents are creating and constructing a giant information space, work space, and museum" (Loertscher 2009).

In this vision, the school library's role goes far beyond delivery of or access to electronic items. Central to the mission is delivery of instructional technology facilitation for students and staff by the librarian and other support staff both online and in person. That changing role for librarians is clearly reflected in the School Librarians Count 2010 survey results, with 54 percent of elementary librarians and a whopping 72 percent of high school librarians providing professional development on digital content. And librarians are embracing new technologies at faster rates than other campus personnel, even teachers, according to Multimedia Schools' *Survey of K–12 Educators on Social Networking and Content-Sharing Tools* (edWeb .net et al. 2009). Consequently, in both physical and virtual spaces, librarians take the lead in assisting students using technology in the library for a variety of purposes, from accessing book content, responding to books in online forums, or creating book trailers, to conducting research, collaborating, and creating content of their own. And their leadership matters because the changing array of web tools involved can be dizzying—from video tools like Animoto, to note-taking tools like Evernote, to document sharing tools like Google Docs.

WHY E-BOOKS?

When students and librarians begin to consider e-books, they are also faced with a bewildering array of choices. E-book content can be web based or device based; housed in apps, databases, or free online sites; or provided by a wide assortment of library/book vendors. Consequently, librarians play a crucial role in helping define the best tools for their students, in providing guidance for students using these tools, in helping teachers learn how to incorporate them into instruction, and in giving feedback to vendors on how e-book content can be effectively delivered in school environments.

Why include e-books in a library collection in the first place? Obviously, for one, libraries need to be responsive to the wave of sales of e-book devices and be proactive in contemplating how that will come to impact their schools and their library services. Students are increasingly expecting to use e-books; according to a 2009 Project Tomorrow survey, 48 percent of students envision using their own mobile devices to access online textbooks (Project Tomorrow 2010). E-books fit the vision of a virtual learning space perfectly—providing students access to books on a twenty-four-hour basis, use of a single published title by multiple students at one time, and increased access to materials that might not fit physically into a brick-and-mortar library. And increasingly, schools who are moving to 1:1 computing platforms find that e-books become a convenient and embedded part of the curriculum throughout the school. In terms of student learning, studies are also beginning to show the advantages to struggling readers of e-books with read-aloud features (Gonzales 2010). In an article in *School Library Journal,* "The Kindles Are Coming," librarians speak to other advantages as well. Buffy Hamilton, librarian at Creekview High School in Georgia, notes that e-books provide privacy for teen readers, while Joanne Hammond, librarian in Chambersburg School District in Pennsylvania, points out that e-books may encourage students to tackle more challenging titles because the size and length of a book isn't so obvious (Barack 2011). Some e-book services offer the possibility of sharing books or commenting on books as well. Beyond all the above practical reasons for implementing them, e-books do offer a certain element of delight to some readers. In his book *Enchantment: The Art of Changing Hearts, Minds, and Actions,* Apple visionary Guy Kawasaki (2011) writes about the importance of enchantment in adoption of new technologies, describing how his own enchantment with the new Macintosh computer first led to his decision to go to work for Apple decades ago. Devices like the NookColor or the iPad or other web-based reading formats are exciting to use for many students. Pages that turn with the press of a finger, beautiful animation, lush and colorful screen covers, and books that read themselves aloud can all be very engaging to reluctant readers as well as nonreluctant readers. And after all, providing e-books is ultimately about encouraging student reading.

LEADERSHIP AND OVERCOMING OBSTACLES

However, in the school environment, oftentimes before you can even begin to "enchant" your students, you may have to enchant decision makers who could impact or restrict the use of electronic devices or e-book sites. Kawasaki's book offers a number of helpful strategies for overcoming what he calls "embedded" beliefs and for persuading others about the values of a vision. First, he identifies a few reasons why people may be reluctant about change, like inertia, wanting to maintain the status quo, a fear of mistakes, a lack of other role models using the technology, and more. He suggests useful strategies for overcoming that reluctance, such as

- Providing social proof
- Creating the perception of ubiquity for the product, and alternatively creating the perception of scarcity ("We only have a few, so get in while you can")
- Showing people the "magic"
- Finding one powerful example to share, instead of overwhelming with too many
- Observing users and letting them identify the key benefits for you
- Using data
- Identifying other possible "influencers" and enchanting them with your vision (Kawasaki 2011)

Aside from local obstacles the librarian may have to deal with, there are industry-based obstacles as well, as any librarians who have considered adding e-books to their own collections have already experienced. The authors of a 2010 *Library Journal/School Library Journal* survey comment that "one of the factors that has impeded e-book adoption in the book-buying population as a whole is the plethora of mutually incompatible formats and often draconian digital rights management (DRM) schemes"

(*LJ/SLJ* 2010). The market is in a state of flux, and librarians have to play the role of forecasters, trying to determine which way the market is going to go. Librarian leadership in communicating library concerns to vendors is critically important as the e-book market evolves. With digital rights management also shifting, some publishers are reluctant to allow libraries unlimited use of their products; for example, HarperCollins is restricting e-book use through OverDrive's platform to twenty-six circulations per book, and some publishers allow only one reader at a time, while e-book device vendors are grappling with the issues of electronic book "sharing." As Shonda Brisco points out in the first volume of this series, both this general complexity as well as a lack of understanding about the technologies may lead to hesitance on the part of librarians. "Despite the enthusiasm that is often linked to new technologies and the ability to access various e-book formats, school librarians may also be somewhat apprehensive in deciding how to go about selecting, managing, and maintaining the hardware and software needed to make these resources available to their students. Others may be waiting for a standardized format to be selected before they invest in these resources for their libraries" (Brisco 2011, 38). Partly for these reasons, according to the *Library Journal/School Library Journal* survey, librarians are moving into the e-book format gradually. Thirty-three percent of the school libraries surveyed offered e-books, with high schools offering more e-books than elementary schools, but the average size of collections was only about fifty e-books. However, another 25 percent of those surveyed are considering offering e-books in the future (*LJ/SLJ* 2010).

MAKING CHOICES

E-books might arrive in your library in several formats. One is web-based e-book content, via vendors such as Gale, Follett, Mackin, Permabound, and many others. These e-books can be accessed from any computer, laptop, netbook, smartphone, or tablet (particularly if they are not Flash based). A second route for accessing e-books is through a library-purchased service like OverDrive. The library purchases an OverDrive collection, and then OverDrive's software or apps can be downloaded by the student, allowing them to temporarily check out the books in the library's collection to their mobile device (although this service is rather costly and perhaps cumbersome for school students, especially if they don't have a device). A third method involves the library purchasing books for the device itself (Kindle, iPad, iPod Touch, Nook, Sony tablet, and the like). Of course the device that offers the most flexibility is the iPad or iPod Touch—it can run apps for services like OverDrive, can access web-based e-books, and has Kindle and Nook apps. However, the cost of providing the devices can be an issue (although prices are coming down rapidly), and the maintenance of an ample number of devices can be time consuming. Perhaps this is why libraries are venturing slowly into offering e-devices for checkout; when it comes to delivery of e-books via devices, the *Library Journal/School Library Journal* survey points out that in 2010 only 6 percent of schools offered e-readers, though with prices coming down, 36 percent were considering it (*LJ/SLJ* 2010).

With so many publishers offering different versions of e-books, librarians have to assess how many different ways of accessing e-books can students adapt to. Sometimes decision makers aren't the only ones that may need to be enchanted about e-books. Knowing our students is important. In his book *The Five Most Important Questions You Will Ever Ask about Your Organization,* Peter Drucker (2008) and his coauthors outline five questions that can help librarians with initial e-book decisions. They recommend considering the following:

- What is your mission?
- Who is your customer?
- What does your customer (student) value?
- What are your results?
- What is your plan?

Using a student survey designed with a tool like Polldaddy, PollEverywhere, or SurveyMonkey allows the librarian to assess student needs and decide which type of e-books students are most interested in to begin with. If there are too many delivery methods or the methods are too complicated, it may be a barrier to students embracing e-books provided in the school library. Fortunately, at least e-book formats are standardizing, which makes things less complex. Many e-book publishers are embracing the EPUB format. The plethora of websites delivering free e-books primarily use either EPUB or PDF formats of books that are copyright free, like Project Gutenberg.

How will you decide which delivery method is appropriate for your school library? Begin with the instructional goals in mind. Do you want to provide e-books mostly for research purposes? Gale's Virtual Reference Library and EBSCO's eBooks on EBSCOhost permit key word searching much like databases do, invaluable for student researchers. Like these, other web-based e-books like Follett's can be embedded in the MARC records of the online catalog, making them easily accessible from any-where via the library catalog. A new feature allows users to open Follett e-books with or without the Flash viewer. If you are more interested in providing e-books for leisure reading, books on a Kindle or Nook can be highly motivational and are portable, and new titles can be quickly added. Services like OverDrive also offer fiction titles that can be down-loaded to student devices. If the goal is to make the reading experience more exciting and helpful for reluctant readers, then offering e-books on a device like the iPad can be highly interactive, fun, and dynamic and may prove more enchanting to discouraged readers. And increasingly the model may change to a more interactive one—where students can share, comment upon, and even "add to" the books they are reading. E-book vendors are already beginning to add interactive features. At the 2011 South by Southwest Interactive conference, Andrew Lewellen of Razorfish envisioned how, increasingly, even sites like Twitter and Facebook are creating the future of fiction, where narratives can become interactions between author and readers (Lewellen 2011). Whatever the benefit of any particular format, most important, e-books extend the book-related services of libraries beyond four walls, allowing libraries to create a 24/7 connection with students.

ISSUES AND CONCERNS

The movement to e-books, whatever the format or platform, could affect virtually everything about what libraries and schools do in terms of col-lecting, sharing, and promoting reading materials. Librarians may fear that their library might be dissolved for an electronic one or may themselves feel more comfortable with a print-only environment. However, as the

Library Journal/School Library Journal survey points out, this isn't necessarily an either/or situation for libraries:

> It's not unusual to see the print vs. e-book issue presented as a kind of
> "war," that the choice is between one or the other. But the reality is a bit
> more complicated. Today, users—be they child, teen, or adult—are frag-
> mented among so many different media, that producers of content find
> themselves having to be in all the places that users can be found, if only
> to aggregate a sizable audience. Books are no different. Some users still
> (and some will always) prefer print books, while others favor e-books.
> Some prefer a combination of print and electronic, depending upon spe-
> cific circumstance (print while reading at home, electronic when travel-
> ing, for example) (*LJ/SLJ* 2010).

On the other hand, an increasingly digital student body armed with smart-phones has come to expect information on demand. And as more and more students begin carrying their own technology devices—whether those devices are provided by the school or by the student—the way students interact with literature is changing and becoming ever more personal, which also has to enter the planning equation.

There are other issues associated with e-books that libraries have to think through. For example, how do we address weeding e-book collections, especially when many e-books are owned in perpetuity? Is there a need to weed them because they don't take up shelf space? Do we need to establish an annual process for reviewing e-books, or annually review various call number areas in our e-book collections? What about books loaded on devices? And how does one get rid of e-books once they are weeded? Will you have to consult each vendor? Is this a process you as the librarian are able to do yourself? All important questions to ask vendors as well. It's difficult to think through weeding questions when you are just building a new e-book collection, but by setting up processes, school librarians will be less overwhelmed when it does come time to weed. (More information on weeding practices for e-books can be found in chapter 6.)

Yet another issue that can be of concern to schools is filtering. How do we address issues of filtering when more and more devices come with wireless access as well? If a sample chapter of a book can be easily downloaded on a Kindle, how do you address student downloads? One way a growing number of school librarians are addressing this is through acceptable use forms for students checking out e-book devices. For example, librarians Buffy Hamilton and Kathy Parker created a form for Kindle checkouts that my own library has also modified, and many other libraries are using these models or creating their own forms. The policy can indicate anything from rules for whose responsibility it is to add book content (limiting it to staff, for example) to other concerns (like device replacement). Defining an acceptable use policy for e-book devices is a way to set expectations for students at the outset of the implementation and deal with some issues that the device might pose for schools bound by e-rate funding.

Equity is yet another issue to be considered. How do librarians balance the needs of the many (using web-based e-books that any student can access) with the needs of fewer students (having a small collection of iPads or e-book readers to circulate, for example)? And how do we address the issue of students' own personal devices coming into the schools being used to access e-books, as budget shortfalls across the nation are driving many schools in the direction of utilizing more BYOD device policies? How will library purchasing choices regarding e-books be affected by those decisions? And how can we provide equitable access to e-books if not all students own their own "devices"? Questions of equity need to be thought through as well; providing a limited number of devices for checkout, or using only web-based e-books that any student can use from any location are ways to guarantee equitable access.

Fortunately, a number of library organizations are working to iron out issues related to e-books. The American Library Association has an E-book Task Force—working on issues surrounding e-books and publishers. *School Library Journal* and *Library Journal* held a joint summit in 2010 on "E-books: Libraries at the Tipping Point" to begin to collect discussions regarding e-book use in libraries. The second event, "E-books: The New Normal," is scheduled for October 2011. Library Renewal (library renewal.org) is a collaborative nonprofit forum dedicated to discussions of e-content and the future of libraries. Harvard's Berkman Center has already embarked on planning for a national digital library, and the blog Library City (librarycity.org) furthers the discussion of digital libraries. But with librarians already engaged in using e-books, many details and best practices are already being developed by librarians around the country, in the "libratory" itself. And documenting these decisions in blog posts and articles is an important contribution that practicing school librarians can make to the discussions.

As time passes, e-books will inevitably become as ubiquitous as print books, as invisible as Chris Lehmann posits in the epigraph to this chapter. As librarians acquire e-book technologies for their libraries, the focus needs to be on what works most effectively for teaching and learning, not on the technology itself. But at the same time, librarians have to make the detailed decisions about how this technology will live in the library—determine which formats work best, how e-book collection development will work, what to do about equity issues, and how to remove barriers to using them. To provide some guidance, in the three chapters that follow, three educators will share how they are using e-book devices in their libraries and classrooms to support reading and instruction and how they are addressing the challenges and opportunities of e-books as they seek to define a new model for themselves and their students.

REFERENCES

ALA. 2010. "ALA School Librarians Count! 2010: AASL's National Longitudinal Survey of School Library Programs." www.ala.org/ala/mgrps/divs/aasl/researchandstatistics/slcsurvey/2010/slc2010.cfm.

Barack, Lauren. 2011. "The Kindles Are Coming: E-readers and Tablets Are Springing Up in Schools—And Librarians Are Leading the Way." *School Library Journal,* March 1. www.libraryjournal.com/slj/home/889110-312/the_Kindles_are_coming.html.csp.

Brisco, Shonda. 2011. "E-books in the School Library." From *No Shelf Required: E-books in Libraries,* Sue Polanka, ed., 37–54. Chicago: American Library Association.

Drucker, Peter. 2008. *The Five Most Important Questions You Will Ever Ask about Your Organization.* San Francisco: Jossey-Bass.

edWeb.net, MCH Inc., and MMS Education. 2009. *A Survey of K–12 Educators on Social Networking and Content-Sharing Tools.* www.edweek.org/media/k-12socialnetworking.pdf.

Gonzales, Michelle R., 2010. "The Effect of Interactive eBooks on the Reading Comprehension of Struggling Readers and Students with Reading Disabilities." PhD diss., Walden University.

Kawasaki, Guy. 2011. *Enchantment: The Art of Changing Hearts, Minds, and Actions.* New York: Portfolio.

Lehmann, Chris. 2010. "10 Tips on Creating a School 2.0." *Learning Today* (blog), April 23, http://blog.learningtoday.com/blog/?Tag = Chris%20 Lehmann.

Lewellen, Andrew, 2011. "Interactive Narratives: Creating the Future of Storytelling." Panel presentation at South by Southwest Interactive Conference, March 14.

Library Journal/School Library Journal. 2010. "Survey of E-book Penetration and Use in U.S. School Libraries." http://c0003264.cdn2.cloudfiles .rackspacecloud.com/School%20Library%20Ebook%20Report_2.pdf.

Loertscher, David. 2009. "The Virtual Learning Commons." *School Libraries,* http://davidloertscher.wordpress.com/.

Project Tomorrow. 2010. *Creating Our Future: Students Speak Up about Their Vision for 21st Century Learning.* www.tomorrow.org/speakup/pdfs/SU09Nat ionalFindingsStudents&Parents.pdf.

Tapscott, Don. 2011. "Grown Up Digital: About the Book." www.grownupdigital .com/archive/index.php/about.

Valenza, Joyce. 2008. "Library as Domestic Metaphor." *Never-Ending Search* (blog), *School Library Journal,* August 25, http://blog.schoollibraryjournal .com/neverendingsearch/2008/08/25/library-as-domestic-metaphor/.

14

E-reader Adoption in the School Library Media Center
A Journey of Collaboration and Discovery

JENNIFER LAGARDE AND
CHRISTINE JAMES

T he year 2010 seemed to be the year of the e-reader. It was hard to swing the proverbial dead cat without smacking a Kindle out of somebody's hand. So, it's not surprising that for individuals who spend much of their time connecting kids to books, the summer of 2010 was one of nervous contemplation. Even as the whole world seemed poised and ready to jump on the e-reader bandwagon, school librarians—and the classroom teachers with whom they collaborate—faced big questions regarding these little devices. From identifying the instructional needs that an e-reader can meet to selecting the right device from the plethora of choices, this chapter represents the philosophical and procedural journey to e-reader adoption by the library media program at Myrtle Grove Middle School in Wilmington, North Carolina. Together, the school library media specialist and seventh-grade English teacher will answer both the frequently and not so frequently asked questions that shaped a successful and impactful collaboration that, ultimately, put e-readers in the hands of their students.

CONTEXT

Myrtle Grove Middle School is a suburban middle school, serving approximately 750 students, in southeastern North Carolina. The student population of Myrtle Grove changed in 2010 when the school district lines were redrawn to accommodate a new middle school. These changes included Myrtle Grove's federal designation as a Title 1 school, a designation reserved for schools with large concentrations of low-income students. In response to these changes, the library media center needed to grow its practice in order to engage these new students while also addressing their unique instructional needs, which included a larger group of reluctant and below-grade-level readers as well as a significant number of ESL learners. The confluence of these factors (the change in student demographics coupled with the emergence of e-readers as a possible instructional tool) resulted in the perfect storm of opportunity to explore the timely question of whether or not e-readers represented the answer to the instructional questions facing the library/school/reading program.

WHY E-READERS?

The number of reasons to incorporate e-readers into a library program (in any setting) are as varied and numerous as the patrons being served. What is essential, however, is that there *be* a reason. Simply buying e-readers because they're "the next big thing" is not good enough. The first thing anyone considering this journey must do is figure out what problems and needs faced by their patrons can be addressed by e-readers. And in the school setting, that question must include a focus on impacting student learning.

At Myrtle Grove, the immediate challenge was to engage a population of students for whom reading just doesn't come easily. This meant providing instructional scaffolding—in the shape of text interaction—along with a delivery method that is easily adapted to pique student interests, while also speaking directly to today's twenty-first-century learners. New ways of delivering literacy curricula and helping students see themselves as readers were needed, and e-readers fit this bill in several ways.

First, e-readers present opportunities for text interaction that simply are not possible with traditional, school-owned print materials—be they student textbooks, class novels, or library books. E-readers allow students to highlight and annotate text while also affording them the ability to look up unfamiliar words along with instant access to the Internet and all its related resources. Additionally, many e-readers offer a text-to-speech function, which provides students the opportunity to hear unfamiliar words being spoken—a wonderful tool for impacting fluency, particularly among ESL learners. Further, because selecting and downloading an e-book can literally be done in seconds, e-readers provide the rare opportunity for library personnel to respond instantly to observed student needs. Whether library staff are responding to a student's social/emotional needs, the struggles a student faces as a reader, or simply an expressed interest in a particular title, the speed in which the e-reader allows staff to modify this ongoing assessment lends greater weight and meaning to each and every student interaction—creating greater opportunity to engage in conversations for learning.

Ultimately, the only "right answer" to the question of why adopt e-readers is the answer that identifies specific student needs that can best be met by e-readers. Once those needs are identified, it's time to take the next step.

HOW DO YOU PICK THE RIGHT E-READER?

There are lots of things to ponder when selecting an e-reader. As with any major purchase, factors such as cost, content, available features, and ease of use must be considered. Luckily, there are just as many really good resources available out there to help narrow down the choices. From digital product reviews, to social networks dedicated to e-readers in libraries (specifically the eBook Educators Group's EduKindle Ning, http://eduKindle .ning.com/), the published work of other e-reader pioneers, such as Buffy Hamilton and Kathy Parker, provide a wealth of information and experiences to explore while trying to figure out which device will best serve the needs of your students and staff. There's no need to reinvent the wheel. Not only can diving into the work of others prevent missteps, but these library leaders are also incredibly generous when it comes to sharing materials, documentation, and procedural how-tos.

In the end, the e-reader that proved to be the right fit for Myrtle Grove was the Barnes & Noble Nook. The factor that most influenced this decision was, in a word, support. At the time of purchase, there was not a color/ touch version available, so to be frank, the differences between the biggest contenders were nominal. On the other hand, Barnes & Noble provided three separate trainings for Myrtle Grove's staff and also offered on-site technical support. This ability to speak to a real person, watch them manipulate the e-reader to its greatest capacity, or simply hand the thing over if something went wrong proved to be extremely comforting, in part because of the learning curve that always exists when piloting something for the first time.

One thing to consider when exploring e-reader options is the school district's interpretation of the Children's Internet Protection Act (CIPA), which requires K–12 schools and libraries to install "a technology protection measure such as a web filter, on any of its computers with Internet access that protects against access to materials that might be harmful to minors. Such a technology protection measure must be employed during any use of such computers by minors" (FCC n.d.). The North Carolina Department of Public Instruction interprets this to mean that any Internet-ready, school-owned device must have a web filter installed on it in order for said device to go home with students. Because the Nook does provide Wi-Fi access that cannot be filtered, the Nooks at Myrtle Grove Middle School are not checked out by students. Rather, they are used as part of collaborative literacy instruction on-site only. While this fact has not diminished their instructional impact, it is incredibly important that anyone considering implementing an e-reader program understand their school district's policies in regard to CIPA so that the device chosen not only best meets student needs but also maintains school compliance to district policy.

HOW DO YOU PAY FOR IT?

In these tough economic times, libraries have less money than ever to fund their programs, so the important thing is to make sure that every dollar spent will have a direct impact on student learning. The first set of thirty Nooks purchased at Myrtle Grove were paid for using the basic instructional funds that are allotted to schools. This chunk of the ever-shrinking instructional budget was apportioned to this project because of its clear focus on student learning. When pitching the benefits of purchasing e-readers, be sure to plan for formative and summative assessments of the project, provide examples of research that supports student impact, describe how impact at your school will be measured, and outline ways that the program can be sustained if funding dries up. Additionally, don't forget that the money provided to the library for e-readers might be perceived as meaning less money going toward classroom purchases. So be sure to partner with the instructional staff to let them know that this purchase is designed to further schoolwide initiatives and to assist them in meeting their goals for student achievement. Paint the purchase as what it is: an opportunity for successful and meaningful collaboration designed to positively impact student achievement. Ultimately, if the pedagogy behind the purchase is sound and student learning is the focus, the money will be there—whether it comes from the general budget, a grant, or a philanthropic donation.

HOW DO E-READERS FIT WITH INSTRUCTIONAL GOALS?

Because a large sum of general instructional funds had been used to purchase the Nooks, maintaining the fidelity of the initiative was imperative. It was vital that the e-readers be more than just a gimmick to grab students' attention. Nooks being a new electronic device would keep students focused only for a short time and wouldn't guarantee that learning ensued. It was clear that without intentional planning and solid content, the Nooks would quickly lose credibility, as would the media specialist and teachers who had pushed for their purchase. Creating a strong curriculum connection was essential and became the first step teachers needed to fulfill to use the e-readers in their classrooms. A form was created that teachers completed to establish that the proposed unit's goals were closely tied to the state's learning standards. It also asked the educators to find interdisciplinary connections that would enable students to extend their learning to other classrooms. To make best use of the e-readers' capabilities, teachers were asked to incorporate both fiction and nonfiction titles.

HOW DO YOU PICK THE BOOKS?

One of the most exciting aspects of including e-readers in any library collection is the potential to customize the reading experience for the specific patron. Because e-books are relatively inexpensive, it's possible to make the emotional, social, and academic needs of the individual student the primary concern when purchasing titles. It's like being able to give each child their very own library, which is incredibly powerful. Initially, the plan was to use the library media center's existing general collection development policy as a guideline for selecting e-books, but this quickly proved inadequate. While reading reviews and considering the ways in which a title fits into the overall collection are still important and relevant steps in the process, being able to customize an e-reader to the individual takes a lot of the guesswork out of it. Instead of relying on the influence of third-party analysis (such as professional reviews) to guide purchasing decisions, the ability to tailor the reading experience opens up the doors for meaningful conversations between the school librarian, the student, and/or the classroom teacher.

WHAT DO YOU DO BEFORE THE STUDENTS TOUCH THE E-READERS?

In education everyone knows the importance of "CYA," so Myrtle Grove's adventure with the Nooks had to begin with paperwork and documentation—the e-reader permissions and acceptable use form. It is a form borrowed from Buffy Hamilton's high school e-reader lending program in Georgia and modified to reflect a middle school's needs. Parents and students were required to sign the form verifying that the families understood the e-readers were being used for educational purposes in the classroom and that any damage incurred would be their responsibility. The replacement value included the cost of the e-reader device and the downloaded content. The form served as communication between home and school, helping to bring parents on board to support this new program. The completed forms were kept on file in the media center, ensuring that families had to fill out the form only once, regardless of how many of the child's classes used the e-readers over the course of the school year. While most school districts have established acceptable use policies for staff and students that act as an agreement between these individuals and the school district providing Internet access, it seemed appropriate to have additional documentation that emphasized the privilege of using these devices and the expectation that students be good stewards of the new technology. In response, students took this responsibility seriously and treated their Nooks with lots of TLC.

There are other practical concerns to think about when preparing to launch an e-reader program in the school library setting. In addition to cataloging and processing the devices, it's important to map out a plan for the mundane, such as the mere storage and charging of the e-readers, which will be getting a lot of use. Most e-readers have a long battery life (twelve-plus hours of reading time) but will still need to be charged on a nightly basis so that they are ready for heavy student use the next day. While there are certainly plenty of commercial storage options out there, unused laptop carts or even old school card catalogs can be adapted to house brand-new e-readers. The important thing to is to make a plan that affords teachers and students easy access to the content on each device. Additionally, whether utilizing a mobile cart or fixed storage, be sure to consider both the physical constraints of the library media center as well as the frequency and proximity of use. As we all know, ease and efficiency are often key to the success of adopting any new technology.

WHAT DO STUDENTS NEED TO KNOW BEFORE USING THE E-READERS?

For teachers, the initial concern was that students understand the educational purpose of including Nooks in the classroom. There was actually a need to back up a step further. When e-readers and Nooks were mentioned, about half of the class had blank looks on their faces. Apparently, a device that allows them to read in an electronic format wasn't in the same category as devices that allow them to listen to music, play video games, or send text messages. After a brief explanation of what an e-reader was, the students were curious why e-books on the Nooks were better than traditional bound books. It was discussed that it wasn't an issue of one format necessarily being better than the other but which format would best suit their needs and prepare them as twenty-first-century learners. The Nooks would allow these students to interact with the text extensively and switch between related texts with the press of a button.

To make sure the e-readers could easily be used by students, a cheat sheet was created that listed the basic features and controls of the Nook: power, choosing books, adding highlights and notes, and so on. Additionally, the teacher displayed the Nook to the classroom using a document camera to demonstrate the features before the devices were passed out to the assigned students. Immediately the students were turning the Nooks on and opening their e-books. When it came time to add reader response notes, most students were quickly navigating their way and showing their tablemates shortcuts they'd discovered. None of them referenced the carefully crafted cheat sheet. The e-reader interface was intuitive for the students. They are part of a generation of digital natives who are accustomed to exploring new technology and devices and are eager to help one another. Most adults found the Nooks easy to operate, but the students mastered them even more quickly.

HOW DO YOU TEACH ADDITIONAL STUDENTS TO USE E-READERS?

A class of seventh-grade students was the first in the building to have access to the Nooks. From day one, they adopted the mantra of "first in the nation with Nooks." While it can't be verified that they were truly the premiere users in the entire country, it did add a sense of pride and proved to be a catchy slogan. The students also understood that with the thrill of being first came the responsibility to pass their e-reader knowledge to other students. They created a short promotional video with pictures of students reading their e-books and interacting with one another set to upbeat music. As students finished their e-books, a number of them volunteered to create video segments showing how to operate the Nooks and use the basic functions in kid-friendly language. The links for both the promotional and instructional videos were e-mailed to the teacher scheduled to use the Nooks next. The day before he distributed the e-readers, he showed the promotional video to pique students' interest. The instructional video was shown the following day. Along with the videos, between three and five students experienced with using the Nooks volunteered to serve as Nook experts and provide hands-on support in each of the classes of novice users. This arrangement was well received by students and the teacher.

The videos are now on the media center website to serve as resources for our students and teachers.

WHAT DO E-READERS LOOK LIKE IN CLASSROOM INSTRUCTION?

The ability to purchase one e-book and load it on six devices* lends itself to using the Nooks in a number of ways in the classroom: whole group, small group, or independent novel study. This also makes it extremely affordable to buy multiple texts related to one topic, including interesting and current nonfiction texts in varying reading levels. In the seventh-grade classroom, students chose between six different novels, all related to a common theme. The element of choice increased the student buy-in to the instructional activities, as well as opportunities to make use of active reading strategies. Many of the students didn't fully grasp the social aspect of reading until they used the e-readers. The Nooks facilitated discussion among students since they could easily access the portions of the text they'd highlighted and the notes they'd made. Using e-readers also aided the teacher in the individual reading conferences with students. The students were able to make deeper comparisons and cite text evidence from various sources on the Nooks. Their notes and conversations became the basis of many extended discussion threads on the unit wiki.

Additionally, the ability to customize the reading experience for the individual student played a role in selecting titles for independent novel study. While students were able to choose the text they read from the preloaded library, the teacher was able to select the novels in the library based not only on the student's instructional goals but also on their social and emotional needs. For example, during a unit in which students all read novels revolving around the common theme of "tough choices," students were able to select from texts that were handpicked to address many of the issues they faced at home—ranging from domestic violence to drug use to teen pregnancy and so on. To extend the experience, each Nook library was stocked with several nonfiction texts related to teens and making

---

* In summer 2011 Barnes & Noble launched the Barnes and Noble Managed Program for schools. It may impact the ability to share content on six devices.

good choices. These were used as common texts in conjunction with the individual reading initiatives.

In another situation, a teacher requested the Nooks in order to conduct a unit on dystopian societies. In this instance, students conducted research on what a dystopian society is and created a bibliography of young adult literature with a dystopian theme. Once the list was narrowed down (based on a set of criteria established in collaboration by the media specialist and classroom teacher), the books that the students requested were loaded on the Nooks.

In both instances, students were able to highlight and annotate the text in ways that they are taught strong readers do, but that simply cannot be done with traditional print materials that are owned by the school and must be reused. Furthermore, in both cases, students were highly engaged in these projects in large part because they had a voice in crafting their own customized reading experience. By engaging students in the conversation, providing opportunities for them to think about their own learning, and guiding the direction of that learning, all students moved beyond typical literacy goals of comprehension and analysis to that of metacognition and evaluation—all of which was made possible by the adoption and purposeful implementation of this technology.

WHAT LESSONS WERE LEARNED?

One surprising aspect of this adoption was the relative tentativeness of teachers to use the Nooks. This was in stark contrast to the students, who couldn't wait to get their hands on them. Aside from the students being quick learners and excellent ambassadors, they were also the best promoters of the Nooks to teachers, far better than either the media specialist or initial teacher ever could have been. Students were so excited to have the e-readers at their school and assumed that teachers would be just as enthusiastic. For the first two months the Nooks were available, only one teacher requested to use them. Even after the very positive training experiences with Barnes & Noble, few teachers were eager to include the e-readers in their classroom instruction. The tide turned, however, as students started talking to their friends in other classes, and those students in turn started asking their teachers when they would get to use the Nooks. The more students who used the Nooks, the more interested the teachers became.

From a teaching perspective, the Nooks presented a new type of time management issue. While assigning the Nooks to students was relatively simple, distributing them from the Nook cart on a daily basis was a constant experiment in inefficiency. The Nook cart allowed for all the e-readers to be stored, charged, and easily transported between the media center and classrooms. Because the Nooks were all plugged in to charge, each one needed to be disconnected individually. With practice and student help, the process became smoother but never quick.

Finally, one lesson that presented itself repeatedly throughout this process was the fact that school libraries are not the target consumers of e-book vendors. Barnes & Noble and Amazon will not change their purchasing procedures to accommodate the idiosyncratic nature of buying stuff with school money.* That said, just as e-readers opened up a floodgate of opportunities for conversations regarding student learning and literacy instruction, so too do they provide the same opportunity for dialogue with district-level finance and purchasing staffs whose assistance will be integral to making the buying process work. The important thing is to make sure these conversations happen. There is nothing more heartbreaking than being ready to roll out some shiny new e-readers only to realize purchasing protocols prohibit purchasing e-books.

WHAT'S NEXT?

At Myrtle Grove Middle School, the e-reader journey continues with the purchase of thirty-five Sony Pocket readers. These new additions to the e-reader collection do not provide Wi-Fi access and therefore allow for student checkout while maintaining school compliance to CIPA. While some of the steps in the process are known thanks to a successful Nook pilot during the 2010–11 school year, the same "butterflies in the tummy" are reappearing now that new conversations about how these devices will

---

* The Barnes & Noble Managed Program, launched in mid-2011, allows for purchase orders and accommodates tax-exempt institutions, simplifying the process for schools.

impact student learning begin. This journey will continue to be chronicled at The Adventures of Library Girl (http://lib-girl.blogspot.com).

CONCLUSION

Now more than ever, school library media programs must provide evidence to support the fact that they change students' lives and impact academic growth. Adopting e-readers as a new way to inform literacy instruction and shape the way students view reading and/or themselves as readers offers an opportunity to do just that—provided that the process is fueled, from start to finish, by the desire to answer the big instructional questions facing schools and students.

It may be tempting to consider e-readers as the ultimate brush by which to paint a library program as digitally relevant, but such an approach is shortsighted. Rather, the hype surrounding these devices provides all school librarians with the opportunity to initiate some important discussions regarding targeted reading instruction, purposeful technology integration, and the impact that collaboration between the school librarian and the classroom teacher (in all areas) can have on student achievement. These conversations will help cultivate the knowledge that is necessary to decide how and if e-readers provide the solution to the needs facing your students.

REFERENCE

Federal Communications Commission (FCC). N.d. "Guide: Children's Internet Protection Act," www.fcc.gov/guides/childrens-internet-protection-act.

15

Give Them Something to Talk About
The Kindle Pilot Program at the Unquiet Library

BUFFY HAMILTON

The Unquiet Library at Creekview High School—a high school of 1,800 students serving grades nine through twelve about fifty miles north of Atlanta—officially rolled out its Kindle e-reader program for students in November 2010. It was decided to offer Kindles to provide students with another "container" and experience of reading; we also saw this program as a way to close the participation gap for students who do not have access to a Kindle. Students can check out one of ten Kindle e-readers for a loan period of one week; in addition, students are encouraged to submit an e-book request form with their Kindle acceptable use and parental permission form so that the library can purchase and load Kindle e-books of interest to students and create a customized reading experience. As of March 2011 over 120 e-book titles were either purchased or donated to the library's e-reader program. All Kindle program resources, program updates, and videos are available to view and use under a Creative Commons license at http://theunquietlibrary.libguides.com/Kindles.

People frequently ask why we chose to start with Kindles rather than the Barnes & Noble Nook or Sony Reader. While other libraries were piloting programs with Nooks and Sony Readers, it never failed that when students inquired about the possibility of our library providing e-readers, Kindle was always the specific device teens mentioned by name. The primary reason for beginning with Kindle though was the format. Library staff were comfortable with the format and felt it was an affordable entry point into the e-book/e-reader market. Despite Kindle being the library's only e-reader at this time, it won't be exclusive. We plan to eventually add Nooks and are exploring options for e-book delivery to non-Kindle devices from other vendors.

WHY DO HIGH SCHOOL STUDENTS NEED KINDLES?

The impetus for implementing the Kindle program was to provide Creekview High students access to reading a text in a different "container" as part of our effort to meet the learning and reading styles of all students. The circulation of Kindles to students through the library gives students the opportunity to read on a device that they otherwise might not be able to access. In addition, our Kindle program meets the "three Ps of librarianship": the reading experience is portable, participatory, and personal (Hamilton 2010). Through the Kindle program, students can access and read as many books as they want on a lightweight device that will not add additional pounds to their already oversized book bags. Students participate in the collection development of our Kindle e-book library by submitting specific titles and authors they would like to read, consequently contributing to a collection for the Kindles that truly provides a personalized reading experience. The library follows the standard district selection policy (http://goo.gl/CSDwN) for purchasing e-books as it would for any other material purchase.

Another benefit of using e-readers in a high school is the ability to purchase student-requested books and to put those books in students' hands within a matter of minutes as opposed to days or weeks with traditional purchasing of print materials. Being able to fulfill a student book request so quickly leaves a positive and memorable impression on the teen patron who doesn't have to wait a few weeks to see that her input is truly valued by the library.

Kindles help the library to encourage and support teens' tendency to read multiple books by an author or to feed their voracious reading appetites for books in a series. Students love that the Kindle can house a mini library of their favorite authors or series in one space without having to worry about keeping up with multiple copies of a print book. Additionally, the Kindle affords teen readers privacy because no one can see what they are reading.

CIRCULATION PROCEDURES AND CHALLENGES

Students first take home and review a Kindle acceptable use policy we adapted from school librarian Kathy Parker of Seneca Grade School in Seneca, Illinois. This form, which requires a parent signature, states that the student will be responsible for the Kindle and agrees to not purchase or download any books or other content. The student also takes home a Kindle e-book request form and can request up to ten titles he'd like the library to purchase for the Kindle. Once the form is returned with student and parent signatures, the student is placed on the waiting list. Once a library staff member makes sure he does not have any fines exceeding one dollar or outstanding overdue materials, the student is contacted through his English teacher and/or by e-mail as soon as a Kindle is available. When the student comes to check out the Kindle, a library staff member reviews basic Kindle operating procedures if he hasn't used one in the past so that he feels confident enough to operate the Kindle once he leaves the library. Students have caught on to the basic operating procedures of the Kindle quickly and have not demonstrated any hesitance or apprehension about reading on the Kindle.

The student then enjoys the Kindle for a one-week loan period and may renew the loan immediately if enough Kindles are available to meet the current demand; if the demand exceeds the supply at the time of renewal, the student goes back on the waiting list and may check it out again once the current waiting list has been exhausted. If the student does not return the Kindle within the seven-day loan period, a fine of ten cents is assessed for each day past the due date. With the exception of one student, those who have checked out the Kindle have been punctual and responsible with returning the Kindle on time. While the power supply was initially circulated with the device, we now are not doing so, because the battery life lasts easily over a week with the wireless disabled on the Kindle. We discovered we need to keep the wireless turned off on the Kindles even when they are not in use because the battery drains rapidly trying to either find the 3G signal or to connect to the wireless network. Because the Kindle wireless configuration does not work with the school's wireless setup, compliance with CIPA was not an issue; although students could have enabled wireless off campus, CIPA does not extend to any networks off campus.

The process of dealing with the cataloging of Kindle e-books had been a process of trial and error. In a nutshell, we are not cataloging the Kindle e-books at this time through the Destiny OPAC for two reasons. One wrinkle is that we do not have rights to edit MARC records, which means we can't update which books are loaded on individual Kindle e-readers. Second, we found that when we did catalog the Kindle e-books, it was somewhat confusing for patrons as well as us, the library staff, to distinguish which copy (print or Kindle edition) was available at first glance, particularly when trying to place a hold for a student, because we do not actually check out the Kindle e-books through Destiny. We do maintain a master list of Kindle e-books that shows the title, author, and the Kindles to which the e-book is assigned; students can access this list in person in the library or on our Kindle LibGuide page.

For internal record-keeping purposes, we maintain two spreadsheets—one spreadsheet tracks the purchases of e-books by device, and the other spreadsheet tracks purchases by gift card. Because our district will not allow us to use a personal credit card and be reimbursed and because our school does not provide a credit or purchasing card for the library, we use American Express gift cards to buy the e-books. We maintain a spreadsheet of all purchases by gift card as well as a hard copy of the receipt for each e-book purchase. In addition, the library also records the information for books that are gifted to the library's Kindle account by friends from our Amazon wish list. Amazon allows users to create public wish lists that can be purchased and given as a virtual gift. Once the gift card is exhausted, copies are made of all paperwork and that documentation is shared with the district purchasing department. Updating the spreadsheets and printing hard copies of receipts at the time of purchase is essential to maintain the integrity of the records; e-book purchases are also pushed to all devices they are assigned to (for us, Kindles 1–6 or Kindles 7–10) at the time of purchase.

A frequently asked question is if there is a way to lock the Kindles so that students cannot purchase unauthorized content. At this time, there is no way to protect the account via password and stop students from downloading content whether it is free or paid. Because the device is registered to the library's Amazon account, anyone using the Kindle device could technically purchase an e-book via the library account. However, the library's Kindle acceptable use policy emphasizes that a student will lose the privilege of using the Kindle if she purchases and/or downloads content; in addition, we verbally remind each student of this policy at the time the Kindle is checked out. Because the library emphasizes we will buy whatever titles the students want to read and because we exhaust the gift card balance in a short time so that no money is available on the card, we have not had any issues at this point with unauthorized purchases or downloads. However, I would like to have the option to protect the device with a password and account so that this potential issue is then a nonissue. We do not de-register the devices because we own 130 titles; in a school library setting in which most of our day is spent on instruction, it would be too time consuming to de-register and re-register the books because we want to keep a set list of titles assigned to each group of Kindles.

In terms of marketing, the library has utilized several strategies to advertise this new service. In the library, the Kindle cart—a book cart with copies of the acceptable use form, book request form, and current list of books for each set of devices—is available for students to browse throughout the day. In addition, English teachers were given flyers to hang in their room, and they took time to share the Kindle information with their classes. The library's website (http://theunquietlibrary.wordpress .com) and YouTube channel (www.youtube.com/user/theunquietlibrary) were also utilized to create buzz about the Kindle program.

Because the current collection of Kindle devices is small (ten), they are stored in the library office. Additional power supply strips have been purchased for charging the devices between load periods.

STUDENT RESPONSES TO THE KINDLES

Freshmen and sophomores have been the primary users of the Kindles although we've seen an increase in the number of juniors and seniors requesting to read on them. The majority of Kindle readers at this point have been female, but we've seen a slight increase in the number of male students inquiring about the Kindle and checking them out. The majority of students have requested the Kindle for pleasure reading, but we've seen more students in the last six weeks asking to use the Kindle for required class reading assignments.

Now that the Kindles have been in circulation for approximately five months, preferences and response patterns have emerged. Students:

- expressed extreme satisfaction with the Kindle reading experience;
- are thrilled that we purchase the books they want—the personalized reading experience is very important to our readers;
- like the ability to make adjustments to the page views and font size while reading;
- like the convenience and ease of reading on the Kindle;
- have been consistent and diligent in returning the Kindles on time within the one-week circulation period;
- have requested to use the Kindle again;
- like the leather covers provided with the Kindle by the library;
- have expressed they would love to have one of their own for school reading, including textbooks and independent reading assignments (nonfiction and/or fiction);
- indicated a desire for the Kindle to be backlit and/or for us to purchase reading lights for nighttime reading—most students indicated that reading in bed in the evening was a regular part of their reading routine;
- have indicated they would prefer to see a "visual bookshelf" of book titles rather than just a text listing of titles on the Kindle (similar to what you would see with the iPhone or iPad Kindle app);
- would like a loan period longer than one week (as we acquire more e-reader devices, we plan to extend the loan period to two weeks in 2011–12)

  Additionally, students who are avid series readers or devotees of a particular author benefit from reading on the

Kindle because the device gives them access to multiple books for their reading preferences.

A few students indicated they wished the Kindle had a touch screen option, but the majority of students rated the Kindle as "perfect." In our postreading written survey (see box below) as well as oral interviews, students also expressed they found they could read faster and concentrate more easily while reading on the Kindle. Several students enjoyed the Kindle reading experience so much that their families purchased a Kindle for them as a holiday or birthday gift.

BEST PRACTICES AND RECOMMENDATIONS

Before you purchase any e-reader device, investigate what methods of payment each potential vendor will take; it is equally important to know what methods of payment can be used to purchase the e-books for a specific device and from whom you can purchase the e-books. Some devices,

Post-Kindle Reading Experience Survey

1. On a scale of 1–10 (1 worst, 10 best), how would you rate your reading experience on the Kindle eReader?

2. Is this your first experience reading on a Kindle?

3. What did you enjoy most about reading on the Kindle?

4. What did you enjoy least about reading on the Kindle?

5. Which books did you read on the Kindle?

6. How was the experience of reading on the Kindle similar to and/or different from reading a print book?

7. Would you want to read on a Kindle again? If yes, why? If no, why?

8. What suggestions do you have for Amazon to improve the Kindle?

9. Would you use a cover with a reading light if offered one?

10. What can the library do to improve the Kindle experience for you?

11. Other comments or feedback you want to share:

like the Kindle, are proprietary, and only Kindle e-books can be read on the device (legally). Other devices, like the Nook, not only allow you to download Nook e-books, but you can also borrow a book from a library who uses OverDrive for e-book circulation. Nothing is worse than investing in devices only to discover you do not have a school district–approved means of purchasing the content for the devices. It is also wise to confirm what methods of payment are acceptable and not acceptable with your district purchasing department and to keep all documentation of the correspondence so that everyone is clear on the policies and procedures for documenting the purchases.

I also recommend trying out the devices you're thinking of circulating; take some time to go to your local store and play with them and test the features firsthand. Some hands-on experience will give you a much better context for conceptualizing how your learners/patrons might use the device and how/where the devices fit into your library collection/program as an access point for learning.

You will also want to see if the devices you plan to purchase work on a wireless connection only, or if a 3G connection is an option. We chose to go with the Kindle that offered both 3G and wireless connectivity for two primary reasons. Because our school wireless network is not compatible with the wireless configuration of the Kindle, we could not synchronize our e-book purchases through this method; however, we can pick up a 3G signal just outside the building, so we can easily synchronize and download our e-books on campus. Second, not all students have wireless access at home, and we wanted them to be able to download e-books from the archives in the event we could synchronize their requests on campus, or if they e-mailed a request and we purchased that during the loan period (perhaps through an e-mail or on-the-fly verbal request). If the device is wireless only and is not compatible with your school's wireless network, make sure there is a manual way to download the purchases; this method is usually done via a USB cable provided with the device.

Thanks to Kathy Parker, author of chapter 16, who generously shared her Kindle preparation procedures and forms with us, we found the implementation of the Kindle program fairly seamless. My fellow librarian, Roxanne Johnson, and I took a great deal of time to review Kathy's procedures in detail and broke down her blog posts outlining her procedures into a checklist to ensure we hit every step needed in registering our

Kindles in an organized manner. We also took time to test out the cataloging procedures and to write up those procedures together to see how they would actually work. While we did fine-tune these procedures after we began circulating them to students, this initial groundwork helped us to be methodical in our thinking about how to keep up with the devices and the Kindle e-books.

I found that keeping a spreadsheet for e-book purchases for a set of Kindles (e.g., Kindles 1–6; I recommend groupings of six because you can put each book on up to six devices) rather than individual Kindle devices was the easiest way to maintain accurate records of the purchases. By buying a book and putting it on all six devices in a set, you will also find it easier to keep up with which devices to which you are pushing the e-book. For example, if purchasing *The Hunger Games* by Suzanne Collins, the book is assigned to either Kindles 1–6 or Kindles 7–10. Making purchases and maintaining records at regular points in the day with limited interruptions is recommended in order to decrease mistakes in the record-keeping process.

Finally, be sure to document student responses to the reading experience with the device(s) you pilot. We use a short eleven-question written survey with all students; students may also elect to participate in verbal interviews that we video and share on our library YouTube channel.

FUTURE DIRECTIONS

Our library plans to purchase Nooks for 2011–12 so that students can enjoy the e-reader experience on a different device. In addition, we plan to purchase a subscription from OverDrive for 2011–12 so that students can download books through this subscription service onto the Kindles, Nooks, or their own devices; this subscription to OverDrive will simplify record keeping and allow the library to funnel monies into one central vendor for e-book purchases. We are interested in seeing if students indicate a preference for one specific device, or if we will grow sets of multiple kinds of e-reading devices to meet our students' needs as readers. Our hope is that the additional purchase of e-readers in conjunction with the OverDrive subscription will make reading and access to books more ubiquitous to the teens.

We also hope to get permission to do a deeper ethnographic study of the students using the Kindles and to document how the Kindle informs their identities as readers and perceptions of reading. While I am interested in purchasing slate or tablet devices for instructional and reading purposes as a learning tool for a collaboratively planned instructional unit with a classroom teacher, I see the Kindle as a device that can be used strictly for recreational circulation or one that might be purchased in sets for classes that are engaged in frequent and deep independent reading and/or literature circle readings.

CONCLUSION

The Kindle program at Creekview High's Unquiet Library has provided students an additional access point to reading and to books. This initial small-scale implementation has provided the evidence needed to justify additional purchases of these devices as the library prepares to add a more significant e-book presence to the collection with the subscription to OverDrive. The Kindle program has not only enhanced the library's reputation for cutting-edge service and practice, but it has elevated the school's credibility in the eyes of the students, with one teen observing, "This must be a really good school since it checks out Kindles to students." Another student feels the Kindles help students embrace preferred genres of reading while exposing them to new ones they might not have discovered in the traditional physical stacks because a multitude of diverse readings are right at the user's fingertips on the Kindle. The Unquiet Library sees Kindles as another element of "collection" as we try to honor Dr. Henry Jenkins's call for "[s]chools, libraries, and other educational institutions . . . to be both embracing the potentials and confronting the challenges of this emerging culture not as a replacement for existing print practices but as an expansion of them" (Jenkins 2010).

POSTSCRIPT

On Thursday, July 21, 2011, I received an e-mail from Amazon Kindle Education that stated:

We discovered the FAQ on your Facebook post [author: they actually discovered the post from our LibGuides page through our library's Facebook page] and wanted you to either update the information to be in line with Amazon's End User License Agreement with the attached setup information. Or to remove the information on registering 6 devices per account to share digital content.

The e-mail also pointed me to the Amazon end user license (updated in February, well after we began our Kindle program and that was never brought to my attention in subsequent phone/e-mail conversations with Amazon Kindle Education in June 2011). The e-mail included a PDF attachment of a draft "Kindle Education: Setup Guide" (which reflects a real lack of understanding of the needs of K–12 schools and libraries) and then concluded with this paragraph:

Amazon recommends schools register each Kindle to a single account. If you are looking for a library solution, we are working to include Kindle books in Overdrive.com's offering to libraries before the end of the year.

I e-mailed Amazon Kindle Education to make sure that I understood:

1. They now require a separate e-mail address for each device, and subsequently, for managing e-book content, which is now 1:1 for K–12. I immediately thought of colleagues who have much larger collections of Kindle devices and Kindle books and felt astonished that Amazon could be so ignorant (or indifferent?) of how ridiculously impractical this mandate will make it for librarians to manage those devices and content.

2. The 1:1 rule will now be enforced for K–12 and school libraries, yet the only back-end management tool being offered to us is to purchase a subscription to OverDrive, which is financially impossible for most school libraries. This is also not a feasible solution in terms of ease of accessibility for younger readers or a selection of interactive e-books that are more developmentally appropriate for younger learners. I don't have a problem with the 1:1 aspect, but I do have a problem with Amazon not providing alternatives to help libraries and schools work within the confines of the new licensing agreement that is now apparently being enforced (I was told via

phone that in our case, they were responding to a concern shared
by a publisher who apparently saw our LibGuides Kindle pages).

In a phone conversation with my Amazon Kindle Education rep on
the following Monday, the new terms of the agreement were confirmed.
While the rep stated that Amazon is working on some type of back-end
management tool/system, it will not be available for several months, and
I got the impression it won't be comparable to what Barnes & Noble is
now offering to K–12 schools and libraries. I had already planned to go
with the Nook Simple Touch for 2011–12 because of their K–12–friendly
policies and the new features of the Nook Simple Touch. Nonetheless, it
was disappointing to walk away from this series of conversations feeling
as though Amazon does not seem to value the needs of the K–12 market
and is not being terribly responsive to our needs as institutional consumers.
While we will continue to utilize our existing fleet of ten Kindles, we will
not invest any additional monies in the devices or e-book content under
the current limitations that will not work for our environment.

REFERENCES

Hamilton, B. 2010. "Applying the Three Ps to Libraries," June 8, http://
   theunquietlibrarian.wordpress.com/2010/06/08/applying-the-three-ps-to
   -libraries/.

Jenkins, H. 2010. "Learning in a Participatory Culture: A Conversation about
   New Media and Education (Part Three)." *Confessions of an Aca-fan* (blog),
   February 12, http://henryjenkins.org/2010/02/learning_in_a_participatory_
   cu.html.

16

Using E-books with Reluctant Readers

KATHY PARKER

What is the difference between an obstacle
and an opportunity? Our attitude toward it.
Every opportunity has a difficulty, and every
difficulty has an opportunity.

J. Sidiow Baxter

As head librarian in a rural school system, it has been a privilege to share a passion for reading with students of all grade levels and colleagues alike. Naturally, the enthusiasm of those who enjoy reading is motivating and a career highlight. Unfortunately, there are a number of students who are not all that excited by the written word, although over thirty-five years of librarianship I've had the nagging suspicion that low reading enjoyment was linked more to a lack of reading skills than to the book itself. As e-book reading devices were introduced to the commercial market—most notably the Amazon Kindle 2 wireless device in 2008—it was easy for me to become an early user of and a quick convert to this particular device. The design and presentation of text was so intuitive and appealing to this experienced reader that I began to wonder how this new technology might change the habits of reluctant readers. In various discussions with teachers and administrators alike, the concept of utilizing the Amazon Kindle 2 wireless device in teaching emerged as a practical solution to an ongoing concern with a number of our students.

With consensus that the Kindle could be a valuable adjunct to the reading curriculum, we submitted a proposal for funding to the administrators of the school outlining the advantages to better learning by merging the device into the curriculum. Knowing that personal use was not a convincing argument to promote the Kindle for classroom reading, I researched how other school systems were utilizing the technology. Surprisingly, the research revealed nothing on school systems adopting e-books entirely, although there were a few individual teachers and librarians already attempting enhanced teaching techniques through the use of the Amazon Kindle 2 technology. In the presentation to the board of education and administrators, I highlighted the experiences and reported successes of these early users, as well as the promising features that the Kindle 2 could have for Seneca's students. Seneca Grade School District 170, located in rural LaSalle County, Illinois, has historically been in the forefront of educational quality, especially in the area of technology, so this Kindle concept was of great interest to the audience. After an extensive presentation, the concept of incorporating the device for supplemental learning was convincing enough for them to agree upon a trial run. The board ultimately approved a pilot program to use the Amazon Kindle 2 to be launched in 2009 for two of Seneca's middle school programs: the literature classes and the Response to Intervention Reading classes. As thrilling as it was to think of the prospects digital learning had on curriculum improvement, there was much work to be done to design and implement this initiative.

The first order of business for the project was the acquisition of eighteen new Kindle 2 e-readers. There were no stumbling blocks incurred during the purchasing process of the Kindle 2 e-readers, nor were there any challenges while downloading the content onto the Kindles. While charting new territory in technology-based curriculum in this initial pilot, we received positive feedback from all stakeholders: the students, their parents, and the teachers who adapted to the new technology. In the preliminary pilot program the three teachers involved were given six Kindles to use with their students. The two seventh- and eighth-grade language arts teachers rotated the use of the e-readers with their students on a three-week basis. This enabled each student to read a book on the Kindle 2 throughout the course of the school year. The Response to Intervention Reading teacher used her six Kindle 2 e-readers for group reading of a particular book with a smaller class size. The pilot program soon grew into a second-stage pilot project, a similar technology-based lesson plan to the elementary level.

The second phase of the project involved the top five readers in second grade, out of a class of eighteen students; all five top readers were female students. The second-grade class was specifically chosen for the pilot as a way to mirror current research showing improved learning through adaptation of technology and text with this particular age group. As Larson (2010A) found in her study, the ability to manipulate text in digital reading devices promotes literacy and new ways for students to connect to the material. The strong readers of the group were specifically chosen for the pilot based on the mutual decision of the K–4 principal, the second-grade teacher, and myself. Because we had never used e-books with younger students we felt it best to experiment with the high reading group. We did not know what to anticipate with youth using this type of technology as described in Larson's lesson plan, "Going Digital: Using E-book Readers to Enhance the Reading Experience" (2010B). In addition to Larson's insightful study on the merits of e-book reading in the formative years of education, her published ReadWriteThink online lesson plan—targeted for second- through fourth-grade students—proved invaluable for Seneca's Kindle 2 project. Of particular interest was the chapter "Going Digital: Using E-book Readers to Enhance the Reading Experience." This lesson plan offered straightforward and uncomplicated step-by-step instructions on implementing the use of the Kindle 2 into a new and successful reading encounter for students in the second grade. As librarian of Seneca schools and primarily responsible for the Kindle 2 initiative, it was my task to assist teachers in developing curriculum. As Collier and Berg (2011) point out, librarians are regarded as credible partners in classroom instruction when promoting e-books "to build phonemic awareness, phonics, fluency, vocabulary, and comprehension" (23). As I worked in this capacity with the Kindle 2 project, it was most welcoming and gratifying to observe Larson's inclusion of state standards in the lesson plans, as well as a comprehensive list of objectives, forty-five-minute introductory lessons, and mini lessons. Consequently, Larson's program of study was chosen as the primary tool for assisting Dawn Stuedemann, the teacher in charge of rolling out the Kindle 2 project for the five second-grade students in her classroom at Seneca.

In an article about our second-grade pilot Kindle 2 project, it was reported that within the first week students began showing improvement in the area of comprehension by selecting text to share what they learned with fellow students (Barack 2010). Encouraged by the advanced reading skills acquired by the five talented students through e-book reading, Stuedemann was eager to introduce the initiative to yet another group of students, a group of same-age second graders who were categorized as reluctant readers. The goal was to determine whether they too would benefit from digital reading. Not an entirely lofty goal, as we were aware of the possibilities by a few articles written on the benefits of improved reading through means of technology. The most pertinent to our study was Larson's research, which stated that "digital readers show promise in supporting struggling readers through multiple tools and features, including manipulation of font size, text-to-speech options, expandable dictionary, and note capabilities" (Larson 2010A).

The new group of second-grade students, the reluctant readers, were chosen for the Kindle project based on criteria scores from three sources: (1) Renaissance Learning STAR scores, which is a computer-adapted test that measures comprehension and provides reading grade–level equivalencies and a zone of proximal development; (2) AIMS WebFluency Reading scores, a national reading assessment measuring a child's oral fluency reading; and (3) guided reading level through the use of the A–Z Leveling System. Those five students—whose Renaissance Learning STAR scores placed them into the 1.8 to 2.8 reading levels of the zone of proximal development—were selected for the project. Interestingly, this group was comprised of all male students. Parental permission was granted for all student subject participants. Stuedemann chose *The December Secrets* from the Polk Street Kids series by Patricia Reilly Giff as the class reading assignment. The students displayed much excitement to be chosen for this program, especially because they would be able to read in such a new way. A plan outlining specific Kindle 2 skills was devised for the following Kindle 2 features:

1. Power and sleep/wake button
2. Home screen options
3. Navigating from home screen to selected e-book
4. Differences and similarities of the location feature versus book pages
5. Font size options

6. Standard dictionary found on the Kindle 2
7. Highlighting text
8. Text-to-speech option

During the orientation it was discovered that the young age was less of an obstacle operating the Kindle 2 than we had anticipated. Although a bit anxious to push the buttons, the students settled in quickly once they understood the basic steps. One student in particular had a habit of pushing the button to move the text without reading it first. Stuedemann lent assistance by reviewing the basic steps again, focusing more on the highlighting feature for this student to concentrate on.

Shortly after the orientation period, the five reluctant readers were asked to silently read a few paragraphs from their device. Those students who had difficulty at first received further assistance and instruction from the teacher. Students were encouraged to use the dictionary function if they came across a word they did not know. After the students finished reading the assigned paragraphs, they were asked to reread the material and determine what they found to be the most important sentences and ideas of the paragraphs. This instruction was designed to encourage the use of the highlighting feature on the Kindle. Although our study preceded Collier and Berg's research, they articulated our findings precisely when they stated, "[L]earners must stop and think about what they have read, make connections to what they already know and construct their own meaning" (Collier and Berg 2011, 35).

In an attempt to teach improved reading skills, the highlighting feature was used as a way for the student to answer *why* a particular sentence is relevant to the story. Once the students chose the sentence(s) of importance, the class discussed why they found the sentence to be significant. Students were able to perform this function effectively because they had some ability to explain the story due to the highlighted sections. These findings were accurate in both groups of second graders.

Although high expectations were set for the skilled readers, we observed that reluctant readers displayed some of the same enthusiasm for certain functions of the Kindle. For example, in the My Clippings function, accessed from the home screen, highlighted sentences and phrases are stored for later review. When the second graders retrieved their saved material, they were surprised to find additional information—for example,

date, time, location of the sentences, the number of sentences, and information related to their highlighting. This function had them most intrigued,
and they spent a considerable amount of time reviewing the retrieval
aspect. Through this function students had the ability to discuss the reasons for their highlighted choices and why they thought the sentences
were important to the story. Based on their discussion, it appeared that
My Clippings provided an excellent vehicle in developing comprehension
skills with this group. Based on the students' responses, Stuedemann has
plans to enhance this lesson through the note-taking function of the Kindle
in the future.

As the librarian, I knew that many students judge a book not so much
by the cover but by the physical size of the book and number of pages. With
a Kindle there are location numbers rather than page numbers; therefore,
the length of the story is not easily determined for the new Kindle 2 user. In
addition, the ability to increase the font size results in decreasing the number of words on a page. This feature presents a less intimidating appearance for the reluctant reader. In his research, DeLamater (2010) found
font size to be significant in improving reading rates in all readers when
lessening the crowding of the words by increasing the font size. Counter
to this benefit, however, with a group of readers using different font sizes,
it is difficult to keep the group all on the same page. Stuedemann found
this to be true with her reluctant readers, stating that the use of location
versus page numbers was one of the few challenges in keeping the group in
sync with the lesson plan. To possibly overcome this particular challenge,
Stuedemann suggested having all students use the same font size.

After this pilot, Stuedemann relayed what she found to be successful
with the Kindle 2 project. Her experiences were all positive: the highlighting, text-to-speech, dictionary, and font size functions were all helpful for
grasping the attention of the reluctant readers and for assisting them to
tackle an assignment, enough so that she is excited about the prospects of
adding note taking, typing questions, and integrating meaning to the story.
Stuedemann uses the word connections for comprehension. She found
students who read from a Kindle 2 were making connections to reading.
Stuedemann was delighted that the students showed enthusiasm every
day to read, stating that the reluctant readers asked for the next Kindle
2 assignment. She would have liked more time to see the extent of effec-
tiveness for the project, and this is a chance she is looking for next school

year. For other educators who may be considering the use of e-books/ readers, she recommends that new users choose appropriate reading-level selections and plan for at least two mini lessons to orient the students on the digital technology device.

Introducing the concept of Kindle 2 e-readers to the students at Seneca Grade School is a proud accomplishment for this school librarian. The pilot in developing reading skills through the use of the Kindle 2 has been expanded to a larger number of students in various elementary grade levels. Although it is too soon to attribute Kindle 2 e-readers to improved skills, there is evidence that reluctant readers are showing an increasing interest in reading. Ideally, Seneca Grade School administrators and faculty will embrace the possibilities that can be found in utilizing Kindle 2 devices in other subject matter classrooms. If the Kindle 2 can ignite reluctant readers to reading, imagine the possibilities Kindle could have for reluctant learners.

REFERENCES

Barack, Lauren. 2010. "A Kindle Program of Their Own." *School Library Journal,* 56 (12).

Collier, Jackie, and Susan Berg. 2011. "Student Learning and E-books." In *No Shelf Required: E-books in Libraries,* ed. Sue Polanka, 19–36. Chicago: American Library Association.

DeLamater, William E. 2010. "How Larger Font Size Impacts Reading and the Implications for Educational Use of Digital Text Readers." EReadia, April 29, www.ereadia.com/research/How_Larger_Font_Size_Affects_Reading.pdf.

Larson, Lotta C. 2010A. "Digital Readers: The Next Chapter in E-book Reading and Response." *The Reading Teacher* (International Reading Association), 64 (1): 15–22.

———. 2010B. "Going Digital: Using E-book Readers to Enhance the Reading Experience." Lesson plan, www.readwritethink.org/classroom-resources/ lesson-plans/going-digital-using-book-30623.html.

CONTRIBUTORS

AMELIA BRUNSKILL is currently the electronic resources librarian at DePaul University. Prior to this position, she was the liaison librarian for the sciences at Dickinson College. She received her M.S.I.S. from the University of Texas at Austin in 2006. She enjoys reading paperbacks, hates reading hardbacks, and is increasingly intrigued by the possibilities of e-ink.

ALICE CROSETTO has spent more than thirty years as an educator and librarian at both the high school and university levels in the Cleveland and Youngstown, Ohio, areas. Her academic degrees include a B.A. in Latin, an M.A. in English, an M.Ed. in curriculum and instruction, and an M.L.S. She has been at the University of Toledo since 2005 as the University Libraries coordinator for collection development. Her publications include articles in the areas of collection development and children's literature as well as the 2009 book *Disabilities and Disorders in Literature for Youth: A Selective Annotated Bibliography for K–12* (Scarecrow, 2009). Crosetto was also a contributor in the first volume of this series.

CAROLYN FOOTE is the district librarian for Eanes Independent School District in Austin, Texas. A former English teacher, she has presented at library and technology conferences since 1991 and published numerous articles on e-books, iPads, and other library technologies in journals such as *School Library Journal, Library Media Connection, Multimedia Schools,* and *TechEdge.* She is a two-time finalist for the Texas Computer Educator Librarian of the Year Award, and her blog *Not So Distant Future* (http://futura.edublogs.org) has been recognized in the Edublogs awards and Salem Press Blog awards. Her passions include technology in libraries, library design, and legislative action.

ALLISON GALLAHER has been head of circulation at Oberlin College Library since 1987. She started her library career as a reference librarian at Oberlin, following assistant positions at the Center for Research Libraries and the University of Chicago.

JESSICA GRIM is collection development and management librarian at Oberlin College Library. She has served as a reference and instruction librarian at Oberlin for twenty years and as a reference librarian at the UC Berkeley undergraduate library and the New York Public Library.

BUFFY HAMILTON is the founding librarian of the Unquiet Library at Creekview High School in Canton, Georgia. Hamilton, a nineteen-year veteran educator, is passionate about creating learning experiences for her students that will encourage them to be lifelong learners; she blogs at *The Unquiet Library* (theunquietlibrary.wordpress.com). Buffy is one of *Tech and Learning*'s thirty EdTech Leaders of the Future as well as the Georgia School Library Media Specialist of the Year 2010. Her Media 21 program is also an ALA Office for Information Technology Policy (OITP) 2011 Cutting Edge Service Award winner. Hamilton is also a 2011 *Library Journal* Mover and Shaker.

CHRISTINE JAMES has taught language arts and social studies in North Carolina and South Carolina for fourteen years. She is currently the Title I literacy coach at Myrtle Grove Middle School. She has worked with the National Writing Project promoting content area literacy as well as providing staff development. James is a former technophobe who is embracing the wonders of technology with her students these days. She earned her undergraduate degree from Drake University in Des Moines, Iowa, and is also a National Board–certified teacher for early adolescence language arts.

STEVE KELLEY is the head of resource services and serials cataloging at the Z. Smith Reynolds Library of Wake Forest University in Winston-Salem, North Carolina. He was previously the cataloging services librarian for serials and government documents at Ball State University. He is a member of the editorial board of *Serials Review* and is very active in NASIG and ALCTS.

AMY KIRCHHOFF has been the archive service product manager for Portico since 2006. She is responsible for creation and execution of archival policy and oversees operation and development of the Portico website. Prior to her work at Portico, Amy was director of technology for JSTOR and also served as a member of the shared software development group at ITHAKA. She has published articles on Portico's preservation methodology and policies in several publications, including *Learned Publishing* and *The Serials Librarian.*

JENNIFER LAGARDE wears many library hats. In addition to being the lead media specialist for the New Hanover County school system in Wilmington, North Carolina, she is also the school librarian at Myrtle Grove Middle School and is a part-time reference librarian for the New Hanover County Public Library. LaGarde is also the current advocacy and governance chair for the North Carolina School Library Media Association and is a founding member of the North Carolina Young Adult Book Award Committee. She earned her undergraduate degree in English education from the University of North Carolina at Wilmington and her graduate degree in library information sciences from Appalachian State University. LaGarde is a National Board–certified school librarian and the author of the blog The Adventures of Library Girl (http://lib-girl .blogspot.com).

SYLVIA K. MILLER has twenty-five years' experience in publishing scholarly books for libraries, including ten Dartmouth Medal–winning reference works. At Scribner Reference, she was involved in some of the earliest digital reference publishing, and she spearheaded online publishing as a publishing director at Routledge. She brought the ten-volume *Encyclopedia of World Dress and Fashion* to Berg Publishers (Oxford, UK) and Oxford University Press, which they copublished and which recently won the 2011 Dartmouth Medal. She took the directorship of the Mellon-funded collaborative project "Publishing the Long Civil Rights Movement" at UNC Chapel Hill in 2008. She holds a B.A. (UC Berkeley) and an M.A. (Columbia University) in comparative literature.

BOBBI NEWMAN is dedicated to helping libraries find their place in the digital age. She is passionate about twenty-first-century literacies and the role of all libraries in equal access and opportunity for all. Her professional interests include digital and technology-based services, the digital divide, and improving existing services through expanding traditional methods while creating innovative new practices. She has won numerous awards and appointments for her work, and her writing and professional activities are regularly cited in national news media. Read more from Newman at librarianbyday.net.

KATHY PARKER has been the school library media specialist at Seneca Grade School for thirty-four years, and for the past four years she has also held the same position at Seneca High School, both in Seneca, Illinois. She has presented at the local and national level in the area of e-book program development. She is an avid blogger and is often found discussing the latest in literature for all age levels on her blog: http://marianslibrary.wordpress.com/.

THOMAS PETERS currently serves as the assistant dean for strategic technology initiatives at Milner Library at Illinois State University in Normal. Prior to that, Peters was the CEO of TAP Information Services, a company he founded in 2003. Peters also has worked at the Committee on Institutional Cooperation (CIC, the academic consortium of the Big Ten universities and the University of Chicago), Western Illinois University in Macomb, Northern Illinois University in DeKalb, Minnesota State University at Mankato, and the University of Missouri at Kansas City. Peters holds a bachelor's in English and philosophy from Grinnell College, a, library science degree from the University of Iowa, and a master's in English from the University of Missouri at Kansas City. His library experience includes reference service, library instruction, collection management, information technology, and administration.

KEN PETRI has been the director of the Ohio State University Web Accessibility Center since 2005 and holds a B.S. in computer science and an M.A.

in English. Among his accessibility-related tasks at the university, Petri works with the Office for Disability Services exploring new alternative media technologies. He also has performed accessibility evaluations of e-book products for the Ohio Board of Regents. Thus his interest in e-book accessibility is both practical and technical. Outside of work, Ken enjoys spending time with his lovely wife and daughter and the menagerie of animals the family has inadvertently amassed.

MICHAEL PORTER is a librarian, presenter, author, practical technology fan, and PEZ collector. He has twenty years of experience working in Libraryland and has presented hundreds of times to library staff around the world. His writings regularly appear in major library journals around the world. In 2009 he was selected as a *Library Journal* Mover and Shaker, in 2010 was elected to the American Library Association's governing council, and in 2011 was also elected to the ALA Executive Board. He previously worked with the Bill and Melinda Gates Foundation, OCLC, WebJunction, and the Allen County Public Library. Porter currently serves as CEO of the Library Renewal, an organization dedicated to research, partnerships, and grassroots support for libraries as they struggle to offer electronic content to their users in competitive ways. Read more from Porter at www.libraryman.com and www.libraryrenewal.org.

JOSEPH SANCHEZ completed his M.L.I.S. in 2006 at San Jose State University. Currently he is the instructional design librarian for the University of Colorado at Denver. He is pursuing a doctorate at the University of Denver with an emphasis in information literacy. He began his library career in 2000 at the Georgina Cole public library in Carlsbad, California, working on the reference desk. He has since served as the library director at Red Rocks Community College in Lakewood, Colorado. His interests include classic cars, skateboarding, book collecting, videography, and e-content management. His website can be found at www.thebookmyfriend.com.

LISA CARLUCCI THOMAS is a nationally recognized librarian, author, and speaker, known for her leadership, innovation, and expertise on mobile and social technologies. Her research includes e-books, mobile culture, social media, technology trends, and training and career development for information professionals. Thomas is a 2010 *Library Journal* Mover and Shaker, a 2009 ALA Emerging Leader, and a graduate of the Syracuse University School of Information Studies. Thomas's experience includes project and services management at the Yale University Library and library systems, technology, and digital initiatives at Southern Connecticut State University. Thomas leads a library technology and creative services firm in Connecticut (www.lisacarlucci.com). Follow Thomas on Twitter @lisacarlucci.

SARAH E. TWILL, PhD, MSW, is a professor of social work at Wright State University in Dayton, Ohio. Prior to becoming a faculty member, Twill was a practicing social worker. She worked with low-income individuals as a mental health therapist, a juvenile probation officer, and the assistant director of a poverty outreach center. Her research interests include juvenile justice sentencing and treatment, economic human rights violations, and student success.

MATT WEAVER is a board member for the nonprofit Library Renewal and the Web librarian at Westlake Porter Public Library. As part of his day job, he has always worked to help staff and patrons learn to use e-book and other e-content services, especially by making screencast tutorials. He has an M.S-L.I.S. from Syracuse University and is a member of the Pi Lambda Sigma chapter of the international library and information studies honor society Beta Phi Mu. He has been published in *Library Hi-Tech*. His professional interests are electronic content, social media, and open source software in libraries (especially Drupal).

INDEX